DR. JAMES DOBSON
—On Parenting—

DR. JAMES DOBSON
—On Parenting—

Two Bestselling Works Complete in One Volume

THE
STRONG–WILLED CHILD

PARENTING
ISN'T FOR COWARDS

DR. JAMES DOBSON

Inspirational Press • New York

First Inspirational Press edition published in 1997.

Inspirational Press
A division of BBS Publishing Corporation
386 Park Avenue South
New York, NY 10016

Inspirational Press is a registered trademark of BBS Publishing Corporation.

Published by arrangement with Tyndale House Publishers and Word Inc.

Library of Congress Catalog Card Number: 97-73419

ISBN: 0-88486-177-5

Printed in the United States of America.

Contents

THE STRONG-WILLED CHILD

Birth through Adolescence

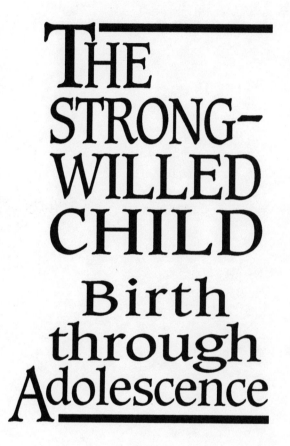

This book is affectionately dedicated to my own mother, who was blessed with a brilliant understanding of children. She intuitively grasped the meaning of discipline and taught me many of the principles which I've described on the following pages. And, of course, she did an incredible job of raising me, as everyone can plainly see today. But I've always been puzzled by one troubling question: Why did my fearless mother become such a permissive pushover the moment we made her a grandmother?

Contents

Introduction

A woman with seven rambunctious children boarded a Los Angeles bus and sat in the seat behind me. Her hair was a mess and the gaunt look on her face revealed a state of utter exhaustion. As she stumbled past me with her wiggling tribe, I asked, "Do all these children belong to you, or is this some kind of picnic!"

She looked at me through sunken eyes and said, "They're all mine, and believe me, it's *no* picnic!"

I smiled to myself, understanding fully what she meant. Small children have an uncanny ability to unravel an adult nervous system. They are noisy and they make incredible messes and they bicker with one another and their noses drip and they scratch the furniture and they have more energy in their fat little fingers than mama has in her entire weary body.

7

There's no doubt about it: children are expensive little people. To raise them properly will require the *very best* that you can give of your time, effort, and financial resources. However, to those who have never experienced parenthood, the job may appear ridiculously simple. Such people remind me of a man watching the game of golf for the first time, thinking, "That looks easy. All you have to do is hit that little white ball out there in the direction of the flag." He then steps up to the tee, draws back his club, and dribbles the "little white ball" about nine feet to the left. Accordingly, I should warn those who have not yet assumed the responsibilities of parenthood: the game of raising kids is more difficult than it looks.

So parenthood is costly and complex. Am I suggesting, then, that newly married couples should remain childless? Certainly not! The family that loves children and wants to experience the thrill of procreation should not be frightened by the challenge of parenthood. Speaking from my own perspective as a father, there has been no greater moment in my life than when I gazed into the eyes of my infant daughter, and five years later, my son. What could be more exciting than seeing those tiny human beings begin to blossom and grow and learn and love? And what reward could be more meaningful than having my little boy or girl climb onto my lap as I sit by the fire, hug my neck and whisper, "I love you, Dad." Oh, yes, children are expensive, but they're worth the price. Besides, nothing worth having comes cheap.

Furthermore, many of the frustrations of parenthood occur because we have no well-designed model or "game plan" to follow in response to the inevitable circumstances that develop. Then when the routine, predictable problems occur, we try to muddle through by random trial and error. Such parents remind me of a friend who flew his single-engine airplane toward a small country airport. He arrived as the sun had dropped behind a mountain at the close of the day, and by the time he had maneuvered his plane into position to land, he could not see the hazy field below. He had no lights on his plane and there was no one on duty at the airport. He circled the runway for another attempt to land, but the darkness had then become even more impenetrable. For two hours he flew his plane around and around in the blackness of night, knowing that he faced certain death when his fuel was expended. Then as greater panic gripped him, a miracle occurred. Someone on the ground heard the continuing drone of his engine and realized his predicament. That merciful man drove his car back and forth on the runway to show my friend the location of the airstrip, and then let his lights cast their beam from the far end while the plane landed.

I think of that story whenever I am descending at night in a commercial airliner. As I look ahead, I can see the green lights bordering the runway which tell the captain where to direct the plane. If he stays between those lighted boundaries, all will be well. There is safety in that illuminated zone, but disaster lies to the left or right.

Isn't that what we need as parents? There should be clearly marked boundaries that tell us where to steer the family ship. We require some guiding *principles* which will help us raise our children in safety and health. It should be apparent by now that my purpose in this book is to provide some of those understandings which will contribute to competent parenthood. We will deal particularly with the subject of discipline as it relates to the "strong-willed child." Most parents have at least one such youngster who seems to be born with a clear idea of how he wants the world to be operated and an intolerance for those who disagree. Even in infancy, he fairly bristles when his dinner is late and he insists that someone hold him during every waking hour. Later, during toddlerhood he declares total war on all forms of authority, at home or abroad, and his greatest thrill comes from drawing on the wall and flushing kitties down the toilet. His parents are often guilt-ridden and frustrated people who wonder where they've gone wrong and why their home life is so different than they were led to expect.

We'll be investigating this self-propelled youngster during his progression through childhood, including infancy, toddlerhood, early and late elementary school years, and (brace yourselves) during adolescence. Our discussion will also consider his behavior as it relates to sibling rivalry, hyperactivity, and the foundations of self-esteem.

It is my firm conviction that the strong-willed child usually possesses more creative potential and strength of character than his compliant siblings, provided his parents can help him channel his impulses and gain control of his rampaging will. My writings are dedicated to this purpose.

In short, this book is designed to provide *practical* advice and suggestions to parents who may be reacting to these more difficult challenges without design or fore-thought. And if I've been successful, this discourse may offer a lighted runway to pilots who circle in the darkness above.

James Dobson, Ph.D.

The Wild and Woolly Will

The Dobson household consists of a mother and father, a boy and a girl, one hamster, a parakeet, one lonely goldfish, and two hopelessly neurotic cats. We all live together in relative harmony with a minimum of conflict and strife. But there is another member of our "family" who is less congenial and cooperative. He is a stubborn twelve-pound dachshund named Sigmund Freud (Siggie), who honestly believes he owns the place. All dachshunds tend to be somewhat independent, I'm told, but Siggie is a confirmed revolutionary. He's not vicious or mean; he just wants to run things—and the two of us have been engaged in a power struggle for the past twelve years.

Siggie is not only stubborn, but he doesn't pull his own weight in the family. He won't bring in the newspaper on cold mornings; he refuses to "chase a ball" for the children; he doesn't keep the gophers out of the garden; and he can't do any of the usual tricks that most cultured dogs perform. Alas, Siggie has refused to participate in any of the self-improvement programs I have initiated on his behalf. He is content just to trot through life, watering and sniffing and stopping to smell the roses.

Furthermore, Sigmund is not even a good watchdog. This suspicion was confirmed the night we were visited by a prowler who had entered our backyard at three o'clock in the morning. I suddenly awoke from a deep sleep, got out of bed, and felt my way through the house without turning on the lights. I knew someone was on the patio and Siggie knew it too, because the coward was crouched behind me! After listening to the thumping of my heart for a few minutes, I reached out to take hold of the rear doorknob. At that moment, the backyard gate quietly opened and closed. Someone had been standing three feet from me, and that "someone" was now tinkering in my garage. Siggie and I held a little conversation in the darkness and decided that he should be the one to investigate the disturbance. I opened the back door and told my dog to "attack!" But Siggie just *had* one! He stood there throbbing and shaking so badly that I couldn't even push him out the back door. In the noise and confusion that ensued, the intruder escaped, (which pleased both dog *and* man).

Please don't misunderstand me; Siggie is a member of our family and we love him dearly. And despite his anarchistic nature, I have finally taught him to obey a few simple commands. However, we had some classic battles before he reluctantly yielded to my authority. The greatest confrontation occurred a few years ago when I had been in Miami for a three-day conference. I returned to observe that Siggie had become boss of the house while I was gone. But I didn't realize until later that evening just how strongly he felt about his new position as Captain.

At eleven o'clock that night, I told Siggie to go get into his bed, which is a permanent enclosure in the family room. For six years I had given him that order at the end of each day, and for six years Siggie had obeyed. On that occasion, however, he refused to budge. You see, he was in the bathroom, seated comfortably on the furry lid of the toilet seat. That is his favorite spot in the house, because it allows him to bask in the warmth of a nearby electric heater. Incidentally, Siggie had to learn the hard way that it is extremely important that the lid be *down* before he leaves the ground. I'll never forget the night he learned that lesson. He came thundering in from the cold, sailed through the air—and nearly drowned before I could get him out.

When I told Sigmund to leave his warm seat and go to bed, he flattened his ears and slowly turned his head toward me. He deliberately braced himself by placing one paw on the edge of the furry lid, then hunched his shoulders, raised his lips to reveal the molars on both sides, and uttered his most threatening growl. That was Siggie's way of saying, "Get lost!"

I had seen this defiant mood before, and knew there was only one way to deal with it. The *only* way to make Siggie obey is to threaten him with destruction. Nothing else works. I turned and went to my closet and got a small belt to help me "reason" with Mr. Freud. My wife, who was watching this drama unfold, tells me that as soon as I left the room, Siggie jumped from his perch and looked down the hall to see where I had gone. Then he got behind her and growled.

When I returned, I held up the belt and again told my angry dog to go get into his bed. He stood his ground so I gave him a firm swat across the rear end, and he tried to bite the belt. I hit him again and he tried to bite *me*. What developed next is impossible to describe. That tiny dog and I had the most vicious fight ever staged between man and beast. I fought him up one wall and down the other, with both of us scratching and clawing and growling and swinging the belt. I am embarrassed by the memory of the entire scene. Inch by inch I moved him toward the family room and his bed. As a final desperate maneuver, Siggie jumped up on the couch and backed into the corner for one last snarling stand. I eventually got him to bed, but only because I outweighed him 200 to 12!

The following night I expected another siege of combat at Siggie's bedtime. To my surprise, however, he accepted my command without debate or complaint, and simply trotted toward the family room in perfect submission. In fact, that fight occurred more than four years ago, and from that time to this, Siggie has never made another "go for broke" stand.

It is clear to me now that Siggie was saying in his canine way, "I don't think you're tough enough to make me obey." Perhaps I seem to be humanizing the behavior of a dog, but I think not. Veterinarians will confirm that some breeds of dogs, notably dachshunds and shepherds, will not accept the leadership of their masters until human authority has stood the test of fire and proved itself worthy.

But this is not a book about the discipline of dogs; there is an important moral to my story which is highly relevant to the world of children. *Just as surely as a dog will occasionally challenge the authority of his leaders, a little child is inclined to do the same thing, only more so.* This is no minor observation, for it represents a characteristic of human nature which is rarely recognized (or admitted) by the "experts" who write books on the subject of discipline. I have yet to find a text for parents or teachers which acknowledges the struggle—the exhausting confrontation of wills—which most parents and teachers experience regularly with their children. Adult leadership is rarely accepted unchallenged by the next generation; it must be "tested" and found worthy of allegiance by the youngsters who are asked to yield and submit to its direction.

The Hierarchy of Strength and Courage

But why are children so pugnacious? Everyone knows that they are lovers of justice and law and order and secure boundaries. The writer of the book of Hebrews in the Bible even said that an undisciplined child feels like an illegitimate son or daughter, not even belonging to his family. Why, then, can't parents resolve all conflicts by the use of quiet discussions and explanations and gentle pats on the head? The answer is found in this curious value system of children which respects strength and courage (when combined with love). What better explanation can be given for the popularity of the mythical Superman and Captain Marvel and Wonder Woman in the folklore of children? Why else do children proclaim, "My dad can beat up your dad!"? (One child replied to that statement, "That's nothing, my *mom* can beat up my dad, too!")

You see, boys and girls care about the issue of "who's toughest." Whenever a youngster moves into a new neighborhood or a new school district, he usually has to fight (either verbally or physically) to establish himself in the hierarchy of strength. Anyone who understands children knows that there is a "top dog" in every group, and there is a poor little defeated pup at the bottom of the heap. And every child between those extremes knows where he stands in relation to the others.

Recently my wife and I had an opportunity to observe this social hierarchy in action. We invited the fourteen girls in our daughter's fifth-grade class to our home for a slumber party. It was a noble gesture, but I can tell you with sincerity that we will never do that again. It was an exhausting and sleepless night of giggling and wiggling and jumping and bumping. But it was also a very interesting evening, from a social point of view. The girls began arriving at five o'clock on Friday night, and their parents returned to pick them up at 11 o'clock Saturday morning. I met most of them for the first time that weekend, yet during those seventeen hours together, I was able to identify every child's position in the hierarchy of respect and strength. There was one queen bee who was boss of the crowd. Everyone wanted to do what she suggested, and her jokes brought raucous laughter. Then a few degrees below her was the number two princess, followed by three, four, and five. At the bottom of the list was a harassed little girl who was alienated and rejected by the entire herd. Her jokes were as clever (I thought) as those of the leader, yet no one laughed when she clowned. Her suggestions of a game or event were immediately condemned as stupid and foolish. I found myself defending this isolated girl because of the injustice of her situation. Unfortunately, there is a similar outcast or loser in every group of three or more kids (of either sex). Such is the nature of childhood.

This respect for strength and courage also makes children want to know how "tough" their leaders are. They will occasionally disobey parental instructions for the precise purpose of testing the determination of those in charge. Thus, whether you are a parent or grandparent or Boy Scout leader or bus driver or Brownie leader or a schoolteacher, I can guarantee that sooner or later one of the children under your authority will clench his little fist and challenge your leadership. Like Siggie at bedtime, he will convey this message by his disobedient manner: "I don't think you are tough enough to make me do what you say."

This defiant game, called Challenge the Chief, can be played with surprising skill by very young children. Only yesterday a father told me of taking his three-year-old daughter to a basketball game. The child was, of course, interested in everything in the gym except the athletic contest. The father permitted her to roam free and climb on the bleachers, but he set up definite limits regarding how far she could stray. He took her by the hand and walked with her to a stripe painted on the gym floor. "You can play all around the building, Janie, but don't go past this line," he instructed her. He had no sooner returned to his seat than the toddler scurried in the direction of the forbidden territory. She stopped at the border for a moment, then flashed a grin over her shoulder to her father, and deliberately placed one foot over the line as if to say, "Whacha gonna do about it?" Virtually every parent the world over has been asked the same question at one time or another.

The entire human race is afflicted with the same tendency toward willful defiance that this three-year-old exhibited. Her behavior in the gym is not so different from the folly of Adam and Eve in the Garden of Eden. God had told them they could eat *anything* in the Garden except the forbidden fruit ("do not go past this line"). Yet they challenged the authority of the Almighty by deliberately disobeying His commandment. Perhaps this tendency toward self-will is the essence of "original sin" which has infiltrated the human family. It certainly explains why I place such stress on the proper response to willful defiance during childhood, for that rebellion can plant the seeds of personal disaster. The thorny weed which it produces may grow into a tangled briar patch during the troubled days of adolescence.

When a parent refuses to accept his child's defiant challenge, something changes in their relationship. The youngster begins to look at his mother and father with disrespect; they are unworthy of his allegiance. More important, he wonders why they would let him do such harmful things if they really loved him. The ultimate paradox of childhood is that boys and girls want to be led by their parents, but insist that their mothers and fathers earn the right to lead them.

It is incredible to me that this aspect of human nature is so poorly recognized in our permissive society. Let me repeat my observation that the most popular textbooks for parents and teachers fail even to acknowledge that parenthood involves a struggle or contest of wills. Books and articles written on the subject of discipline usually relate not to willful defiance but to *childish irresponsibility*. There is an enormous difference between the two categories of behavior.

A 1975 article in *Family Circle* magazine[1] is typical of the watery stuff fed to parents. The title proclaimed "A Marvelous New Way to Make Your Child Behave," which should have been the first clue as to the nature of its content. (If its recommendations were so fantastic, why weren't the insights observed in more than 5000 years of parenting?) The subtitle was even more revealing, however, and it stated, "Rewards and Punishment Don't Work." Those two pollyanna-ish headlines revealed the primrose path down which the authors were leading us. Never once did they admit that a child is capable of spitting in his parent's face, or running down the middle of a busy street, or sawing a leg off the dining room table, or trying to flush baby brother down the toilet. There was no acknowledgement that some mothers and fathers go to bed at night with a pounding, throbbing headache, wondering how parenthood became such an exhausting and nerve-wracking experience. Instead, the examples given in the article focused on relatively minor incidents of childish irresponsibility: how to get your child to wash his hands before dinner, or wear the proper clothing, or take out the garbage. Responsible behavior is a noble objective for our children, but let's admit that the heavier task is shaping the child's *will!*

Strength of the Will

I have been watching infants and toddlers during recent years, and have become absolutely convinced that at the moment of birth there exists in children an inborn temperament which will play a role throughout life.

Though I would have denied the fact fifteen years ago, I am now certain that the personalities of newborns vary tremendously, even before parental influence is exercised. Every mother of two or more children will affirm that each of her infants had a different personality—a different "feel"—from the first time they were held. Numerous authorities in the field of child development now agree that these complex little creatures called babies are far from "blank slates" when they enter the world. One important study[2] by Chess, Thomas, and Birch revealed nine kinds of behaviors in which babies differ from one another. These differences tend to persist into later life and include level of activity, responsiveness, distractibility, and moodiness, among others.

Another newborn characteristic (not mentioned by Chess) is most interesting to me and relates to a feature which can be called "strength of the will." Some children seem to be born with an easygoing, compliant attitude toward external authority. As infants they don't cry very often and they sleep through the night from the second week and they goo at the grandparents and they smile while being diapered and they're very patient when dinner is overdue. And, of course, they never spit up on the way to church. During later childhood, they love to keep their rooms clean and they especially like to do their homework and they can entertain themselves for hours. There aren't many of these supercompliant children, I'm afraid, but they are known to exist in some households, (not my own).

Just as surely as some children are naturally compliant, there are others who seem to be defiant upon exit from the womb. They come into the world smoking a cigar and yelling about the temperature in the delivery room and the incompetence of the nursing staff and the way things are run by the administrator of the hospital. They expect meals to be served the instant they are ordered, and they demand every moment of mother's time. As the months unfold, their expression of willfulness becomes even more apparent, the winds reaching hurricane force during toddlerhood.

In thinking about these compliant and defiant characteristics of children, I sought an illustration which would explain the vastly differing thrust of human temperaments. I found an appropriate analogy in a supermarket shortly thereafter. Imagine yourself in a grocery store, pushing a wire cart up the aisle. You give the basket a small shove and it glides at least nine feet out in front, and then comes to a gradual stop. You walk along happily tossing in the soup and ketchup bottles and loaves of bread. Marketing is such an easy task, for even when the cart is burdened with goods, it can be directed with one finger.

But buying groceries is not always so blissful. On other occasions, you select a shopping cart which ominously awaits your arrival at the front of the market. When you push the stupid thing forward, it tears off to the left and knocks over a stack of bottles. Refusing to be outmuscled by an empty cart, you throw all of your weight behind the handle, fighting desperately to keep the ship on course. It seems to have a mind of its own as it darts toward the eggs and careens back in the direction of the milk and almost crushes a terrified grandmother in green tennis shoes. You are trying to do the same shopping assignment that you accomplished with ease the day before, but the job feels more like combat duty today. You are exhausted by the time you herd the contumacious cart toward the check stand.

What is the difference between the two shopping baskets? Obviously, one has straight, well-oiled wheels which go where they are guided. The other has crooked, bent wheels that refuse to yield. Do you recognize how this illustration relates to children? We might as well face it, some kids have "crooked wheels"! They do not want to go where they are led, for their own inclinations would take them in other directions. Furthermore, the mother who is "pushing the cart" must expend seven times the energy to make it move, compared with the parent of a child with "straight, well-oiled wheels." (Only mothers of strong-willed children will *fully* comprehend the meaning of this illustration.)

But how does the "typical" or "average" child respond? My original assumption was that children in the Western world probably represented a "normal" or bell-shaped curve with regard to strength of the will. In other words, I presumed there were a few very compliant kids and an equally small number who were defiant, but the great majority of youngsters were likely to fall somewhere near the middle of the distribution. (See Fig. 1.)

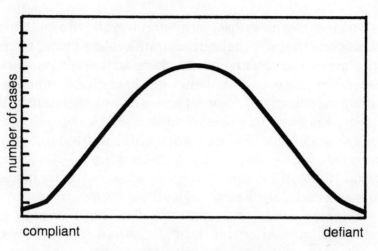

FIG. 1   STRENGTH OF THE WILL

However, having talked to at least 25,000 harried parents, I'm convinced that my supposition was wrong. The true distribution probably is depicted in Fig. 2, below:

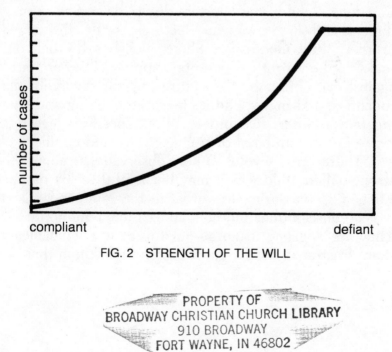

FIG. 2   STRENGTH OF THE WILL

Don't take this observation too literally, for perhaps it only *seems* that the majority of toddlers are trying to conquer the world. Furthermore, there is another phenomenon which I have never been able to explain, relating to sibling relationships. When there are two children in the family, it is likely that one youngster will be compliant and the other defiant. The easygoing child is often a genuine charmer. He smiles at least sixteen hours a day and spends most of his time trying to figure out what his parents want and how he can make them happy. In reality, he *needs* their praise and approval; thus his personality is greatly influenced by this desire to gain their affection and recognition.

The second child is approaching life from the opposite vantage point. He is sliding all four brakes and trying to gain control of the family steering mechanism. And don't you see how these differences in temperament lay the foundation for serious sibling rivalry and resentment? The defiant child faces constant discipline and hears many threats and finger-wagging lectures, while his angelic brother, little Goody-Two-Shoes, polishes his halo and soaks up the warmth of parental approval. They are pitted against each other by the nature of their divergent personalities, and may spend a lifetime scratching and clawing one another. (Chapter 4 offers specific suggestions regarding the problem of sibling rivalry and conflict.)

There are several other observations about the strong-willed child which may be helpful to his parents. First, it is reassuring to verbalize the guilt and anxiety which conscientious mothers and fathers commonly feel. They are engaged in an all-out tug of war which leaves them frustrated and fatigued. No one told them that par-

enthood would be this difficult, and they blame themselves for the tension that arises. They had planned to be
such loving and effective parents, reading fairy stories to
their pajama-clad angels by the fireplace. The difference
between life as it is and life as it ought to be is a frightening and distressing bit of reality.

Furthermore, I have found that the parents of compliant children don't understand their friends with defiant
youngsters. They intensify guilt and anxiety by implying,
"If you would raise your kids the way I do it, you wouldn't
be having those awful problems." May I say to both
groups that the willful child can be difficult to control
even when his parents handle him with great skill and
dedication. It may take several years to bring him to a
point of relative obedience and cooperation within the
family unit. While this training program is in progress, it is
important not to panic. Don't try to complete the transformation overnight. Treat your child with sincere love
and dignity, but require him to follow your leadership.
Choose carefully the matters which are worthy of confrontation, then accept his challenge on those issues and
win decisively. Reward every positive, cooperative gesture
he makes by offering your attention, affection, and verbal
praise. Then take two aspirin and call me in the morning.

But the most urgent advice I can give the parents of
an assertive, independent child concerns the importance
of beginning to shape his will during the *early* years. I
honestly believe, though the assumption is difficult to
prove, that the defiant youngster is in a "high risk" category for antisocial behavior later in life. He is more likely
to challenge his teachers in school and question the values
he has been taught and shake his fist in the faces of those

who would lead him. I believe he is more inclined toward sexual promiscuity and drug abuse and academic difficulties. This is not an inevitable prediction, of course, because the complexities of the human personality make it impossible to forecast behavior with complete accuracy. I must also stress that the overall picture is not negative. It would appear that the strong-willed child may possess more character and have greater potential for a productive life than his compliant counterpart. However, the realization of that potential may depend on a firm but loving early home environment. Thus, I repeat my admonition: begin shaping the will of that child while he is in toddlerhood. (Notice that I did not say *crush* the will, or destroy it, or snuff it out. The "how to" of that recommendation will provide the subject matter of subsequent chapters.)

Questions

Question: I'm still not sure if I understand the difference between willful defiance and childish irresponsibility. Could you explain it further?

Answer: Willful defiance, as the name implies, is a *deliberate* act of disobedience. It occurs *only* when the child knows what his parents expect and then chooses to do the opposite in a haughty manner. In short, it is a refusal to accept parental leadership, such as running away when called, screaming insults, acts of outright disobedience, etc. By contrast, childish irresponsibility results from forgetting, accidents, mistakes, a short attention span, a low frustration tolerance, immaturity, etc. In the first instance, the child knows he was wrong and is waiting to see what his parent can do about it; in the second, he has simply blundered into a consequence he did not plan. It is wrong, in my view, to resort to corporal punishment for the purpose of instilling responsibility (unless, of course, the child has defiantly refused to accept it).

Ultimately, the appropriate disciplinary reaction by a mother or father should be determined entirely by the matter of *intention*. Suppose my three-year-old son is standing in the doorway and I say, "Ryan, please shut the door." But in his linguistic immaturity he misunderstands my statement and *opens* the door even further. Will I punish him for disobeying me? Of course not, even though he did the opposite of what I asked. He may never even know that he failed the assignment. My tolerance is dictated by his intention. He honestly tried to obey me. However, when I ask Ryan to pick up his toys, but he stamps his little foot and screams "NO!" before throwing a Tonka truck in my direction—then I am obligated to accept his challenge. In short, my child is never so likely to be punished as when I'm sure *he knows* he deserves it. And our Creator has warned of the consequences of this rebellion, stating in Proverbs 29:1, "He that being often reproved hardeneth his neck, shall suddenly be destroyed, and that without remedy" (KJV). Thus, we should teach our children to submit to our loving leadership as preparation for their later life of obedience to God.

Question: Should my child be permitted to say, "I hate you!" when he is angry?

Answer: Not in my opinion. Other writers will tell you that all children hate their parents occasionally and should be permitted to ventilate that hostility. I believe it is possible (and far more healthy) to encourage the expression of negative feelings without reinforcing temper tantrums and violent behavior. If my child screamed his hatred at me *for the first time* in a moment of red-faced anger, I would probably wait until his passion had cooled and then convey this message in a loving, sincere manner: "Charlie, I know you were very upset earlier today when we had our disagreement, and I think we should talk about what you were feeling. *All* children get angry at their parents now and then, especially when they feel unfairly treated. I understand your frustration and I'm sorry we got into such a hassle. But that does not excuse you for saying, 'I hate you!' You'll learn that no matter how upset I become over something you've done, I'll *never* tell you that I hate you. And I can't permit you to talk that way to me. When people love each other, as you and I do, they don't want to hurt one another. It hurt me for you to say that you hated me, just as you would be hurt if I said something like that to you. You can, however, tell me what angers you, and I will listen carefully. If I am wrong, I will do my best to change the things you dislike. So I want you to understand that you are free to say *anything* you wish to me as always, even if your feelings are not very pleasant. But you will never be permitted to scream and call names and throw temper tantrums. If you behave in those childish ways, I will have to punish you as I would a little child. Is there anything you need to say to me now? (If not, then put your arms around my neck because I love you!)"

My purpose would be to permit the ventilation of negative feelings without encouraging violent, disrespectful, manipulative behavior.

Question: Would you, then, go so far as to apologize to a child if you felt you had been in the wrong?

Answer: I certainly would—and indeed, I have. Approximately one year ago I was burdened with pressing responsibilities which made me fatigued and irritable. One particular evening I was especially grouchy and short-tempered with my ten-year-old daughter. I knew I was not being fair, but was simply too tired to correct my manner. Through the course of the evening, I blamed Danae for things that were not her fault and upset her needlessly several times. After going to bed, I felt bad about the way I had behaved and I decided to apologize the next morning. After a good night of sleep and a tasty breakfast, I felt much more optimistic about life. I approached my daughter before she left for school and said, "Danae, I'm sure you know that daddies are not perfect human beings. We get tired and irritable just like other people, and there are times when we are not proud of the way we behave. I know that I wasn't fair with you last night. I was terribly grouchy, and I want you to forgive me."

Danae put her arms around me and shocked me down to my toes. She said, "I knew you were going to have to apologize, Daddy, and it's okay; I forgive you."

Can there be any doubt that children are often more aware of the struggles between generations than are their busy, harassed parents?

Shaping the Will

The young mother of a defiant three-year-old girl approached me in Kansas City recently, to thank me for my books and tapes. She told me that a few months earlier her little daughter had become increasingly defiant and had managed to "buffalo" her frustrated mom and dad. They knew they were being manipulated but couldn't seem to regain control. Then one day they happened to see a copy of my first book, *Dare to Discipline*, on sale in a local bookstore. They bought the book and learned therein that it is appropriate to spank a child under certain well-defined circumstances. My recommendations made sense to these harassed parents, who promptly spanked their sassy daughter the next time she gave them reason to do so. But the little girl was just bright enough to figure out where they had picked up that new idea. When the mother awoke the next morning, she found her copy of *Dare to Discipline* floating in the toilet! That darling little girl had done her best to send my writings to the sewer, where they belonged. I suppose that is the strongest editorial comment I've received on any of my literature!

This incident with the toddler was not an isolated case. Another child selected my book from an entire shelf of possibilities and threw it in the fireplace. I could easily become paranoid about these hostilities. Dr. Benjamin Spock is loved by millions of children who have grown up under his influence, but I am apparently resented by an entire generation of kids who would like to catch me in a blind alley on some cloudy night.

It is obvious that children are aware of the contest of wills between generations, and that is precisely why the parental response is so important. When a child behaves in ways that are disrespectful or harmful to himself or others, his hidden purpose is often to verify the stability of the boundaries. This testing has much the same function as a policeman who turns doorknobs at places of business after dark. Though he tries to open doors, he hopes they are locked and secure. Likewise, a child who assaults the loving authority of his parents is greatly reassured when their leadership holds firm and confident. He finds his greatest security in a structured environment where the rights of other people (and his own) are protected by definite boundaries.

Our objective, then, is to *shape the will* during the early years of childhood. But how is that to be accomplished? I have talked to hundreds of parents who recognize the validity of the principle but have no idea how it can be implemented in their homes. Consequently, the remainder of this chapter has been devoted to specific suggestions and recommendations. We will begin with six broad guidelines which are paraphrased from my previous writings, followed by practical examples at each age level.

First: Define the Boundaries Before They Are Enforced

The most important step in any disciplinary procedure is to establish reasonable expectations and boundaries *in advance*. The child should know what is and what is not acceptable behavior *before* he is held responsible for those rules. This precondition will eliminate the overwhelming sense of injustice that a youngster feels when he is slapped or punished for his accidents, mistakes, and blunders. If you haven't defined it—don't enforce it!

Second: When Defiantly Challenged, Respond with Confident Decisiveness

Once a child understands what is expected, he should then be held accountable for behaving accordingly. That sounds easy, but as we have seen, most children will assault the authority of their elders and challenge their right to lead. In a moment of rebellion, a little child will consider his parents' wishes and defiantly choose to disobey. Like a military general before a battle, he will calculate the potential risks, marshal his forces and attack the enemy with guns blazing. When that nose-to-nose confrontation occurs between generations, it is *extremely* important for the adult to win decisively and confidently. The child has made it clear that he's looking for a fight, and his parents would be wise not to disappoint him! *Nothing* is more destructive to parental leadership than for a mother or father to disintegrate during that struggle. When the parent consistently loses those battles, resorting to tears and screaming and other evidence of frustration, some dramatic changes take place in the way they are "seen" by their children. Instead of being secure and confident leaders, they become spineless jellyfish who are unworthy of respect or allegiance.

Third: Distinguish between Willful Defiance and Childish Irresponsibility

A child should not be spanked for behavior that is not willfully defiant. When he forgets to feed the dog or make his bed or take out the trash—when he leaves your tennis racket outside in the rain or loses his bicycle—remember that these behaviors are typical of childhood. It is, more than likely, the mechanism by which an immature mind is protected from adult anxieties and pressures. Be gentle as you teach him to do better. If he fails to respond to your patient instruction, it then becomes appropriate to administer some well-defined consequences (he may have to work to pay for the item he abused or be deprived of its use, etc.). However, childish irresponsibility is very different from willful defiance, and should be handled more patiently.

Fourth: Reassure and Teach After the Confrontation Is Over

After a time of conflict during which the parent has demonstrated his right to lead, (particularly if it resulted in tears for the child), the youngster between two and seven (or older) may want to be loved and reassured. By all means, open your arms and let him come! Hold him close and tell him of your love. Rock him gently and let him know, again, why he was punished and how he can avoid the trouble next time. This moment of communication builds love, fidelity, and family unity. And for the Christian family, it is extremely important to pray with the child at that time, admitting to God that we have *all* sinned and no one is perfect. Divine forgiveness is a marvelous experience, even for a very young child.

Fifth: Avoid Impossible Demands

Be absolutely sure that your child is *capable* of delivering what you require. Never punish him for wetting the bed involuntarily or for not becoming potty-trained by one year of age, or for doing poorly in school when he is incapable of academic success. These impossible demands put the child in an unresolvable conflict: there is no way out. That condition brings inevitable damage to human emotional apparatus.

Sixth: Let Love Be Your Guide!

A relationship that is characterized by genuine love and affection is likely to be a healthy one, even though some parental mistakes and errors are inevitable.

To Spank or Not to Spank

With those six guidelines providing our background, let's turn our attention now to the more specific tools and techniques for shaping the will. We'll begin by discussing the practice of spanking, which has been the subject of heated controversy in recent years. More foolishness has been written on this subject than all other aspects of child rearing combined. Consider the views of Dr. John Valusek, a psychologist with whom I appeared on the Phil Donahue television show:

> The way to stop violence in America is to stop spanking children, argues psychologist John Valusek. In a speech to the Utah Association for Mental Health some weeks ago, Valusek declared that parental spanking promotes the thesis that violence against others is acceptable.
> "Spanking is the first half-inch on the yardstick of violence," said Valusek. "It is followed by hitting and ultimately by rape, murder, and assassination. The modeling behavior that occurs at home sets the stage: 'I will resort to violence when I don't know what else to do.'"[1]

To Dr. Valusek and his permissive colleagues I can only say, "Poppycock!" How ridiculous to blame America's obsession with violence on the disciplinary efforts of loving parents! This conclusion is especially foolish in view of the bloody fare offered to our children on television each day. The average sixteen-year-old has watched 18,000 murders during his formative years, including a daily bombardment of knifings, shootings, hangings, decapitations, and general dismemberment. Thus, it does seem strange that the psychological wizards of our day search elsewhere for the cause of brutality—and eventually point the finger of blame at the parents who are diligently training our future responsible citizens. Yet this is the kind of "press" that has been given in recent years to parents who believe in spanking their disobedient children.

Opposition to corporal punishment can be summarized by four common arguments, all of them based on error and misunderstanding. The first is represented by Dr. Valusek's statement, and assumes that spankings teach children to hit and hurt others. It depicts corporal punishment as a hostile physical attack by an angry parent whose purpose is to damage or inflict harm on his little victim. Admittedly, that kind of violence does occur regularly between generations and is tremendously destructive to children. (It is called child abuse and is discussed in the following chapter.) However, corporal punishment in the hands of a loving parent is altogether different in purpose and practice. It is a teaching tool by which harmful behavior is inhibited, rather than a wrathful attempt by one person to damage another. One is an act of love; the other is an act of hostility, and they are as different as night and day.

I responded to Dr. Valusek's argument in *Hide or Seek*, showing the place of minor pain in teaching children to behave responsibly:

> "Those same specialists also say that a spanking teaches your child to hit others, making him a more violent person. Nonsense! If your child has ever bumped his arm against a hot stove, you can bet he'll never deliberately do that again. He does not become a more violent person because the stove burnt him. In fact, he learned a valuable lesson from the pain. Similarly, when he falls out of his high chair or smashes his finger in the door or is bitten by a grumpy dog, he learns about the physical dangers in his world. These bumps and bruises throughout childhood are nature's way of teaching him what to treat with respect. They do not damage his self-esteem. They do not make him vicious. They merely acquaint him with reality. In like manner, an appropriate spanking from a loving parent provides the same service. It tells him there are not only physical dangers to be avoided, but he must steer clear of some social traps as well (selfishness, defiance, dishonesty, unprovoked aggression, etc.)."[2]

The second rationale against corporal punishment can also be found in Dr. Valusek's concluding sentence, "I will resort to violence (spankings) when I don't know what else to do." Do you see the subtlety of this quotation? It characterizes a spanking as an absolute last resort—as the final act of exasperation and frustration. As such, it comes on the heels of screaming, threatening, hand-wringing, and buckets of tears. Even those authorities who recommend corporal punishment often fall into this trap, suggesting that it be applied only when all else has failed. I couldn't disagree more strongly.

A spanking is to be reserved for use in response to willful defiance, *whenever it occurs.* Period! It is much more effective to apply it early in the conflict, while the parent's emotional apparatus is still under control, than after ninety minutes of scratching and clawing. In fact, child abuse is more likely to occur when a little youngster is permitted to irritate and agitate and sass and disobey and pout for hours, until finally the parent's anger reaches a point of explosion where anything can happen (and often does). Professionals like Dr. Valusek have inadvertently contributed to violence against children, in my view, because they have stripped parents of the right to correct children's routine behavior problems while they are of minor irritation. Then when these small frustrations accumulate, the parent does (as Valusek said) "resort to violence when he doesn't know what else to do."

The third common argument against spanking comes from the findings of animal psychology. If a mouse is running in a maze, he will learn much faster if the experimentor rewards his correct turns with food than he will if his incorrect choices are punished with a mild electric shock. From this and similar studies has come the incredible assumption that punishment has little influence on human behavior. But human beings are not mice, and it is naive to equate them simplistically. Obviously, a child is capable of rebellious and defiant attitudes which have no relevance to a puzzled mouse sitting at a crossroads in a maze. I agree that it would not help a boy or girl learn to read by shocking them for each mispronounced word. On the other hand, deliberate disobedience involves the child's perception of parental authority and his obligations to accept it (whereas the mouse does not even know the experimentor exists).

If punishment doesn't influence human behavior, then why is the issuance of speeding citations by police so effective in controlling traffic on a busy street? Why, then, do homeowners rush to get their tax payments in the mail to avoid a 6 percent penalty for being late? If punishment has no power, then why does a well-deserved spanking often turn a sullen little troublemaker into a sweet and loving angel? Rat psychology notwithstanding, both reward and punishment play an important role in shaping human behavior, and neither should be discounted. Leonardo da Vinci hadn't heard about the mouse in the maze when he wrote, "He who does not punish evil commands it to be done!"

The fourth argument against the judicious practice of spanking comes from those who see it as damaging to the dignity and self-worth of the child. This subject is so important that an entire chapter has been devoted to preserving the spirit (see Chapter 4). Suffice it to say at this point that a child is fully capable of discerning whether his parent is conveying love or hatred. This is why the youngster who knows he deserves a spanking appears almost relieved when it finally comes. Rather than being insulted by the discipline, he understands its purpose and appreciates the control it gives him over his own impulses.

This childish comprehension was beautifully illustrated by a father who told me of a time when his five-year-old son was disobeying in a restaurant. This lad was sassing his mother, flipping water on his younger brother, and deliberately making a nuisance of himself. After four warnings which went unheeded, the father took his son by the arm and marched him to the parking lot where he proceeded to administer a spanking. Watching this episode was a meddling woman who had followed them out of the restaurant and into the parking lot. When the punishment began, she shook her finger at the father and screamed, "Leave that boy alone! Turn him loose! If you don't stop I'm going to call the police!" The five-year-old, who had been crying and jumping, immediately stopped yelling and said to his father in surprise, "What's wrong with that woman, Dad?" He understood the purpose for the discipline, even if the "rescuer" didn't. I only wish that Dr. Valusek and his contemporaries were as perceptive as this child.

Let me hasten to emphasize that corporal punishment is not the only tool for use in shaping the will, nor is it appropriate at all ages and for all situations. The wise parent must understand the physical and emotional characteristics of each stage in childhood, and then fit the discipline to a boy's or girl's individual needs. Perhaps I can assist in that process now by listing specific age categories and offering a few practical suggestions and examples for the various time frames. Please understand that this discussion is by no means exhaustive, and merely suggests the general nature of disciplinary methods at specific periods.

Birth to Seven Months

No *direct* discipline is necessary for a child under seven months of age, regardless of behavior or circumstance. Many parents do not agree, and find themselves "swatting" a child of six months for wiggling while being diapered or for crying in the midnight hours. This is a serious mistake. A baby is incapable of comprehending his "offense" or associating it with the resulting punishment. At this early age, he needs to be held, loved, and most important, to hear a soothing human voice. He should be fed when hungry and kept clean and dry and warm. In essence, it is probable that the foundation for emotional and physical health is laid during this first six-month period, which should be characterized by security, affection, and warmth.

On the other hand, it is possible to create a fussy, demanding baby by rushing to pick him up every time he utters a whimper or sigh. Infants are fully capable of learning to manipulate their parents through a process called reinforcement, whereby any behavior that produces a pleasant result will tend to recur. Thus, a healthy baby can keep his mother hopping around his nursery twelve hours a day (or night) by simply forcing air past his sandpaper larynx. To avoid this consequence, it is important to strike a balance between giving your baby the attention he needs and establishing him as a tiny dictator. Don't be afraid to let him cry a reasonable period of time (which is thought to be healthy for the lungs) although it is necessary to listen to the tone of his voice for the difference between random discontent and genuine distress. Most mothers learn to recognize this distinction in time.

Before leaving this first age category, I feel I must say again what has been implied before: Yes, Virginia, there *are* easy babies and there are difficult babies! Some seem determined to dismantle the homes into which they were born; they sleep cozily during the day and then howl in protest all night; they get colic and spit up the vilest stuff on their clothes (usually on the way to church); they control their internal plumbing until you hand them to strangers, and then let it blast. Instead of cuddling into the fold of the arms when being held, they stiffen rigidly in search of freedom. And to be honest, a mother may find herself leaning sockeyed over a vibrating crib at 3 A.M., asking the eternal question, "What's it all about, Alfie?"* A few days earlier she was wondering, "Will he survive?" Now she is asking, "Will *I* survive?!" But believe it or not, both generations will probably recover and this disruptive beginning will be nothing but a dim memory for the parents in such a brief moment. And from that demanding tyrant will grow a thinking, loving human being with an eternal soul and a special place in the heart of the Creator. To the exhausted and harassed new mother, let me say, "Hang tough! You are doing *the* most important job in the universe!"

Eight to Fourteen Months

Many children will begin to test the authority of their parents during the second seven-month period. The confrontations will be minor and infrequent before the first birthday, yet the beginnings of future struggles can be seen. My own daughter, for example, challenged her mother for the first time when she was nine months old.

---

*Someone has suggested that babies be fed a combination of oatmeal and garlic for dinner each evening. The stuff tastes terrible, of course, but it does help parents locate their kids in the dark! (Please don't take this suggestion literally.)

My wife was waxing the kitchen floor when Danae crawled to the edge of the linoleum. Shirley said, "No, Danae," gesturing to the child not to enter the kitchen. Since our daughter began talking very early, she clearly understood the meaning of the word *no*. Nevertheless, she crawled straight onto the sticky wax. Shirley picked her up and sat her down in the doorway, while saying, "No," more firmly. Not to be discouraged, Danae scrambled onto the newly mopped floor. My wife took her back, saying, "No" even more strongly as she put her down. Seven times this process was repeated, until Danae finally yielded and crawled away in tears. As far as we can recall, that was the first direct collision of wills between my daughter and wife. Many more were to follow.

How does a parent discipline a one-year-old? Very carefully and gently! A child at this age is extremely easy to distract and divert. Rather than jerking a china cup from his hands, show him a brightly colored alternative— and then be prepared to catch the cup when it falls. When unavoidable confrontations do occur, as with Danae on the waxy floor, win them by firm persistence but not by punishment. Again, don't be afraid of the child's tears, which can become a potent weapon to avoid naptime or bedtime or diapertime. Have the courage to lead the child without being harsh or mean or gruff.

Compared to the months that are to follow, the period around one year of age is usually a tranquil, smooth-functioning time in a child's life.

Fifteen to Twenty-four Months

It has been said that all human beings can be classified into two broad categories: those who would vote
"yes" to the various propositions of life, and those who
would be inclined to vote "no." I can tell you with confidence that each toddler around the world would definitely
cast a negative vote! If there is one word that characterizes the period between fifteen and twenty-four months of
age, it is *No!* No, he doesn't want to eat his cereal. No, he
doesn't want to play with his dump truck. No, he doesn't
want to take his bath. And you can be sure, no, he doesn't
want to go to bed anytime at all. It is easy to see why this
period of life has been called "the first adolescence," because of the negativism, conflict, and defiance of the age.

Dr. T. Berry Brazelton has written a beautiful description of the "terrible twos" in his excellent book *Toddlers and Parents.* (I enthusiastically recommend this
book to anyone wanting to understand this fascinating and
challenging age.) Quoted below is a classic depiction of a
typical eighteen month old boy named Greg.[3] Although I
have never met the fellow, I know him well . . . as you
will when your child becomes a toddler.

When Greg began to be negative in the second year,
his parents felt as if they had been hit with a sledge hammer. His good nature seemed submerged under a load of
negatives. When his parents asked anything of him, his
mouth took on a grim set, his eyes narrowed, and, facing
them squarely with his penetrating look, he replied simply
"no!" When offered ice cream, which he loved, he pre-

ceded his acceptance with a "no." While he rushed to get his snowsuit to go outside, he said "no" to going out.

His parents' habit of watching Greg for cues now began to turn sour. He seemed to be fighting with them all of the time. When he was asked to perform a familiar chore, his response was, "I can't." When his mother tried to stop him from emptying his clothes drawer, his response was, "I have to." He pushed hard on every familiar imposed limit, and never seemed satisfied until his parent collapsed in defeat. He would turn on the television set when his mother left the room. When she returned, she turned it off, scolded Greg mildly, and left again. He turned it on. She came rushing back to reason with him, to ask him why he'd disobeyed her. He replied, "I have to." The intensity of her insistence that he leave it alone increased. He looked steadily back at her. She returned to the kitchen. He turned it on. She was waiting behind the door, swirled in to slap his hands firmly. He sighed deeply and said, "I have to." She sat down beside him, begging him to listen to her to avoid real punishment. Again he presented a dour mask with knitted brows to her, listening but not listening. She rose wearily, walked out again. Just as wearily, he walked over to the machine to turn it on. As she came right back, tears in her eyes, to spank him, she said, "Greg, why do you want me to spank you? I hate it!" To which he replied, "I have to." As she crumpled in her chair, weeping softly with him across her lap, Greg reached up to touch her wet face.

After this clash, Mrs. Lang was exhausted. Greg sensed this and began to try to be helpful. He ran to the kitchen to fetch her mop and her dustpan, which he dragged in to her as she sat in her chair. This reversal made her smile and she gathered him up in a hug.

Greg caught her change in mood and danced off gaily to a corner, where he slid behind a chair, saying "hi and see." As he pushed the chair out, he tipped over a lamp which went crashing to the floor. His mother's reaction was a loud "No, Greg!" He curled up on the floor, his hands over his ears, eyes tightly closed, as if he were trying to shut out all the havoc he had wrought.

As soon as he was put into his high chair, he began to whine. She was so surprised that she stopped preparation of his food, and took him to change him. This did not settle the issue, and when she brought him to his chair again, he began to squirm and twist. She let him down to play until his lunch was ready. He lay on the floor, alternately whining and screeching. So unusual was this that she felt his diaper for pins which might be unclasped, felt his forehead for fever and wondered whether to give him an aspirin. Finally, she returned to fixing his lunch. Without an audience Greg subsided.

When she placed him in his chair again, his shrill whines began anew. She placed his plate in front of him with cubes of food to spear with his fork. He tossed the implement overboard, and began to push his plate away, refusing the food. Mrs. Lang was nonplussed, decided he didn't feel well, and offered him his favorite ice cream. Again, he sat helpless, refusing to feed himself. When she offered him some of the mush, he submissively allowed himself to be fed a few spoonfuls. Then he knocked the spoon out of her hand and pushed the ice cream away. Mrs. Lang was sure he was ill.

Mrs. Lang extracted Greg from his embattled position, and placed him on the floor to play while she ate her own lunch. This, of course, wasn't what he wanted either. He continued to tease her, asking for food off her plate, which he devoured greedily. His eagerness disproved her theory of illness. When she ignored him and continued to eat, his efforts redoubled. He climbed under the sink to find the bleach bottle which he brought to her on command. He fell forward onto the floor and cried loudly as if he'd hurt himself. He began to grunt as if he were having a bowel movement and to pull on his pants. This was almost a sure way of drawing his mother away from her own activity, for she'd started trying to "catch" him and put him on the toilet. This was one of his signals for her attention, and she rushed him to the toilet. He smiled smugly at her, but refused to perform. Mrs. Lang felt as if she were suddenly embattled on all fronts—none of which she could win.

When she turned to her own chores, Greg produced the bowel movement he'd been predicting.

The picture sounds pretty bleak, and admittedly, there are times when a little toddler can dismantle the peace and tranquility of a home. (My son Ryan loved to blow bubbles in the dog's water dish—a game which still horrifies me.) However, with all of its struggles, there is no more thrilling time of life than this period of dynamic blossoming and unfolding. New words are being learned daily, and the cute verbal expressions of that age will be remembered for a half century. It is a time of excitement over fairy stories and Santa Claus and furry puppy dogs. And most important, it is a precious time of loving and warmth that will scurry by all too quickly. There are millions of older parents today with grown children who would give all they possess to relive those bubbly days with their toddlers.

Let me make a few disciplinary recommendations which will, I hope, ease some of the tension of the toddler

experience. I must hasten to say, however, that the negativism of this turbulent period is both normal and healthy,
and *nothing* will make an eighteen-month-old child act
like a five-year-old.

First, and for obvious reasons, it is extremely important for fathers to help discipline and participate in the
parenting process when possible. Children need their fathers and respond to their masculine manner, of course,
but wives need their husbands, too. This is especially true
of housewives, such as Greg's mother, who have done
combat duty through the long day and find themselves in
a state of battle fatigue by nightfall. Husbands get tired
too, of course, but if they can hold together long enough
to help get the little tigers in bed, nothing could contribute more to the stability of their homes. I am especially
sympathetic with the mother who is raising a toddler or
two and an infant at the same time. There is no more
difficult assignment on the face of the earth. Husbands
who recognize this fact can help their wives feel understood, loved and supported in the vital jobs they are doing. (Don't ask me, please, how to convince husbands to
accept that responsibility. I'm like the mouse who recommended that a bell be put around the neck of the cat, but
had no idea how to get it there!)

With regard to specific discipline of the strong-willed
toddler, mild spankings can begin between fifteen and
eighteen months of age. They should be relatively infrequent, and must be reserved for the kind of defiance Greg
displayed over the television set. He clearly knew what his
mother wanted, but refused to comply. He should *not*
have been spanked for knocking over the lamp or for the
bowel movement episode or for refusing to eat his ice

cream. A heavy hand of authority during this period causes the child to suppress his need to experiment and test his environment, which can have long lasting consequences. To repeat, the toddler should be taught to obey and yield to parental leadership, but that end result will not be accomplished overnight.

When spankings occur, they should be administered with a neutral object; that is, with a small switch or belt, but rarely with the hand. I have always felt that the hand should be seen by the child as an object of love rather than an instrument of punishment. Furthermore, if a parent commonly slaps a youngster when he is not expecting to be hit, then he will probably duck and flinch whenever Father suddenly scratches his ear. And, of course, a slap in the face can reposition the nose or do permanent damage to the ears or jaw. If all spankings are administered with a neutral object, applied where intended, then the child need never fear that he will suddenly be chastised for some accidental indiscretion. (There are exceptions to this rule, such as when a child's hands are slapped or thumped for reaching for a stove or other dangerous object.) Incidentally, I mentioned in *Dare to Discipline* that my mother once spanked me with a girdle for being sassy and rude. One man read that story and became so angry that he refused to come and hear me speak the next time I was in his city. I found out later why he was so incensed. He had misread my explanation and thought my mother had hit me with a griddle! There is a difference between the two, although girdles in 1940 weighed about sixteen pounds and were riveted with steel bolts down both sides. It was also equipped with dozens of straps and buckles that dangled ominously from the bottom. In some ways, a griddle would have been easier to duck than this abominable undergarment which was flung in my direction.

Should a spanking hurt? Yes, or else it will have no influence. A swat on the behind through three layers of wet diapers simply conveys no urgent message. However, a small amount of pain for a young child goes a long way; it is certainly not necessary to lash or "whip" him. Two or three stinging strokes on the legs or bottom with a switch are usually sufficient to emphasize the point, "You must obey me." And finally, it is important to spank *immediately* after the offense, or not at all. A toddler's memory is not sufficiently developed to permit even a ten-minute delay in the administration of justice. Then after the episode is over and the tears subsided, the child might want to be held and reassured by his mother or father. By all means, let him come. Embrace him in the security of your loving arms. Rock him softly. Tell him how much you love him and why he must "mind his mommie." This moment can be the most important event in the entire day.

I caution parents not to punish toddlers for behavior which is natural and necessary to learning and development. Exploration of their environment, for example, is of great importance to intellectual stimulation. You and I as adults will look at a crystal trinket and obtain whatever information we seek from that visual inspection. A toddler, however, will expose it to all of his senses. He will pick it up, taste it, smell it, wave it in the air, pound it on the wall, throw it across the room, and listen to the pretty sound that it makes when shattering. By that process he learns a bit about gravity, rough versus smooth surfaces, the brittle nature of glass, and some startling things about mother's anger.

Am I suggesting that children be allowed to destroy a home and all of its contents? No, but neither is it right to expect a curious child to keep his hands to himself. Parents should remove those items that are fragile or particularly dangerous, and then strew the child's path with fascinating objects of all types. Permit him to explore everything possible and do not ever punish him for touching something that he *did not know was off limits*, regardless of its value. With respect to dangerous items, such as electric plugs and stoves, as well as a few untouchable objects, such as the knobs on the television set, it is possible and necessary to teach and enforce the command, "Don't touch!" After making it clear what is expected, a thump on the fingers or slap on the hands will usually discourage repeat episodes.

Entire books have been written on the subject which I have only touched here. Nevertheless, I hope this brief introduction will give the "flavor" of discipline for the young toddler.

Before leaving this dynamic time of life, I must share with my readers the results of an extremely important ten-year study of children between eight and eighteen months of age. This investigation, known as Harvard University's Preschool Project, has been guided by Dr. Burton L. White and a team of fifteen researchers between 1965 and 1975. They studied young children intensely during this period, hoping to discover which experiences in the early years of life contribute to the development of a healthy, intelligent human being. The conclusions from this exhaustive effort are summarized below, as reported originally in the *APA Monitor*.[4]

1. It is increasingly clear that the origins of human competence are to be found in a critical period of development between eight and eighteen months of age. The child's experiences during these brief months do more to influence future intellectual competence than any time before or after.

2. The single most important environmental factor in the life of the child is his mother. "She is on the hook," said Dr. White, and carries more influence on her child's experiences than any other person or circumstance.

3. The amount of *live* language directed to a child (not to be confused with television, radio, or overheard conversations) is vital to his development of fundamental linguistic, intellectual, and social skills. The researchers concluded, "Providing a rich social life for a twelve- to fifteen-month-old child is the best thing you can do to guarantee a good mind."

4. Those children who are given free access to living areas of their homes progressed much faster than those whose movements are restricted.

5. The nuclear family is the most important educational delivery system. If we are going to produce capable, healthy children, it will be by strengthening family units and by improving the interactions that occur within them.

6. The best parents were those who excelled at three key functions:
   (1) They were superb designers and organizers of their children's environments.
   (2) They permitted their children to interrupt them for brief thirty-second episodes, during which

personal consultation, comfort, information, and enthusiasm were exchanged.
(3) "THEY WERE FIRM DISCIPLINARIANS WHILE SIMULTANEOUSLY SHOWING GREAT AFFECTION FOR THEIR CHIL-DREN." (I couldn't have said it better myself.)

Do these results speak dramatically to anyone but me? I hear within them an affirmation and validation of the concepts to which I have devoted my professional life.

Two to Three Years

Perhaps the most frustrating aspect of the "terrible twos" is the tendency of kids to spill things, destroy things, eat horrible things, fall off things, flush things, kill things, and get into things. They also have a knack for doing embarrassing things, like sneezing on a nearby man at a lunch counter. During these toddler years, any unexplained silence of more than thirty seconds can throw an adult into a sudden state of panic. What mother has not had the thrill of opening the bedroom door, only to find Tony Tornado covered with lipstick from the top of his pink head to the carpet on which he stands? On the wall is his own artistic creation with a red handprint in the center, and throughout the room is the aroma of Chanel No. 5 with which he has anointed his baby brother. Wouldn't it be interesting to hold a national convention sometime, bringing together all the mothers who have experienced that exact trauma?

When my daughter was two years of age, she was fascinated the first time she watched me shave in the morning. She stood captivated as I soaped my face and began using the razor. That should have been my first clue that something was up. The following morning, Shirley came into the bathroom to find our dachshund, Siggie, sitting in his favorite spot on the furry lid of the toilet seat. Danae had covered his head with lather and was systematically shaving the hair from his shiny skull! Shirley screamed, "Danae!" which sent Siggie and his barber scurrying for safety. It was a strange sight to see the frightened dog with nothing but ears sticking up on the top of his bald head.

When Ryan was the same age, he had an incredible ability to make messes. He could turn it over or spill it faster than any kid I've ever seen, especially at meal time. (Once while eating a peanut butter sandwich he thrust his hand through the bottom side. When his fingers emerged at the top they were covered with peanut butter, and Ryan didn't recognize them. The poor lad nearly bit off his index finger.) Because of his destructive inclination, Ryan heard the word "mess" used repeatedly by his parents. It became one of the most important words in his vocabulary. One evening while taking a shower I left the door ajar and got some water on the floor. And as you might expect, Ryan came thumping around the corner and stepped in it. He looked up at me and said in the gruffest voice he could manage, "Whuss all this mess in hyere?"

You *must* keep a sense of humor during the twos and threes in order to preserve your own sanity. But you must also proceed with the task of instilling obedience and respect for authority. Thus, most of the comments written in the preceding section also apply to the child between twenty-two and thirty-six months of age. Although the "older" toddler is much different physically and emotionally than he was at eighteen months, the tendency to test and challenge parental authority is still very much in evidence. In fact, when the young toddler consistently wins the early confrontations and conflicts, he becomes even more difficult to handle in the second and third years. Then a lifelong disrespect for authority often begins to settle into his young mind. Therefore, I cannot overemphasize the importance of instilling two distinct messages within your child before he is forty-eight months of age: (1) "I love you more than you can possibly understand. You are precious to me and I thank God every day that He let me raise you!" (2) "Because I love you, I must teach you to obey me. That is the only way I can take care of you and protect you from things that might hurt you. Let's read what the Bible tells us: 'Children, obey your parents, for this is what God wants you to do.'" (Ephesians 6:1)

Healthy parenthood can be boiled down to those two essential ingredients, love and control, operating in a system of checks and balances. Any concentration on love to the exclusion of control usually breeds disrespect and contempt. Conversely, an authoritarian and oppressive home atmosphere is deeply resented by the child who feels unloved or even hated. To repeat, the objective for the toddler years is to strike a balance between mercy and justice, affection and authority, love and control.

Specifically, how does one discipline a "naughty" two- or three-year-old child? One possible approach is to require the boy or girl to sit in a chair and think about what he has done. Most children of this age are bursting with energy, and absolutely hate to spend ten dull minutes with their wiggly posteriors glued to a chair. To some individuals, this form of punishment can be even more effective than a spanking, and is remembered longer.

Parents to whom I have made that recommendation have often said, "But what if he won't stay in the chair?" The same question is asked with reference to the child's tendency to pop out of bed after being tucked in at night. These are examples of the direct confrontations I have been describing. The parent who cannot require a toddler to stay on a chair or in his bed is not yet in command of the child. There is no better time than now to change the relationship.

I would suggest that the youngster be placed in bed and given a little speech, such as, "Johnny, this time Mommie means business. Are you listening to me? *Do not* get out of this bed. Do you understand me?" Then when Johnny's feet touch the floor, give him one swat on the legs with a small switch. Put the switch on his dresser where he can see it, and promise him one more stroke if he gets up again. Walk confidently out of the room without further comment. If he rebounds again, fulfill your promise and offer the same warning if he doesn't stay in bed. Repeat the episode until Johnny acknowledges that you are the boss. Then hug him, tell him you love him, and remind him how important it is for him to get his rest so that he won't be sick, etc. Your purpose in this painful exercise (painful for both parties) is not only to keep li'l John in bed, but to confirm your leadership in his mind. It is my opinion that too many American parents lack the courage to win this kind of confrontation, and are off-balance and defensive ever after. Dr. Benjamin Spock wrote in 1974, "Inability to be firm is, to my mind, the commonest problem of parents in America today." I agree.

Four to Eight Years

By the time a child reaches four years of age, the focus of discipline should be not only on his behavior, but also on the *attitudes* which motivate it. This task of shaping the personality can be relatively simple or incredibly difficult, depending on the basic temperament of a particular child. Some youngsters are naturally warm and loving and trusting, while others sincerely believe the world is out to get them. Some enjoy giving and sharing, whereas their siblings are consistently selfish and demanding. Some smile throughout the day while others complain and bellyache about everything from toothpaste to turnip greens.

Furthermore, these attitudinal patterns are not consistent from one time to the next. They tend to alternate cyclically between rebellion and obedience. In other words, a time of intense conflict and defiance (if properly handled) gives way to a period of love and cooperation. Then when Mom and Dad relax and congratulate themselves for doing a super job of parenting, their little chameleon changes colors again.

Some might ask, "So what? Why should we be concerned about the attitudes of a boy or girl?" Indeed, there are many child-rearing specialists who suggest that parents ignore negative attitudes, including those which are unmistakably defiant in tone. Consider the naive recommendations of Dr. Luther Woodward, as paraphrased in the book for parents, *Your Child from Two to Five.*

> What do you do when your preschooler calls you a "big stinker" or threatens to flush you down the toilet? Do you scold, punish . . . or sensibly take it in your stride? . . .
>
> Dr. Woodward recommends a positive policy of understanding as the best and fastest way to help a child outgrow this verbal violence. When parents fully realize that all little tots feel angry and destructive at times, they are better able to minimize these outbursts. Once the preschooler gets rid of his hostility, the desire to destroy is gone and instinctive feelings of love and affection have a chance to sprout and grow. Once the child is six or seven, parents can rightly let the child know that he is expected to be outgrowing sassing his parents.

In conclusion, Dr. Woodward reveals the permissive implications of his recommendation by warning those who try to apply it:

> But this policy takes a broad perspective and a lot of composure, especially when friends and relatives voice disapproval and warn you that you are bringing up a brat.[5]

In this case, your friends and relatives will probably be right. This suggestion (published during the permissive 1950s and so typical of other writings from that era) is based on the simplistic notion that children will develop sweet and loving attitudes if we adults will permit and encourage their temper tantrums during childhood. According to the optimistic Dr. Woodward, the tot who has been calling his mother a "big stinker" for six or seven years can be expected to embrace her suddenly in love and dignity. That outcome is most improbable. Dr. Woodward's creative "policy of understanding" (which means, stand and do nothing) offers a one-way ticket to emotional and social disaster, in my view.

I expressed my contrasting opinion in my earlier book *Dare to Discipline:*

> If it is desirable that children be kind, appreciative, and pleasant, those qualities should be taught—not hoped for. If we want to see honesty, truthfulness, and unselfishness in our offspring, then these characteristics should be the conscious objectives of our early instructional process. If it is important to produce respectful, responsible young citizens, then we should set out to mold them accordingly.
>
> The point is obvious: heredity does not equip a child with proper attitudes; children will learn what they are taught. We cannot expect the desirable attitudes and behavior to appear if we have not done our early homework. It seems clear that many of the parents of the post-war crop of American babies failed in that critical assignment.[6]

But *how* does one shape the attitudes of children? Most parents find it easier to deal with outright disobedience than with unpleasant characteristics of temperament or personality. Let me restate two age-old suggestions for parents, and then I'll offer a system which can be used with the especially disagreeable child.

1. There is no substitute for parental modeling of the attitudes we wish to teach. Someone wrote, "The footsteps a child follows are most likely to be the ones his

parents thought they covered up." It is true. Our children are watching us carefully, and they instinctively imitate our behavior. Therefore, we can hardly expect them to be kind and giving if we are consistently grouchy and selfish. We will be unable to teach appreciativeness if we never say "please" or "thank you" at home or abroad. We will not produce honest children if we teach them to lie to the bill collector on the phone by saying, "Dad's not home." In these matters, our boys and girls instantly discern the gap between what we say and what we do. And of the two choices, they usually identify with our behavior and ignore our empty proclamations.

2. Most of the favorable attitudes which should be taught are actually extrapolations of the Judeo-Christian ethic, including honesty, respect, kindness, love, human dignity, obedience, responsibility, reverence, etc. And how are these time-honored principles conveyed to the next generation? The answer was provided by Moses as he wrote more than 4000 years ago in the book of Deuteronomy. "You must teach them to your children and talk about them when you are at home or out for a walk; at bedtime, and the first thing in the morning. Tie them on your finger, wear them on your forehead, and write them on the doorposts of your house." (Deut. 6:7–9, TLB) In other words, we can't instill these attitudes during a brief, two-minute bedtime prayer, or during formalized training sessions. We must *live* them from morning to night. They should be reinforced during our casual conversation, being punctuated with illustrations, demonstrations, compliments, and chastisement. This teaching task is, I believe, *the* most important assignment God has given to us as parents.

Finally, let me offer a suggested approach for use with the strong-willed or negative child (age six or older) for whom other forms of instruction have been ineffective. I am referring specifically to the sour, complaining child who is making himself and the rest of the family miserable. He may slide his brakes for weeks and criticize the efforts of everyone nearby. The problem with such an individual is in defining the changes that are desired and then reinforcing the improvements when they occur. Attitudes are abstractions that a six- or eight-year-old may not fully understand, and we need a system that will clarify the "target" in his mind.

Toward this end, I have developed an Attitude Chart (see illustration) which translates these subtle mannerisms into concrete mathematical terms. Please note: This system which follows would *not* be appropriate for the child who merely has a bad day, or displays temporary unpleasantness associated with illness, fatigue, or environmental circumstances. Rather, it is a remedial tool to help change persistently negative and disrespectful attitudes by making the child conscious of his problem.

The Attitude Chart should be prepared and then reproduced, since a separate sheet will be needed every day. Place an X in the appropriate square for each category, and then add the total points "earned" by bedtime. Although this nightly evaluation process has the appearance of being objective to a child, it is obvious that the parent can influence the outcome by considering it in advance (it's called cheating). Mom or Dad may want Junior to receive eighteen points on the first night, barely missing the punishment but realizing he must stretch the following day. I must emphasize, however, that the system

MY ATTITUDE CHART _____

	1 EXCELLENT	2 GOOD	3 OKAY	4 BAD	5 TERRIBLE
My Attitude Toward Mother					
My Attitude Toward Dad					
My Attitude Toward Sister					
My Attitude Toward Friends					
My Attitude Toward Work					
My Attitude At Bedtime					

TOTAL POINTS _____

CONSEQUENCES

6–9 POINTS	THE FAMILY WILL DO SOMETHING FUN TOGETHER
10–18 POINTS	NOTHING HAPPENS, GOOD OR BAD
19–20 POINTS	I HAVE TO STAY IN MY ROOM FOR ONE HOUR
21–22 POINTS	I GET ONE SWAT WITH BELT
23+ POINTS	I GET TWO SWATS WITH BELT

will fail miserably if a naughty child does not receive the punishment he deserves, or if he hustles to improve but does not obtain the family fun he was promised. This approach is nothing more than a method of applying reward and punishment to attitudes in a way that children can understand and remember.

For the child who does not fully comprehend the concept of numbers, it might be helpful to plot the daily totals on a cumulative graph, such as the one provided on page 71.

I don't expect everyone to appreciate this system or to apply it at home. In fact, parents of compliant, happy children will be puzzled as to why it would ever be needed. However, the mothers and fathers of sullen, ill-tempered children will comprehend more quickly. Take it or leave it, as the situation warrants.

Nine to Twelve Years

Ideally, the foundation has been laid during the first nine years which will then permit a general loosening of the lines of authority. Every year that passes should bring fewer rules, less direct discipline, and more independence for the child. This does not mean that a ten-year-old is suddenly emancipated; it does mean that he is permitted to make more decisions about his daily living than when he was six. It also means that he should be carrying more responsibility each year of his life.

Physical punishment should be relatively infrequent during this period immediately prior to adolescence. Of course, some strong-willed children absolutely demand to be spanked, and their wishes should be granted. How-

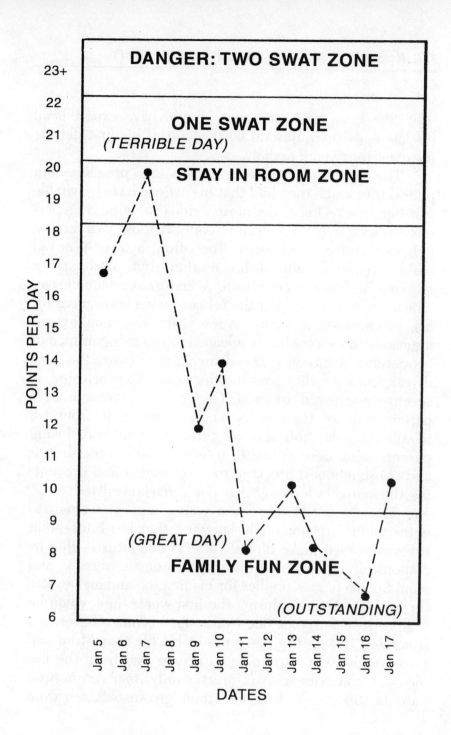

ever, the compliant youngster should have experienced his last woodshed episode by the end of his first decade (or even four years earlier).

The overall objective during this final preadolescent period is to teach the child that his actions have inevitable consequences. One of the most serious casualties in a permissive society is the failure to connect those two factors, behavior and consequences. Too often, a three-year-old child screams insults at his mother, but Mom stands blinking her eyes in confusion. A first-grader launches an attack on his teacher, but the school makes allowances for his age and takes no action. A ten-year-old is caught stealing candy in a store, but is released to the recognizance of his parents. A fifteen-year-old sneaks the keys to the family car, but his father pays the fine when he is arrested. A seventeen-year-old drives his Chevy like a maniac and his parents pay for the repairs when he wraps it around a telephone pole. You see, all through childhood, loving parents seem determined to intervene between behavior and consequences, breaking the connection and preventing the valuable learning that could have occurred.

Thus, it is possible for a young man or woman to enter adult life, not really knowing that life bites—that every move we make directly affects our future—that irresponsible behavior eventually produces sorrow and pain. Such a person applies for his first job and arrives late for work three times during the first week; then, when he is fired in a flurry of hot words, he becomes bitter and frustrated. It was the first time in his life that Mom and Dad couldn't come running to rescue him from the unpleasant consequences. (Unfortunately, many American parents still try to "bail out" their grown children even

when they are in their twenties and live away from home.)
What is the result? This overprotection produces emotional cripples who often develop lasting characteristics of
dependency and a kind of perpetual adolescence.

How does one connect behavior with consequences?
By being willing to let the child experience a reasonable
amount of pain when he behaves irresponsibly. When
Jack misses the school bus through his own dawdling, let
him walk a mile or two and enter school in midmorning
(unless safety factors prevent this). If Janie carelessly loses
her lunch money, let her skip a meal. Obviously, it is
possible to carry this principle too far, being harsh and
inflexible with an immature child. But the best approach
is to expect boys and girls to carry the responsibility that is
appropriate for their age, and occasionally to taste the
bitter fruit that irresponsibility bears.

Let me offer a concluding illustration that may be
read to an eleven- or twelve-year-old child. The following
story was published by United Press International a few
days after an eclipse of the sun had occurred.[7]

'JUST KEPT STARING'
'I WAS FASCINATED,' GIRL SAYS
OF ECLIPSE—NOW SHE'S BLIND

TIPTON, Ind. (UPI)—Ann Turner, 15, is living
proof of the danger of trying to watch a solar eclipse with
the naked eye. Now she is blind.

On March 7, despite the warnings she had read, Ann
"took a quick look through the window" at her home at
the solar eclipse in progress.

"For some reason, I just kept staring out of the window," she told Pat Cline, a reporter for the Tipton Daily

Tribune. "I was fascinated by what was taking place in the sky.

"There was no pain or feeling of discomfort as I watched. I stood there perhaps four or five minutes when mom caught me and made me turn away from the window."

Ann said she "saw spots before my eyes but I didn't think much about it." Shortly afterward, she walked downtown and suddenly realized when she looked at a traffic signal that she could not read signs.

Frightened, Ann turned around and headed home. As she neared the porch, she said, she found she was "walking in darkness."

She was too scared to tell her family until the next day, although she "had an intuition or suspicion that something terrible was happening."

"I cried and cried," she said. "I didn't want to be blind. God knows I didn't want to live in darkness the rest of my life.

"I kept hoping the nightmare would end and I could see again but the darkness kept getting worse. I was scared. I had disobeyed my parents and the other warnings. I could not go back and change things. It was too late."

When Mr. and Mrs. Coy Turner learned what had happened, they took Ann to specialists. But the doctors shook their heads and said they could not help Ann regain her sight. They said she is 90% blind and can make out only faint lines of large objects on the periphery of what used to be her normal sight field.

With the help of a tutor, Ann is going ahead with her education. She is learning to adjust to the world of darkness.

After reading this dramatic story to your boy or girl, it might be wise to say, "Paul, this terrible thing happened to Ann because she didn't believe what she was told by her parents and other adults. She trusted her own judgment, instead. And the reason I read this to you is to help you understand that you might soon be in a situation that is similar to Ann's. As you go into your teen years, you will have many opportunities to do some things that we have told you are harmful. For example, someone could give you some drugs which don't seem dangerous at all, even after you take them. Just like Ann, you may not realize the consequences until it is too late. That is why it will be so important for you to *believe* the warnings that you've been taught, rather than trust your own judgment. Many young people make mistakes during the teen-age years that will affect the rest of their lives, and I want to help you avoid those problems. But the truth of the matter is, only you can set your course and choose your pathway. You can accept what your eyes tell you, like Ann, or you can believe what your mother and I have said, and more important, what we read in God's Word. I have confidence that you will make the right decisions, and it's going to be fun watching you grow up."

There is so much that should be said about this late childhood era, but time and space limitations force me to move on. In conclusion, the period between ten and eleven years of age often represents a final time of great closeness and unpretentious love between parent and child. Enjoy it to the maximum, for believe me, there are more tumultuous days coming! (I have chosen to reserve the discussion of adolescent discipline for a separate chapter, because of the significance of the topic.)

Final Comment

I was accompanied on a recent speaking trip by my wife, Shirley, which required us to leave our two children with their grandparents for a full week. My wife's mother and father are wonderful people and dearly love Danae and Ryan. However, two bouncing, jumping, giggling little rascals can wear down the nerves of *any* adult, especially those who are approaching the age of retirement. When we returned home from the trip I asked my father-in-law how the children behaved and whether or not they caused him any problems. He replied in his North Dakota (Lawrence Welk) accent, "Oh no! Dere good kids. But the important thing is, yu jus' got to keep 'em out in da open."

That was probably the best disciplinary advice ever offered. Many behavioral problems can be prevented by simply avoiding the circumstances that create them. And especially for boys and girls growing up in our congested cities, perhaps what we need most is to "get 'em out in da open." It's not a bad idea.

Questions

Question: Isn't it our goal to produce children with *self*-discipline and *self*-reliance? If so, how does your approach to *external* discipline by parents get translated into internal control?

Answer: You've asked a provocative question, but one that reveals a misunderstanding of children, I believe. There are many authorities who suggest that parents not discipline their children for the reason implied by your question: they want their kids to discipline themselves.

But since young people lack the maturity to generate that self-control, they stumble through childhood without experiencing *either* internal or external discipline. Thus, they enter adult life having never completed an unpleasant assignment, or accepted an order that they disliked, or yielded to the leadership of their elders. Can we expect such a person to exercise self-discipline in young adulthood? I think not. He doesn't even know the meaning of the word.

My concept is that parents should introduce their child to discipline and self-control by the use of external influences when he is young. By being required to behave responsibly, he gains valuable experience in controlling his *own* impulses and resources. Then as he grows into the teen years, the transfer of responsibility is made year by year from the shoulders of the parent directly to the child. He is no longer forced to do what he has learned during earlier years. To illustrate, a child should be *required* to keep his room relatively neat when he is young. Then somewhere during the midteens, his own self-discipline should take over and provide the motivation to continue the task. If it does not, the parent should close his door and let him live in a dump, if necessary.

Question: I'm never completely certain how to react to the behavior of my children. Can you give some specific examples of misbehaviors that should be punished, as well as others which can be ignored or handled differently?

Answer: Certainly. Let me list a few examples at various age levels, asking you to decide how you would handle each matter before reading my suggestions. (Most of

these items represent actual situations posed to me by
parents.)

1. I get very upset because my two-year-old boy will
not sit still and be quiet in church. He knows he's not
supposed to be noisy, but he hits his toys on the pew and
sometimes talks out loud. Should I spank him for being so
disruptive?

My reply

The mother who wrote this question during one of
my seminars revealed a poor understanding of toddlers.
Most two-year-olds can no more fold their hands and sit
quietly in church than they could swim the Atlantic
Ocean. They squirm and churn and burn every second of
their waking hours. No, this child should not be punished.
He should be left in the nursery where he can shake the
foundations without disturbing the worshipers.

2. My four-year-old son came into the house and told
me he had seen a lion in the back yard. He was not trying
to be funny. He really tried to convince me that this lie
was true and became quite upset when I didn't believe
him. I want him to be an honest and truthful person.
Should I have spanked him?

My reply

Definitely not. There is a *very* thin line between fantasy and reality in the mind of a preschool child, and he
often confuses the two. This occurred when I took my son
to Disneyland at three years of age. He was absolutely
terrified by the wolf who stalked around with the three
pigs. Ryan took one look at those sharp, jagged teeth and
screamed in terror. I have a priceless motion picture of
him scrambling for the safety of his mother's arms. After
we returned home, I told Ryan there was a "very nice

man" inside the wolf suit, who wouldn't hurt anyone. My son was so relieved by that news that he needed to hear it repeatedly.

He would say, "Dad?"

"What, Ryan?"

"Tell me 'bout that nice man!"

You see, Ryan was not able to distinguish between the fantasy character and a genuine threat to his health and safety. I would guess that the lion story related in the question above was a product of the same kind of confusion. The child may well have believed that a lion was in the back yard. This mother would have been wise to play along with the game while making it perfectly clear that she didn't believe the story. She could have said, "My! My! A lion in the back yard. I sure hope he is a friendly old cat. Now, Billy, please wash your hands and come eat lunch."

3. My six-year-old has suddenly become sassy and disrespectful in his manner at home. He told me to "buzz off" when I asked him to take out the trash, and he calls me names when he gets angry. I feel it is important to permit this emotional outlet, so I haven't suppressed it. Do you agree?

My reply

I couldn't disagree more strongly. Your son is aware of his sudden defiance, and he's waiting to see how far you will let him go. This kind of behavior, if unchecked, will continue to deteriorate day by day, producing a more profound disrespect with each encounter. If you don't discourage it, you can expect some wild experiences during the adolescent years to come. Thus, the behavior for which punishment is most necessary is that involving a direct assault on the leadership and personhood of the parent (or teacher), especially when the child obviously knows he shouldn't be acting that way.

With regard to the ventilation of anger, it is possible to let a child express his strongest feelings without being insulting or disrespectful. A tearful charge, "You weren't fair with me and you embarrassed me in front of my friends," should be accepted and responded to quietly and earnestly. But a parent should never permit a child to say, "You are so stupid and you never do anything right!" The first statement is a genuine expression of frustration based on a specific issue; the second is an attack on the dignity and authority of the parent. In my opinion, the latter is damaging to both generations and should be inhibited.

4. My ten-year-old often puts his milk glass too close to his elbow when eating, and has knocked it over at least six times. I keep telling him to move the glass, but he won't listen. When he spilt the milk again yesterday, I jerked him up and gave him a spanking with a belt. Today I don't feel good about the incident. Should I have reacted more patiently?

My reply

It is all too easy to tell a mother she shouldn't have become so upset over something that happened yesterday. After all, I'm not the one who had to clean up the mess. However, your son did not *intend* to spill his milk and he was, in effect, punished for his irresponsibility. It would have been better to create a method of grabbing his attention and helping him remember to return his glass to a safe area. For example, you could have cut an "off limits" zone from red construction paper, and taped it to the side of his plate. If junior placed his glass on that paper, he would have to help wash the dishes after the evening meal. I guarantee you that he would seldom "forget" again. In fact, this procedure would probably sensitize him to the location of the glass, even after the paper was removed.

5. John is in the second grade and is playing around in school. Last month his teacher sent home a note telling us of his misbehavior, and he threw it away. We discovered at Open House the following week that he had lied to us and destroyed the note. What would you have done?
My reply

That was a deliberate act of disobedience. After investigating the facts, I would probably have given John a spanking for his misbehavior in school and for being untruthful to his parents. I would then talk to his teacher about *why* he was cavorting in school and consider why he was afraid to bring home the note.

6. My three-year-old daughter, Nancy, plays unpleasant games with me in grocery stores. She runs when I call her and makes demands for candy and gum and cupcakes. When I refuse, she throws the most embarrassing temper tantrums you can imagine. I don't want to punish her in front of all those people and she knows it. What should I do?
My reply

If there are sanctuaries where the usual rules and restrictions do not apply, then your children will behave differently in those protected zones than elsewhere. I would suggest that you have a talk with Nancy on the next trip to the market. Tell her exactly what you expect, and make it clear that you mean business. Then when the same behavior occurs, take her to the car or behind the building and do what you would have done at home. She'll get the message.

7. Our twenty-four-month-old son is not yet toilet trained, although my mother-in-law feels he should be under control now. Should we spank him for using his pants instead of the potty?

My reply

No. Tell your mother-in-law to cool down a bit. It is entirely possible that your child *can't* control himself at this age. The last thing you want to do is spank a two-year-old for an offense which he can't comprehend. If I had to err on this matter, it would be in the direction of being too late with my demands, rather than too early. Furthermore, the best approach to potty training is with rewards rather than with punishment. Give him a sucker (or sugarless candy) for performing properly. When you've proved that he can comply, then you can hold him responsible in the future.

Summary

In summary, it is impossible to discipline properly until the parent is able to interpret the child's intent. Corporal punishment should occur only in response to deliberate disobedience or defiance.

"But how can you know for sure?" That question has been asked of me hundreds of times. A mother will say, "I think Chuckie was being disrespectful when I told him to take his bath, but I'm not sure what he was thinking."

There is a very straightforward solution to this parental dilemma: use the first occasion for the purpose of clarifying the next. Say to your son, "Chuck, your answer to me just now sounded sassy. I'm not sure how you intended it. But so we will understand each other, don't talk to me like that again." If it occurs again, you'll know it was deliberate.

Most confusion over how to discipline results from parents' failure to define the limits properly. If you're hazy on what is acceptable and unacceptable, then your child will be doubly confused. Therefore, don't punish until you have drawn the boundaries too clearly to be missed. Most children will then accept them with only an occasional indiscretion.

Protecting
the Spirit

There are dangers implicit in what I have stated about discipline of the strong-willed child. The reader could assume that I perceive children as the villains and parents as the inevitable good guys. Of greater concern is the inference that I'm recommending a rigid, harsh, oppressive approach to discipline in the home. Neither statement is even partially accurate.

By contrast, I see small children (even those who challenge authority) as vulnerable little creatures who need buckets of love and tenderness every day of their lives. One of my great frustrations in teaching parents has been the difficulty in conveying a *balanced* environment, wherein discipline is evident when necessary, but where it is matched by patience and respect and affection. Let it never be said that I favor the "slap 'em across the mouth" approach to authoritarianism. That hostile manner not only wounds the spirit, but it's hard on teeth, too.

No subject distresses me more than the phenomenon of child abuse which is so prevalent in America today. There are children all across this country, even while I write, who are suffering untold miseries at the hands of their parents. Some of these pitiful little tots are brought to our hospital in every imaginable condition. They have been burned and bruised and broken and their little minds are permanently warped by the awful circumstances into which they were born.

Every professional who works with hurt children has to learn to cope with his own empathy. I have gained a measure of control over my own emotions; however, I have never been able to observe a battered child without feeling a literal agony within my chest. Diseased children suffer, of course, but most of them experience some measure of parental love which provides an emotional undergirding. But battered children suffer physically *and* emotionally. For them, no one cares. No one understands. There is no one to whom the longings can be expressed. They cannot escape. They cannot explain why they are hated. And many of them are too young to develop defense mechanisms or even call for help.

I dealt this spring with an eight-year-old girl who had been sexually assaulted repeatedly by her alcoholic father since she was fifteen months of age. What an immeasurable tragedy! Another child in Los Angeles was blinded by his mother, who destroyed his eyes with a razor blade. Can you imagine going through life knowing that your handicap resulted from a deliberate act by your own mother? Another small child in our city was pushed from a car on a crowded freeway and left clinging to the chain link divider for eight or nine hours. Another child's feet were held to a hot iron as punishment.

Less than five minutes ago, a radio news summary broadcast through my office intercom told of finding a ten-year-old girl hanging by her heels in her parents' garage. These kinds of horror stories are all too familiar to those of us who work with children. In fact, it is highly probable that some youngster within a mile or two of your house is experiencing destructive abuse in one manner or another. Brian G. Fraser, attorney for the National Center for Prevention and Treatment of Child Abuse and Neglect, has written: "Child abuse . . . once thought to be primarily a problem of the poor and down-trodden . . . occurs in every segment of society and may be the country's leading cause of death in children."

The last thing on earth that I want to do is to provide a rationalization and justification for such parental oppression. Let me say it again: I don't believe in harsh, inflexible discipline, even when it is well intentioned. Children must be given room to breathe and grow and love. But there are also threatening circumstances at the permissive end of the spectrum, and many parents fall into one trap in an earnest attempt to avoid the other. These dual dangers were beautifully described by Marguerite and Willard Beecher, writing in their book *Parents on the Run:*

> The adult-centered home of yesteryear made parents the masters and children their slaves. The child-centered home of today has made parents the slaves and children the masters. There is no true cooperation in any master-

slave relationship, and therefore no democracy. Neither the restrictive-authoritative technique of rearing children nor the newer "anything-goes" technique develop the genius within the individual, because neither trains him to be self-reliant. . . .

Children reared under arbitrary rules become either spineless automatons or bitter revolutionaries who waste their lives in conflict with those around them. But children who know no law higher than their own passing fancy become trapped by their own appetites. In either case, they are slaves. The former are enslaved by leaders on whom they depend to tell them what to do, and the latter are enslaved by the pawnbroker. Neither are (sic) capable of maintaining society on any decent basis. A lifetime of unhappiness may be avoided if the twig is bent so the tree will not incline in either of these mistaken directions.[1]

But how can this be accomplished on behalf of our children? How can parents steer a course between the unpleasant alternatives of permissiveness and oppression? What philosophy will guide our efforts?

Our objective is not only to shape the will of the child, as described in the previous chapters, *but to do so without breaking his spirit*. To accomplish this purpose we must understand the characteristic difference between the will and the spirit.

As I've stated, a child's *will* is a powerful force in the human personality. It is one of the few intellectual components which arrives full strength at the moment of birth. In a recent issue of *Psychology Today*, this heading described the research findings from a study of infancy: "A baby knows who he is before he has language to tell us

so. He reaches deliberately for control of his environment, especially his parents." This scientific disclosure
would bring no new revelation to the parents of a strong-
willed infant. They have walked the floor with him in the
wee small hours, listening to this tiny dictator as he made
his wants and wishes abundantly clear.

Later, a defiant toddler can become so angry that he
is capable of holding his breath until he loses conscious-
ness. Anyone who has ever witnessed this full measure of
willful defiance has been shocked by its power. One headstrong three-year-old recently refused to obey a direct
command from her mother, saying, "You're just my *mommie,* you know!" Another mere mommie wrote me that
she found herself in a similar confrontation with her
three-year-old son over something that she wanted him to
eat. He was so enraged by her insistence that he refused
to eat or drink *anything* for two full days. He became
weak and lethargic, but steadfastly held his ground. The
mother was worried and guilt ridden, as might be expected. Finally, in desperation, the father looked the child
in the eyes and convinced him that he was going to receive a spanking he would never forget if he didn't eat his
dinner. With that maneuver, the contest was over. The
toddler surrendered. He began to consume everything he
could get his hands on, and virtually emptied the refrigerator.

Now tell me, please, why have so few child development authorities recognized this willful defiance? Why
have they written so little about it? My guess is that the
acknowledgement of childish imperfection would not fit
neatly with the humanistic notion that little people are
infused with sunshine and goodness, and merely "learn"

the meaning of evil. To those who hold that rosy view I can only say, "Take another look!"

The will is not delicate and wobbly. Even for a child in whom the spirit has been sandbagged, there is often a will of steel, making him a threat to himself and others as well. Such a person can sit on a bridge threatening to jump, while the entire army, navy, and local fire department try to save his life. My point is that the will is malleable. It can and should be molded and polished—not to make a robot of a child for our selfish purposes, but to give him the ability to control his *own* impulses and exercise self-discipline later in life. In fact, we have a God-given responsibility as parents to shape the will in the manner described in the previous chapter.

On the other hand (and let me give this paragraph the strongest possible emphasis), the *spirit* of a child is a million times more vulnerable than his will. It is a delicate flower that can be crushed and broken all too easily (and even unintentionally). The spirit, as I have defined it, relates to the self-esteem or the personal worth that a child feels. It is *the* most fragile characteristic in human nature, being particularly vulnerable to rejection and ridicule and failure.

How, then, are we to shape the will while preserving the spirit intact? It is accomplished by establishing reasonable boundaries and enforcing them with love, but by avoiding any implication that the child is unwanted, unnecessary, foolish, ugly, dumb, a burden, an embarrassment, or a disastrous mistake. Any accusation that assaults the worth of a child in this way can be costly, such as "You are so stupid!" Or, "Why can't you make decent grades in school like your sister?" Or, "You have been a pain in the neck ever since the day you were born!"

The following letter was sent to me by a mother of three children and illustrates the precise opposite of the principles I am describing. I believe it will be useful to examine this woman's frustrations and the probable causes for her inability to control her defiant son, Billy. (Note: the details of this letter have been changed slightly to conceal the identity of the writer.)

> Dear Dr. Dobson:
>
> More than anything else in this world, I want to have a happy family. We have two girls, ages three and five, and a boy who is ten. They don't get along at all. The boy and his father don't get along either. And I find myself screaming at the kids and sitting on my son to keep him from hitting and kicking his sisters.
>
> His teacher of the past year thought he needed to learn better ways of getting along with his classmates. He had some problems on the playground and had a horrible time on the school bus. And he didn't seem to be able to walk from the bus stop to our house without getting in a fight or throwing rocks at somebody. So I usually pick him up and bring him home myself.
>
> He is very bright but writes poorly and hates to do it. He is impulsive and quick tempered (we all are now). He is tall and strong. Our pediatrician says he has "everything going for him." But Billy seldom finds anything constructive to do. He likes to watch television, play in the water and dig in the dirt.
>
> We are very upset about his diet, but haven't been able to do anything about it. He drinks milk and eats jello and crackers and toast. In the past he ate lots of hot dogs

and bologna, but not much lately. He also craves chocolate and bubble gum. We have a grandma nearby who sees that he gets lots of it. She also feeds him baby food. We haven't been able to do anything about that, either.

Billy's teachers, the neighbor children and his sisters complain about him swearing and name-calling. This is really an unfortunate situation because we're *always* thinking of him in a bad light. But hardly a day goes by when something isn't upset or broken. He's been breaking windows since he was a toddler. One day in June he came home early from school and found the house locked, so he threw a rock through his bedroom window, broke it, and crawled in. Another day recently he tried the glass cutter on our bedroom mirror. He spends a great deal of time at the grandma's who caters to him. We feel she is a bad influence, but so are we when we're constantly upset and screaming.

Anyhow, we have what seems to be a hopeless situation. He is growing bigger and stronger but not any wiser. So what do we do or where do we go?

My husband says he refuses to take Billy anywhere ever again until he matures and "acts like a civilized human being." He has threatened to put him in a foster home. I couldn't send him to a foster home. He needs people who know what to do with him. Please help us if you can.

Yours truly,
Mrs. T.

P.S. Our children are adopted and there isn't much of anything left in our marriage.

This is a very sad plea for help, because the writer is undoubtedly sincere in professing "more than anything else in the world I want to have a happy family." From the tone of her letter, however, it is unlikely that she will *ever* realize her greatest desire. In fact, that specific need for peaceful coexistence and harmony has probably led to many of her problems with Billy. The mother is making two very serious mistakes with her son which are among the most common disciplinary errors.

First, Billy's parents have taken no steps to shape his will, although he is begging for their intervention. It is a terrifying thing to be your own boss at ten years of age— unable to find even one adult who is strong enough to earn your respect. Why else would this lad break every rule and attack every figure of authority? Billy waged war on his teacher at school, but she was baffled by his challenge. All she knew to do was to call his trembling mother and report, "Billy needs to learn better ways of getting along with his classmates." (Didn't she phrase it kindly? You can bet there were some stronger things she could have said about his classroom behavior!)

Billy has been an intolerable brat on the school bus, and he fought with his classmates on the way home, and he broke windows and cut mirrors and used the foulest language and tormented his sisters. He selected the worst possible diet and refused to complete his academic assignments or accept any form of responsibility. Can there be any doubt that Billy was screaming, "Look! I'm doing it all wrong! Doesn't anyone love me enough to care? Can't anyone help me?! I hate the world and the world hates me!"

But Mrs. T's only response to Billy's defiance has been one of utter frustration and distress. She finds herself "screaming at the kids" and "sitting on (her) son" when he misbehaves. Billy is impulsive and quick tempered, but Mrs. T. admits "we all are now." Both she and her husband feel grandma is a bad influence, "but so are we when we are constantly upset and screaming." You see, her only "tool" for control is the use of anger and high-pitched wailing and weeping. There is *no* more ineffective approach to child management than this display of volcanic emotion, as we will see in the following chapter.

Clearly Mrs. T. and her husband have abdicated their responsibilities to provide *leadership* for their family. Note how many times she says, in essence, *we are powerless to act*. These parents were distressed over Billy's poor diet, "but we haven't been able to do anything about it." Billy's grandmother fed him junk food and bubble gum, but "we haven't been able to do anything about that, either." Likewise, they couldn't stop him from swearing or tormenting his sisters or breaking windows or throwing rocks at his peers. We who are observing must wonder, why not? Why is the family ship so difficult to steer? Why is it likely to be dashed to pieces on the rocks or run aground on a sandy beach? The problem is that the ship has no captain! It is drifting aimlessly in the absence of a leader—a decision maker—an authority—who could guide it to safer waters.

Now, please note this second error: instead of shaping Billy's rampaging will, as it desperately needed, *his parents directed their disciplinary efforts at his damaged spirit*. Not only did they scream and cry and wring their hands in despair, but their frustrations gave rise to personal attacks and hostile rejection. Can't you hear his angry father shouting, "Why don't you grow up and act like a civilized human being instead of an intolerable brat?! Well, I'll tell you something! I'm through with you! I'll never take you anywhere again or even let anyone know that you are my son. As a matter of fact, I'm not sure you are going to *be* my son for very long. If you keep acting like a lawless thug we're going to throw you out of this family—we're going to put you in a foster home. Then we'll see how you like it!" And with each accusation, Billy's self-esteem moved down another notch. But did these personal assaults make him sweeter or more cooperative? Of course not! He just became meaner and more bitter and more convinced of his own worthlessness. You see, Billy's spirit had been crushed, but his will raged undiminished at hurricane force. And sadly, he is the kind of individual who, as he grows older, often turns his self-hatred on innocent victims outside his family.

If circumstances permitted, it would be my pleasure to have Billy in our home for a period of time. It's not too late to save him and I would feel challenged by the opportunity to try. How would I approach this defiant youngster? By giving him the following message as soon as his suitcase was unpacked: "Billy, there are several things I want to talk over with you, now that you're a member of our family. First, you'll soon learn how much we love you in this house. I'm glad you're here, and I hope these will be the happiest days of your life. And you should know that I care about your feelings and problems and concerns. We invited you here because we wanted you to come, and you will have the same love and respect our own children receive. If you have something to say to me, you can come right out and say it. I won't get angry or make you regret expressing yourself. Neither my wife nor I will ever intentionally do anything to hurt you or treat you unkindly. You'll see that these are not just empty promises that you're hearing. This is the way people act when they love each other, and we already love you.

"But, Billy, there are some other things you must also understand. There are going to be some definite rules and acceptable ways to behave in this home, and you are going to have to live within these boundaries just as our other children do. You will carry your share of responsibilities and jobs, and your school work will be given high priority each evening. And you need to understand, Billy, that my most important job as your guardian is to see that you behave in ways that are healthy to yourself and others. It may take you a week or two to adjust to this new situation, but you're going to make it and I'm going to be here to help you. And when you refuse to obey, I will punish you immediately. This will help you change some of the harmful, destructive ways you've learned to behave. But even when I must discipline you, I will love you as much as I do right now."

The first time Billy disobeyed what he knew to be my definite instructions, I would react decisively. There would be no screaming or derogatory accusations, although he would soon know that I meant what I had said. He would probably be given a stiff spanking and sent to bed an hour or two early. The following morning we would discuss the issue rationally, reassure him of our continuing love, and then start over. Most delinquent children respond beautifully to this one-two punch of love, and consistent discipline. It's an unbeatable combination!

To repeat, our guiding purpose is to shape the child's will without breaking his spirit. This dual objective is outlined for us throughout the Scriptures, but is specifically stated in two important references:

Shaping the will
> He (the father) must have the proper authority in his own household and be able to control and command the respect of his children. 1 Tim. 3:4, 5 (Phillips)

Preserving the spirit
> And now a word to you parents. Don't keep on scolding and nagging your children, making them angry and resentful. Rather, bring them up with loving discipline the Lord himself approves, with suggestions and godly advice. Ephesians 6:4 (TLB)

Questions

Question: You probably remember the very popular book of a few years ago, entitled *Jonathan Livingston Seagull*. It was about a gull who refused to cooperate with the flock and follow the dictates of his "society." The real meaning of the book, of course, related to the virtues of individuality and independence in the *human* family. Will you comment on the book and its deeper theme.

Answer: This book expressed a damaging philosophy that became popular about eight years ago, which can be summarized by the phrase "Do your own thing." It means, in brief, that I'm protecting my own self-interests and will do whatever suits my fancy, regardless of the needs of others or the moral values of my society. Other words have been used to express the same selfish orientation, including "Looking out for ol' number one," and "If it feels good, do it." This hedonistic viewpoint inspired many other books and songs, including a heart-wrenching ballad by Sammy Davis, Jr. entitled "I've Gotta Be Me." (Who else could he be, pray tell?) It was also responsible for an incredibly brazen recording by Frank Sinatra, titled "I Did It My Way."

It is my conviction that these messages are directly contradictory to the essence of Christianity which puts its emphasis on giving, sharing, caring, loving, turning the other cheek, going the second mile, and accepting God's commandments. Furthermore, extreme selfishness has the power to blow a family (or a society) off the face of the earth. I wonder how many mothers and fathers of that era took flight, as suggested by J. L. Seagull, in search of an individuality at any price? Waiting at home were vulnerable kids who will carry the scars of parental rejection until the day they die! It has been my sad responsibility to treat some of these little victims whose parents were proudly "doing it their way."

Philip Yancey wrote the following statement about sea gulls as related to human behavior:

> It's easy to see why people like the sea gull. I've sat overlooking a craggy harbor and watched one. He exults in freedom. He thrusts his wings backward with powerful strokes, climbing higher, higher until he's above all other gulls, then coasts downward in majestic loops and circles. He constantly performs, as if he knows a movie camera is trained on him, recording.
>
> In a flock, though, the sea gull is a different bird. His majesty and dignity melt into a sordid slough of in-fighting and cruelty. Watch that same gull as he dive-bombs into a group of gulls, provoking a flurry of scattered feathers and

angry squawks, to steal a tiny morsel of meat. The concepts of sharing and manners do not exist among gulls. They are so fiercely competitive and jealous that if you tie a red ribbon around the leg of one gull, making him stand out, you sentence him to execution. The others in his flock will furiously attack him with claws and beaks, hammering through feathers and flesh to draw blood. They'll continue until he lies flattened in a bloody heap.[2]

If we must select a bird to serve as a model for our society the sea gull is not the best choice. Yancey has suggested that we consider the behavior of geese, instead. Have you ever wondered why these remarkable birds fly in "V" formation? Science has recently learned that the flock actually travels up to 71 percent faster and easier by maintaining this pattern. The goose on the point of the "V" has the most difficult assignment, resulting from greater wind resistance. Thus, that lead position is rotated every few minutes in the air, which permits the flock to fly long distances without rest. The easiest flight is experienced at the two rear sections of the formation and, remarkably, the strong geese permit the young, weak, and old birds to occupy those less strenuous positions. It is even believed that the constant "honking" of the flock is a method by which the stronger birds encourage the laggards. Furthermore, if a goose becomes too tired or is ill and has to drop out of the flock, he is never abandoned. A healthy bird will follow the ailing one to the ground and wait with him until he can continue in flight. This cooperation within the social order contributes greatly to the survival and well-being of the flock.

Yancey concludes,

The sea gull teaches me to break loose and fly. But the goose goes farther: he teaches me to fly "in a family." With the support of friends and Christians who care for me, I can far outstrip the aeronautical feats of any sea gulls. I can fly further with the family than I ever could alone. And as I fly, my effort helps each other member of the family.

Alas, there are times when I feel our society consists of 200 million solitary sea gulls, each huffing and puffing to do his own thing, but paying an enormous price in loneliness and stress for his individuality.

Question: Why do children seem to love teachers who are the strongest disciplinarians?

Answer: Well, your statement is only partially true. No one likes a mean old grouch, even if he does maintain strict order and deportment. But you are right in implying that children are drawn to the teacher who can control a class without sacrificing an attitude of love and pleasantness. And that is a highly developed art which most top-notch teachers have discovered.

In answer to your question, children love good disciplinarians primarily because they are afraid of each other and want the security of a leader who can provide a safe atmosphere. *Anything* can happen in the absence of adult leadership.

NOTE: I have deliberately deleted references to classroom discipline in this book. A subsequent book is planned on the subject of discipline for teachers.

Question: Do you think some children are unintentionally cruel to each other?

Answer: I am certain of it. In fact, I lived it. When I was approximately eight years old, I attended a Sunday school class as a regular member. One morning a visitor entered our class and sat down. His name was Fred, and I can still see his face. More important, I can still see Fred's ears. They were curved in the shape of a reversed "C," and protruded noticeably. I was fascinated by the shape of Fred's unusual ears because they reminded me of jeep fenders (we were deep into World War II at the time). Without thinking of Fred's feelings, I pointed out his strange feature to my friends, who all thought Jeep Fenders was a terribly funny name for a boy with bent ears. Fred seemed to think it was funny, too, and he chuckled along with the rest of us. Suddenly, Fred stopped laughing. He jumped to his feet, red in the face (and ears), and rushed to the door crying. He bolted into the hall and ran from the building. Fred never returned to our class.

I remember my shock over Fred's violent and unexpected reaction. You see, I had *no* idea that I was embarrassing him by my little joke. I was a sensitive kid and often defended the underdog, even when I was a youngster. I would *never* have hurt a visitor on purpose—and that is precisely my point. Looking back on the episode, I hold my teachers and my parents responsible for that event. They should have told me what it feels like to be laughed at . . . especially for something different about your body. My mother, who was very wise with children, has since admitted that she should have taught me to feel for others. And as for the Sunday school leaders, I don't remember what their curriculum consisted of at that time, but what better content could they have presented than the *real* meaning of the commandment, "Love thy neighbor as thyself"?

Question: I know that adoption is common today, and children should be able to take the news in stride. But I'm still uneasy about explaining this matter to my toddler and would like some advice on "how to."

Answer: The best answer I've found for that question was written by Dr. Milton I. Levine, as published in *Your Child from 2 to 5.*[3] I'll quote his statement and then comment on his views:

Common-Sense Approaches to Adoption

ADOPTING children has become such an accepted practice these days that the quavering question, *"Shall* I tell him he's *adopted?"* doesn't even qualify as soap-opera dialogue any more. Most parents realize that telling a youngster from the earliest possible moment provides the only solid foundation for his and their security.

However, as Dr. Milton I. Levine, advisory board member of *2-to-5 World News* and Associate Professor of Pediatrics, New York Hospital–Cornell Medical Center, points out: "Even though adoption is no longer regarded as a shameful secret but rightly as a logical matter of fact, the situation still demands delicacy, understanding, and many common-sense decisions on the part of parents."

Parents should tell the child about his adoption from the time he begins to beg for stories, says Dr. Levine. This will spare the youngster serious shock that can accompany the revelation in later years. Parents might treat the story as a wondrous chapter in the family's history. But the tendency to put off a decision sometimes affects even the best-intentioned adoptive parents. "Let's wait until he's old enough to understand," they may say, and delay the explanation until a basic fact turns into a dark secret. In Dr. Levine's opinion, even five- and six-year-olds are too old to be told without resultant emotional damage. He urges parents to:

1. Tell the child about his adoption from the moment he is ready to listen to stories.
2. Use the word "adopted" in the narrative until it becomes a synonym for "chosen" and "selected" and "wanted."
3. Make no attempt to conceal the adoption, even though moving into a new neighborhood might invite concealment.

"Some adoptive parents never seem to outgrow an apologetic attitude based on a feeling that they are merely pinch-hitting for the child's 'own' parents," says Dr. Levine. "For their own mental health, as well as their child's, they must accept the fact that they are, in reality, the youngster's parents. The mother and father who raise a child from infancy, giving him the love and care that enable him to grow freely, *are* the *real* parents; the strangers who produced the baby are merely *biological* parents. The difference can't be stressed strongly enough. By imparting to the child, even unconsciously, an unjustified feeling of loss—a feeling that he *had parents*, but now has substitutes, however loving—these adoptive parents endanger the child's security in his closest relationships and retard his understanding of the true role of parent."

Even professionals are divided over what to tell adopted children about their biological parents, Dr. Levine admits. There are at least three possible approaches, he points out, but not one can qualify as an answer:

1. Tell the child his biological parents are dead.
2. State plainly that the biological parents were unable to care for their baby themselves.
3. Tell the child nothing is known about the biological parents, but that he was secured from an agency dedicated to finding good homes for babies.

"There are pros and cons to all of these solutions," emphasizes Dr. Levine, who prefers the first approach because: "The child who is told that his biological parents are dead is free to love the mother and father he lives with. He won't be tormented by a haunting obligation to search for his biological parents when he's grown.

"Since the possibility of losing one's parents is one of childhood's greatest fears, it is true that the youngster who is told that his biological parents are dead may feel that all parents—including his second set—are pretty impermanent," concedes Dr. Levine. "Nevertheless, I feel that in the long run the child will find it easier to adjust to death than to abandonment. To tell a youngster that his parents gave him up because they were unable to take care of him is to present him with a complete rejection. He cannot comprehend the circumstances which might lead to such an act. But an unwholesome view of himself as an unwanted object, not worth fighting to keep, might be established."

Sex education is another thorny problem for adoptive parents. Any simple, natural explanation of reproduction stresses that a baby is conceived out of his mother's and father's love for each other and their desire to have a child. This explanation is reassuring to other children. But it may, because of the complexity of his situation, cause the adopted child to feel estranged from his adoptive parents, dubious about his own beginnings, and a little out of step with nature in general.

I would disagree with Dr. Levine only in reference to comments made about the biological parents. I am unwilling to lie to my child about anything, and would not tell him that his natural parents were dead if that were not true. Sooner or later, he will learn that he has been misled, which could bring the entire adoption story under suspicion.

Instead, I would be inclined to tell the child that very little is known about his biological parents. Several inoffensive and vague possibilities could be offered to him, such as, "We can only guess at the reasons the man and woman could not take care of a baby. They may have been extremely poor and unable to give you the care you needed; or perhaps the woman was sick; or she may not have had a home. We just don't know. But we *do* know that we're thankful that you could come be our son (or daughter), which was one of the greatest gifts God ever gave to us."

Furthermore, I would add three suggestions to Dr. Levine's comments. First, Christian parents should present the adoptive event as a tremendous blessing (as implied above) that brought great excitement to the household. Tell about praying for a child and waiting impatiently for God's answer. Then describe how the news came that the Lord had answered those prayers, and how the whole family thanked Him for His gift of love. Let your child know your delight when you first saw him lying in a crib, and how cute he looked in his blue blanket, etc. Tell him that his adoption was one of the happiest days of your life, and how you raced to the telephone to call all your friends and family members to share the fantastic news. (Again, I'm assuming that these details are true.) Tell him the story of Moses' adoption by Pharaoh's daughter, and how God chose him for a great work with the children of Israel. Look for other, similar illustrations which convey respect and dignity to the adoptee. You see the child's interpretation of the adoptive event is almost totally dependent on the manner in which it is conveyed during the early years. Most certainly, one does not want to approach the subject sadly, admitting reluctantly that a dark and troublesome secret must now be confessed.

Second, celebrate *two* birthdays with equal gusto each year: the anniversary of his birth, and the anniversary of the day he became your son (or daughter). While other natural children in the family celebrate one birthday, the second hoopla will give the adopted child a compensative edge to offset any differences he might feel relative to his siblings. And use the word "adopted" openly and freely, until it loses its esoteric sting.

Third, when the foundation has been laid and the issue defused, then forget it. Don't constantly remind the child of his uniqueness to the point of foolishness. Mention the matter when it is appropriate, but don't reveal anxiety or tension by constantly throwing adoption in the child's face. Youngsters are amazingly perceptive at "reading" these thinly disguised attitudes.

I believe it is possible, by following these common sense suggestions, to raise an adopted child without psychological trauma or personal insult.

The Common Errors

Dr. Benjamin Spock, noted pediatrician and author, has been severely criticized in recent years for his laissez-faire approach to child rearing. He has been blamed for weakening parental authority and producing an entire generation of disrespectful and unruly children. To the man on the street, Dr. Spock has become a symbol of permissiveness and overindulgence in parent-child relationships.

Despite his wishy-washy reputation, Dr. Spock published an article several years ago in *Redbook* Magazine which was clearly supportive of firm discipline. Consider the following quotations from the surprising publication entitled, "How Not to Bring Up a Bratty Child"[1]:

Inability to be firm is, to my mind, the commonest problem of parents in America today.

A parent says, "Lunch is ready—come in now." The child pretends not to hear and the parent, despite her realization that the child is not going to cooperate on occasions such as this, dodges the issue and goes indoors.

A parent says, "It's cold today; you should wear your snowsuit." The eight-year-old child says, "I don't want to," and the parent doesn't reply. Fifteen minutes later the same conversation is repeated and comes to the same inconclusive ending.

A child says, "I want another piece of candy." The parent says, "You know you are meant to have only one." The child says, "But I want another," and slowly takes it, watching to be sure that the parent doesn't get angry. The parent decides to let it pass.

None of these episodes are at all serious in themselves. If they continue, however, the child's personality will become balkier and peskier as the months and years go by. The wear and tear on the parents from this kind of low-key battling is painful and exhausting.

The commonest reason, I think, why parents can't be firm is that they're afraid that if they insist, their children will resent them or at least won't love them as much. You can see this clearly in an extreme case in which a bratty child can get what she or he wants by shouting, "I hate you!" The parent looks dismayed and gives in promptly.

Of course most of us dislike unpleasantness, and prefer for this reason to accommodate others, including our own children. But that's not a sensible reason for giving in to them unreasonably, since we sense that this only invites more demands and arguments.

And in conclusion, Dr. Spock wrote:

The way to get a child to do what must be done or stop doing what shouldn't be done is to be clear and definite each time. Part of the definiteness consists of keeping an eye on her until she complies. I'm not recommending the overbearing manner of a drill sergeant that would rub anyone the wrong way. The manner can be and should be friendly. A firm, calm approach makes the child much more likely to cooperate—politely, promptly and completely.

I know this is true. I've seen it work not just hundreds but thousands of times. Parental firmness also makes for a happier child.

I found the content of this article to be refreshing and yet confusing. Could these traditional views have been written by Dr. Benjamin Spock—the great paragon of permissiveness? Could the world's most famous anti-disciplinarian actually be recommending parental firmness and authority? I finally concluded that the aging pediatrician must have reevaluated his views and revised some of his earlier recommendations and conclusions.

I was impressed by the courage that was required for Dr. Spock to write such an article. Perhaps the most difficult assignment for any lofty professional is to state publicly, in effect, "I was wrong." It would be even more difficult for the pediatrician to admit his errors, considering the criticism he has received during the past decade. Nevertheless, he confessed in the *Redbook* publication, "We didn't realize, until it was too late, how our know-it-all attitude was undermining the self assurance of parents."[2]

I appreciated his candor and felt compelled to send him a cordial letter to convey my respect. I thanked him for the courage he demonstrated and complimented his views which correlated so well with my own. Then I stated,

> In actuality, neither of us formulated those principles which you expressed so eloquently this month. They were inspired by the Creator of children more than 2000 years ago. Isn't it interesting that He is always right in the final analysis?

Included with my letter to Dr. Spock was a copy of my book *Dare to Discipline*. (That took some gall.) Several weeks later, I received the following reply from his office in New York.

BENJAMIN SPOCK, M. D.
SECRETARIAL ADDRESS (THIRD FLOOR)
538 MADISON AVENUE
NEW YORK, NEW YORK 10022

SECRETARIAL PHONE
(212) 421-1085

April 13, 1974

James Dobson, Ph.D.
Childrens Hospital of Los Angeles
4650 Sunset Boulevard
P.O. Box 54700
Los Angeles, California 90054

Dear Dr. Dobson:
    Thank you for your book and your letter.

    Actually my February article contains nothing that I haven't said again and again

for 25 years. It was those who hadn't read
BABY AND CHILD CARE and my magazine articles but who resented my opposition to the
war in Vietnam who called me a permissivist.

Sincerely,

Benjamin Spock

Whereas I had been unable to harmonize the *Redbook* views with Dr. Spock's reputation, I was even more confused by the content of his letter. His article was definitely self-critical and apologetic in tone, yet he claimed to have said nothing new or unique in that statement. The puzzle appeared to be indecipherable.

Later in 1974, I was granted an opportunity to meet Dr. Spock in person. We were both guests on Barbara Walters' "Not for Women Only" television show, along with two other panel members who write for parents, Dr. Helen Derosis and Dr. Lee Salk. We taped five programs that one day, although the shows were broadcast throughout an entire week. (After a program has been filmed, the hostess and guests retire backstage for a few minutes, change coats and ties or dresses, and return to the set. Thus it appears that five different visits have been made to the studio, when in reality the programs are shot back-to-back.)

I was seated beside Dr. Spock throughout the five-part series, and we ate lunch together. Therefore, I had approximately six hours to get acquainted with the physician whose first book for parents sold 28 million copies and has been published in dozens of languages. We talked about his views on child rearing, and ultimately discussed his article in *Redbook* Magazine.

Based on these conversations, I am firmly convinced that Dr. Benjamin Spock believes in the value of consistent discipline and parental leadership. His reputation for permissiveness is largely unjustified, and is, in fact, a matter that he resents deeply. Dr. Spock blames Dr. Norman Vincent Peale for confusing the public on his views, and believes that the minister's deeper motive was to discredit him for his passivist stance on the Viet Nam war. I can't speak for Dr. Peale, but I do believe Dr. Spock's views have been grossly misrepresented to the American public. I found him to be a very gentle, unassuming man who did not seek the parental influence that fell to him. He told me he agreed to write *Baby and Child Care* only because the publisher assured him that it could be done quickly and "didn't have to be a great book."

It is obvious that Dr. Spock and I are in opposite camps on many issues; he is a political liberal and I tend to be conservative. He is a Freudian and I am most certainly not. He apparently does not share my Christian perspective. However, on the issue of discipline, I do not find myself in disagreement with the views he now expresses. Toward the end of the final "Not for Women Only" program, actress Polly Bergen (filling in for Barbara Walters) asked the panel members, one by one, if we believed in spankings. All four of us endorsed the use of corporal punishment when appropriate, including Dr. Benjamin Spock. And if his earlier writings are examined carefully, one can find the recommendations for parental control represented, but not emphasized, therein. Very little was written which would earn him the title of "Ultimate Permissivist," although he recommended following permissive feeding schedules. (I certainly agree that babies should be fed when they are hungry, regardless of the clock or some arbitrary feeding plan.) Throughout his book, I feel he took a rather reasonable approach to parent-child relationships.

Why have I gone to considerable lengths to set the record straight with regard to Dr. Spock's views? Perhaps I feel I owe the man an apology for having contributed to the confusion in my earlier statements about his work. But also, the American people who are angry over the present permissive trends in this country should know that they are shooting at the wrong target. There are thousands of psychologists, psychiatrists, and self-appointed experts around us who are offering far more foolish recommendations than does the aging pediatrician. One of those writers, educator John Holt, is quoted in a subsequent chapter and makes Dr. Spock appear downright oppressive by comparison.

Another reason for referring to Dr. Spock's article in *Redbook* Magazine is to emphasize one of his observations which I have also found to be extremely important. He stated,

> A child—let's say a girl—instantly detects parental hesitancy, parental guilt, parental crossness. These attitudes challenge her to resist requests and to demand more privileges. Her peskiness in turn makes the parent increasingly resentful inside, until this finally explodes in a display of anger—great or small—that convinces the child she must give in. In other words, parental submissiveness doesn't avoid unpleasantness; it makes it inevitable.[3]

How accurate is this statement by Dr. Spock! The parent who is most anxious to avoid conflict and confrontation often finds himself screaming and threatening and ultimately thrashing the child. Indeed, child abuse may be the end result.

This leads us to *the* most common error in disciplining children, and perhaps the most costly. I am referring to the inappropriate use of *anger* in attempting to control boys or girls. I touched this subject in *Dare to Discipline,* but I feel it must be given greater stress at this point.

There is no more ineffective method of controlling human beings (of all ages) than the use of irritation and anger. Nevertheless, *most* adults rely primarily on their own emotional response to secure the cooperation of children. One teacher said on a national television program, "I like being a professional educator, but I hate the daily task of teaching. My children are so unruly that I have to stay mad at them all the time just to control the classroom." How utterly frustrating to be required to be mean and angry as part of a routine assignment, year in and year out. Yet many teachers (and parents) know of no other way to lead children. Believe me, it is exhausting and it doesn't work!

Consider your *own* motivational system. Suppose you are driving your automobile home from work this evening, and you exceed the speed limit by forty miles per hour. Standing on the street corner is a lone policeman who has not been given the means to arrest you. He has no squad car or motorcycle; he wears no badge, carries no gun, and can write no tickets. All he is commissioned to do is stand on the curb and scream insults as you speed past. Would you slow down just because he shakes his fist in protest?

Of course not! You might wave to him as you streak by. His anger would achieve little except to make him appear comical and foolish.

On the other hand, nothing influences the way Mr. Motorist drives more than occasionally seeing a black and white vehicle in hot pursuit with nineteen red lights flashing in the rear view mirror. When his car is brought to a stop, a dignified, courteous patrolman approaches the driver's window. He is six foot nine, has a voice like the Lone Ranger, and carries a sawed-off shotgun on each hip. "Sir," he says firmly but politely, "our radar unit indicates you were traveling sixty-five miles per hour in a twenty-five-mile zone. May I see your driver's license, please?" He opens his leatherbound book of citations and leans toward you. He has revealed no hostility and offers no criticisms, yet you immediately go to pieces. You fumble nervously to locate the small document in your wallet (the one with the horrible Polaroid picture). Why are your hands moist and your mouth dry? Why is your heart thumping in your throat? Because the course of *action* that John Law is about to take is notoriously unpleasant. Alas, it is his *action* which dramatically affects your future driving habits.

Disciplinary action influences behavior; anger does not. As a matter of fact, I am convinced that adult anger produces a destructive kind of disrespect in the minds of our children. They perceive that our frustration is caused by our inability to control the situation. We represent justice to them, yet we're on the verge of tears as we flail the air with our hands and shout empty threats and warnings. Let me ask: Would *you* respect a superior court judge who behaved that emotionally in administering legal justice? Certainly not. This is why the judicial system is carefully controlled to appear objective, rational, and dignified.

I am not recommending that parents and teachers conceal their legitimate emotions from their children. I am not suggesting that we be like bland and unresponsive robots who hold everything inside. There are times when our boys and girls become insulting or disobedient and our irritation is entirely appropriate. In fact, it *should* be revealed, or else we appear phony and unreal. My point is merely that anger often becomes a *tool* used consciously for the purpose of influencing behavior. It is ineffective and can be damaging to the relationship between generations.

Let's look at a specific illustration that could represent any one of twenty million homes this afternoon. Henry is in the second grade and arrives home from school in a whirlwind of activity. He has been wiggling and giggling since he awakened this morning, but incredibly, he still has excess energy to burn. His mother, Mrs. Gerritol, is not in the same condition. She has been on her feet since staggering out of bed at 6:30 A.M. She fixed breakfast for the family, cleaned the mess, got Dad off to work, and sent Henry to school, and then settled into a long day trying to keep her twin toddlers from killing themselves. By the time Henry blows in from school, she has put in eight hours' work without a rest. (Toddlers don't take breaks, so why should their mothers?)

Despite Mom's fatigue, she can hardly call it a day. She still has at least six hours of work left to do, including going to the grocery store, fixing the evening meal, washing the dishes, giving the twins their baths, putting on their diapers, tucking them in bed, helping Henry with his homework, joining in his prayers, brushing his teeth, reading him a story, saying good-night, and then bringing him four glasses of water throughout the closing forty-five minutes of the evening. I get depressed just thinking about the weary Mrs. Gerritol and her domestic duties.

Henry is not so sympathetic, however, and arrives home from school in a decidedly mischievous mood. He can't find anything interesting to do, so he begins to irritate his uptight mother. He teases one of the twins to the point of tears, and pulls the cat's tail, and spills the dog's water. Mother is nagging by this time, but Henry acts like he doesn't hear her. Then he goes to the toy closet and begins jerking out games and boxes of plastic toys and Pickup Stix. Mom knows that someone is going to have to clean up all that mess and she has a vague notion about who will get the assignment. The intensity of her voice is rising again. She orders him to the bathroom to wash his hands in preparation for dinner. Henry is gone for fifteen minutes, and when he returns his hands are still dirty. Mom's pulse is pounding through her veins by this time, and there is a definite migraine sensation above her left eye.

Finally, the day wears down to its concluding responsibility: Henry's bedtime. But Henry does not *want* to go to bed and he knows it will take his harassed mother at least thirty minutes to get him there. Henry does not do *anything* against his wishes unless his mother becomes very angry and "blows up" at him. Mrs. Gerritol begins the emotional process of coercing her reluctant son to take his bath and prepare for bed. This portion of the story was included in *Dare to Discipline,* and we will quote from that description[4]:

> Eight-year-old Henry is sitting on the floor, playing with his games. Mom looks at her watch and says, "Henry, it's nearly nine o'clock (a thirty minute exaggeration) so gather up your junk and go take your bath." Now Henry knows, and Mom knows, that she doesn't mean for him to go take a bath. She merely meant for him to start *thinking* about going to take his bath. She would have fainted dead away if he had responded to her empty command. Approximately ten minutes later, Mom speaks again, "Now, Henry, it is getting later and you have to go to school tomorrow, and I want those toys picked up; then go get in that tub!" She still does not intend for Henry to obey, and he knows it. Her *real* message is "We're getting closer, Hank." Henry shuffles around and stacks a box or two to demonstrate that he heard her. Then he settles down for a few more minutes of play. Six minutes pass, and Mom issues another command, this time with more passion and threat in her voice. "Now listen, young man, I told you to get a move on, and I meant it." To Henry, this means he must get his toys picked up and meander toward the bathroom door. If his mom pursues him with a rapid step, then he must carry out the assignment posthaste. However, if Mom's mind wanders before she performs the last step of this ritual, Henry is free to enjoy a few more seconds reprieve.
>
> You see, Henry and his mom are involved in a one-act play; they both know the rules and the role being enacted by the opposite player. The entire scene is programmed, computerized, and scripted. Whenever Mom wants Henry to do something he dislikes, she progresses through graduated steps of phony anger, beginning with

calm and ending with a red flush and a threat. Henry does not have to move until she reaches the peak anger point. How foolish this game is! Since Mom controls him by the use of empty threats she has to stay mad all the time. Her relationship with her children is contaminated, and she ends each day with a pounding, throbbing headache. She can never count on instant obedience; it takes her at least 20 minutes to work up a believable degree of anger.

How much better it is to use *action* to get action. There are hundreds of tools which will bring the desired response, some of which involve pain while others offer the child a reward. . . . Minor pain can provide excellent motivation for the child, when appropriate. You see, the parent should have some means of making the child want to cooperate, other than simply obeying because he was told to do so. For those who can think of no such device, I will suggest one: there is a muscle, lying snugly against the base of the neck. Anatomy books list it as the trapezius muscle, and when firmly squeezed, it sends little messengers to the brain saying, "This hurts; avoid recurrence at all costs." The pain is only temporary; it can cause no damage. When the youngster ignores being told to do something by his parent, he should know that Mom has a practical recourse.

Let's return to the bedtime issue between Henry and his Mom; she should have told him that he had fifteen more minutes to play. It then would have been wise to set the alarm clock or the stove buzzer to sound in fifteen minutes. No one, child or adult, likes a sudden interruption to his activity. When the time came, Mom should have quietly told Henry to go take his bath. If he didn't move immediately, the shoulder muscle could have been squeezed. If Henry learns that this procedure is invariably followed, he will move before the consequence is applied.

There will be those among my readers who feel that the deliberate, premeditated application of minor pain to a sweet little child is a harsh and unloving recommendation. I ask those skeptics to hear me out. Consider the alternatives. On the one hand, there is constant nagging and strife between parent and child. When the youngster discovers there is no threat behind the millions of words he hears, he stops listening to them. The only messages he responds to are those reaching a peak of emotion, which means there is much screaming and yelling going on. The child is pulling in the opposite direction, fraying Mom's nerves and straining the parent-child relationship. But the most important limitation of these verbal reprimands is that their user often has to resort to physical punishment in the end, anyway. Thus, instead of the discipline being administered in a calm and judicious manner, the parent has become unnerved and frustrated, swinging wildly at the belligerent child. There was no reason for a fight to have occurred. The situation could have ended very differently if the parental attitude had been one of confident serenity. Speaking softly, almost pleasantly, Mom says, "Henry, you know what happens when you don't mind me; now I don't see any reason in the world why I should have to make you feel pain to get your cooperation tonight, but if you insist, I'll play the game with you. When the buzzer sounds you let me know what your decision is." The child has a choice to make, and the advantages to him of obeying his mother's wishes are clear. She need not scream. She need not threaten to shorten his life. She need not become upset. She is in command. Of course, Mother will have to prove two or three times that she will apply the pain, if necessary, and occasionally throughout the coming months her child will check to see if she is still at the helm. But there is no question in my mind as to which of these two approaches involves the least pain and the least hostility between parent and child.

An understanding of the interaction between Henry and his mother can be very helpful to parents who have become "screamers" and don't know why. Let's look at their relationship during that difficult evening as diagrammed on Figure 3. Note that Henry's mother greeted him at the front door after school, which represented a low

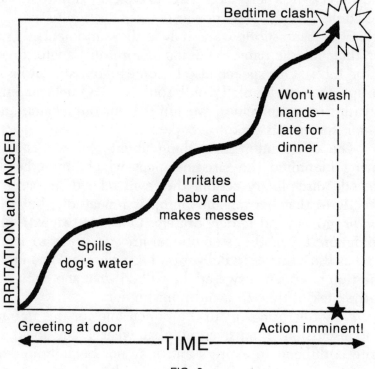

FIG. 3

point of irritation. From that time forward, however, her emotion built and intensified until it reached a moment of explosion at the end of the day.

By her ultimate display of anger at bedtime, Mrs. Gerritol made it clear to Henry that she was through warning and was now ready to take definite action. You see, most parents (even those who are very permissive) have a point on the scale beyond which they will not be pushed; inevitable punishment looms immediately across that line. The amazing thing about children is that they know *precisely* where their parents typically draw the line. We adults reveal our particular points of action to them in at least a dozen subtle ways: only at those moments do we use their middle names (William Thornton Langford, get in the tub!!). Our speech also becomes more staccato and abrupt, (Young! Man! I! Told! You! . . .) Our faces turn red (an important clue), we jump from our chairs, and Junior knows it is time to cooperate.

The other interesting thing about children is that having identified the circumstances which immediately precede disciplinary action, they will take their parents directly to that barrier and bump it repeatedly, but will *seldom* go beyond it deliberately. Once or twice Henry will ignore his mother's emotional fireworks, just to see if she has the courage to deliver on her promise. When that question has been answered, he will do what she demands in the nick of time to avoid punishment.

Now this brings us to the punch line for this important discussion. I must admit that what I am about to write is difficult to express and may not be fully understood by my readers. It can, however, be of value to parents who want to stop fighting with their children.

I have said that parental anger often signals to Junior that he has reached his action line. Therefore, he obeys, albeit reluctantly, only when Mom or Dad "get mad," indicating that they will now resort to punishment. On the other hand, the parents observe that Junior's surrender occurs simultaneously with their anger and inaccurately conclude that their emotional explosion is what forced him to yield. Thus, their anger seems necessary for control in the future. They have grossly misunderstood the situation.

Returning to the story of Henry, his mother told him six or eight times to take his bath. Only when she "blew up" did he get in the tub, leading her to believe that her anger produced his obedience. She is wrong! It was not her anger that sent Hank to the suds—it was the *action* which he believed to be imminent. Her anger was nothing more than a tip-off that Mom was frustrated enough to spank his pink bottom. Henry *cares* about that!

I have written this entire chapter in order to convey this one message: you don't *need* anger to control children. You *do* need action, occasionally. Furthermore, you can apply the action anywhere on the time line that is convenient, and children will live contentedly within that boundary. In fact, the closer the action moves to the front of the conflict the less punishment is required. A pinch of the trapezius muscle would not be a sufficient deterrent at the end of a two-hour struggle, whereas it is more than adequate when the conflict is minimal. (Incidentally, I do not recommend that mothers weighing less than ninety pounds try to squeeze the shoulder muscles of their big teen-agers. There are definite risks involved in that procedure. The general rule to follow is, "If you can't reach it, don't squeeze it.")

Let me return to Dr. Spock's valuable observation, particularly as it applies to the diagram. "Parental submissiveness (by that he refers to parents who have *no action line*, or else it occurs too late) doesn't avoid unpleasantness; it makes it inevitable." (If you don't take a stand early, a child is *compelled* by his nature to push you further.) The child's defiance, then, "makes the parent increasingly more resentful, until it finally explodes in a display of anger." That is precisely what I have been attempting to say for the past thirteen years!

Contained in this statement is an understanding of children which some adults grasp intuitively, while others never quite "feel it." It involves the delicate balance between love and control, recognizing that a reasonable and consistent action-line does not assault self-worth, but represents a source of security for an immature child.

Fathers often comprehend this principle better than mothers, for reasons which escape me. Thus, it is very common for a mother to say to me: "I don't understand my kids. They will do exactly what their father demands, but they won't mind me at all." The behavior of her children is no mystery. They are bright enough to notice that Dad draws his action line earlier than Mother. She screams and argues, while he quietly acts.

Children often understand these forces even better than their parents who are bogged down with adult responsibilities and worries. That is why so many kids are able to win the contest of wills; they devote their *primary* effort to the game, while we grownups play only when we must. One father overheard his five-year-old daughter,

Laura, say to her little sister who was doing something wrong, "Mmmmm, I'm going to tell Mommie on you. No! I'll tell Daddy. He's worse!" Laura had evaluated the disciplinary measures of her two parents, and concluded that one was more effective than the other.

This same child was observed by her father to have become especially disobedient and defiant. She was irritating other family members and looking for ways to avoid minding her parents. Her dad decided not to confront her directly about this change in behavior, but to punish her consistently for every offense until she settled down. Thus, for three or four days, he let Laura get away with nothing. She was spanked, stood in the corner, and sent to her bedroom. At the conclusion of the fourth day, she was sitting on the bed with her father and younger sister. Without provocation, Laura pulled the hair of the toddler who was looking at a book. Her dad promptly thumped her on the head with his large hand. Laura did not cry, but sat in silence for a moment or two, and then said, "Hurrummph! All my tricks are not working!"

If the reader will recall his own childhood years, he will probably remember similar events in which the disciplinary techniques of adults were analyzed consciously and their weaknesses probed. When I was a child, I once spent the night with a rambunctious friend who seemed to know every move his parents were going to make. Earl was like a military general who had deciphered the enemy code, permitting him to outmaneuver his opponents at every turn. After we were tucked into our own twin beds that night, he gave me an astounding description of his father's temper.

Earl said, "When my dad gets very angry, he uses some really bad words that will amaze you." (He listed three or four startling examples from past experience.)

I replied, "I don't believe it!"

Mr. Walker was a very tall, reserved man who seemed to have it all together. I just couldn't conceive of his saying the words Earl had quoted.

"Want me to prove it to you?" said Earl mischievously. "All we have to do is keep on laughing and talking instead of going to sleep. My dad will come and tell us to be quiet over and over, and he'll get madder and madder every time he has to settle us down. Then you'll hear his cuss words. Just wait and see."

I was a bit dubious about this plan, but I did want to see the dignified Mr. Walker at his profane best. So Earl and I kept his poor father running back and forth like a yo-yo for over an hour. And as predicted, he became more intense and hostile each time he returned to our bedroom. I was getting very nervous and would have called off the demonstration, but Earl had been through it all before. He kept telling me, "It won't be long now."

Finally, about midnight, it happened. Mr. Walker's patience expired. He came thundering down the hall toward our room, shaking the entire house as his feet pounded the floor. He burst through the bedroom door and leaped on Earl's bed, flailing at the boy who was safely buried beneath three or four layers of blankets. Then from his lips came a stream of words that had seldom reached my tender ears. I was shocked, but Earl was delighted.

Even while his father was whacking the covers with his hand and screaming his profanity, Earl raised up and shouted to me, "Didja hear em? Huh? Didn't I tell ya? I tolja he would say it!" It's a wonder that Mr. Walker didn't kill his son at that moment!

I lay awake that night thinking about the episode and made up my mind *never* to let a child manipulate me like that when I grew up. Don't you see how important disciplinary techniques are to a child's respect for his parents? When a forty-five-pound bundle of trouble can deliberately reduce his powerful mother or father to a trembling, snarling mass of frustrations, then something changes in their relationship. Something precious is lost. The child develops an attitude of contempt which is certain to erupt during the stormy adolescent years to come. I sincerely wish every adult understood that simple characteristic of human nature.

Near my home in Arcadia, California, is a tan gentleman who certainly understands the way children think. He owns and operates Bud Lyndon's Swim School. Mr. Lyndon must be approaching sixty years of age now, and he has been working with youngsters most of his life. He has a remarkable comprehension of the principles of discipline, and I enjoy sitting at poolside just to watch the man work. However, there are few child developmentalists who could explain why he is so successful with the little swimmers in his pool. He is not soft and delicate in his manner; in fact, he tends to be somewhat gruff. When the kids get out of line he splashes water in their faces and says sternly, "Who told you to move? Stay where I put you until I ask you to swim!" He calls the boys "Men of Tomorrow," and other pet names. His class is regimented and every minute is utilized purposefully. But would you believe it, the children *love* Bud Lyndon. Why? Because they know that he loves them. Within his gruff manner is a message of affection that might escape the adult observer. Mr. Lyndon never embarrasses a child intentionally, and he "covers" for the youngster who swims more poorly. He delicately balances his authority with a subtle affection that attracts children like the Pied Piper. Mr. Bud Lyndon understands the meaning of discipline with love.

When I was in the ninth grade I had an athletic coach who affected me the same way. He was the master of the moment, and no one *dared* challenge his authority. I would have fought wild lions before tackling Mr. Ayers. Yes, I feared him. We all did. But he never abused his power. He treated me courteously and respectfully at a time when I needed all of the dignity I could get. Combined with his acceptance of the individual was an obvious self-confidence and ability to lead a pack of adolescent wolves who had devoured less capable teachers. And that's why my ninth-grade gym coach had a greater influence on me than any other person during my fifteenth year. Mr. Craig Ayers understood discipline with love.

Not every parent can be like Mr. Lyndon or Mr. Ayers, and I would not suggest that they try. Nor would it be wise for a mother to display the same gruffness at home that is appropriate on the athletic field or at the pool. Each person must fit his approach to discipline within his own personality patterns and the responses that feel natural. However, the overriding principle remains the same for men and women, mothers and fathers, coaches and teachers, pediatricians and psychologists: it involves discipline with love, a reasonable introduction to responsibility and self-control, parental leadership with a minimum of anger, respect for the dignity and worth of the child, realistic boundaries that are enforced with confident firmness, and a judicious use of rewards and punishment to those who challenge and resist. It is a system that bears the approval of the Creator Himself.

Questions

Question: It's easy for you to tell me not to get angry at my children, but there are times when they just make me furious. For example, I have a horrible time getting my ten-year-old daughter ready to catch the school bus each morning. She will get up when I insist, but she dawdles and plays as soon as I leave the room. I have to goad and push and warn her every few minutes or else she will be late. So I get more and more angry, and usually end up by screaming insults at her. I know this is not the best way to handle the little brat, but I declare, she makes me want to clobber her. Tell me how I can get her moving without this emotion every day.

Answer: You are playing right into your daughter's hands by assuming the responsibility for getting her ready each morning. A ten-year-old should definitely be able to handle that task on her own steam, but your anger is not likely to bring it about. We had a very similar problem with our own daughter last year. Perhaps the solution we worked out will be helpful to you.

Danae's morning time problem related primarily to her compulsivity about her room. She will not leave for school each day unless her bed is made perfectly and every trinket is in its proper place. This was not something we taught her; she has always been very meticulous about her possessions. (I should add that her brother, Ryan, does not have that problem.) Danae could easily finish these tasks on time if she were motivated to do so, but she was never in a particular hurry. Therefore, my wife began to fall into the same habit you described, warning, threatening, pushing, shoving, and ultimately becoming angry as the clock moved toward the deadline.

Shirley and I discussed the problem and agreed that there had to be a better method of getting through the morning. I subsequently created a system which we called "Check-points." It worked like this. Danae was instructed to be out of bed and standing erect before 6:30 each morning. It was her responsibility to set her own clock-radio and get herself out of bed. If she succeeded in getting up on time (even one minute later was considered a missed item) she immediately went to the kitchen where a chart was taped to the refrigerator door. She then circled "yes" or "no," with regard to the first checkpoint for that date. It couldn't be more simple. She either did or did not get up by 6:30.

The second checkpoint occurred forty minutes later at 7:10. By that time, she was required to have her room straightened to her own satisfaction, be dressed and have her teeth brushed, hair combed, etc., and be ready to begin practicing the piano. Forty minutes was ample time for these tasks, which could actually be done in ten or fifteen minutes if she wanted to hurry. Thus, the only way she could miss the second checkpoint was to ignore it deliberately.

Now, what meaning did the checkpoints have? Did failure to meet them bring anger and wrath and gnashing of teeth? Of course not. The consequences were straightforward and fair. If Danae missed one checkpoint, she was required to go to bed thirty minutes earlier than usual that evening. If she missed two, she hit the "lily whites" an hour before her assigned hour. She was permitted to read during that time in bed, but she could not watch television or talk on the telephone. This procedure took all the morning pressure off Shirley and placed it on our daughter's shoulders, where it belonged. There were occasions when my wife got up just in time to fix breakfast, only to find Danae sitting soberly at the piano, clothed and in her right mind.

This system of discipline can serve as a model for parents who have similar behavioral problems with their children. It was not oppressive; in fact, Danae seemed to enjoy having a target to shoot at. The limits of acceptable performance were defined beyond question. The responsibility was clearly placed on the child. Consequences of noncompliance were fair and easily administered. And it required no adult anger or foot stamping.

There is an adaptation of this concept available to resolve the thorny conflicts in *your* home, too. The only limit lies in the creativity and imagination of the parent.

Question: What other errors do parents commonly make in disciplining their children?

Answer: For one thing, it is very easy to fall into the habit of saying "no" to our children.

"No, you can't go outside."

"No, you can't have a cookie."

"No, you can't use the telephone."

"No, you can't spend the night with a friend." We parents could have answered affirmatively to all of these requests, but chose almost automatically to respond in the negative. Why? Because we didn't take time to stop and think about the consequences; because the activity could cause us more work or strain; because there could be danger in the request; because our children ask for a thousand favors a day and we find it convenient to refuse them all.

While every child needs to be acquainted with denial of some of his more extravagant wishes, there is also a need for parents to consider each request on its own merit. There are so many necessary "no's" in life that we should say "yes" whenever we can.

Dr. Fitzhugh Dodson extended this idea in his book *How to Father.* He wrote of the need for positive interactions with a child when the parent is not demanding anything of him.

Analyze how your child sees you: is 99 percent of your role one in which you are expecting something of him, reminding him to do something, scolding him to stop doing something, or getting after him for misbehaving? If so, you are not building a deep positive emotional relationship. He needs time with you when you are not demanding anything from him, time when the two of you are mutually enjoying yourselves. And he especially needs this time in the first five years of his life, because these are the years for building this kind of relationship with your child. Most abnormal rebellions of adolescents could have been prevented if the father had spent time building a deep and close relationship during the preschool years.[5]

Question: My husband and I are missionaries and have recently been assigned to a remote area of Colombia. Our ministry will be with an Indian culture which can only be reached by horseback or on foot. My concern is for our children, ages seven and nine, and their educational future. There are no schools near our new location, of course, and the nearest boarding facility will be more than 200 miles away. Because of the cost of travel, we would only be able to see them through the summers and perhaps at one other time during the year. Although I could teach them the academic subjects required between now and high school years, they obviously need social contact with their peers and we don't want to deprive them of those experiences. Would you recommend keeping them with us, or sending them away to school?

Answer: "What will we do with the children?" That is often the most difficult question missionaries must answer. I don't propose to have final solutions to this thorny problem, although I do have some definite views on the subject. I've dealt with the children of missionaries, many of whom had become bitter and resentful of the sacrifices they were required to make. They were deprived of a secure home at a critical stage in their development and experienced deep emotional wounds in the process. Consequently, adolescent rebellion was common among these angry young people who resented their parents and the God who sent them abroad.

Based on these observations, it is my firm conviction that the family unit of missionaries should remain intact, if at all possible. I cannot overemphasize the importance of parental support and love during the formative years of life. A child's sense of security and well-being is primarily rooted in the stability of his home and family. Therefore, he is certain to be shaken by separation not only from his parents, but also from his friends and the familiar surroundings of his own culture. He suddenly finds himself in a lonely dormitory in a foreign land where he may face rejection and pressures that threaten to overwhelm him. I can think of no better method of producing emotional (and spiritual) problems in a vulnerable child!

My friend Dr. Paul Cunningham expressed a similar view during a recent conference on family life. His comments were recorded by a court reporter and are quoted below, with Dr. Cunningham's permission:

> I am married to a missionary's daughter who at the age of five and a half was sent to boarding school in Africa, where she saw her parents about three times a year. This represents the most severe kind of sacrifice that a missionary has to face. I have had the privilege of ministering to the children of missionaries, and I think it can be safely said, and I want to say this very carefully, that those children who have had this experience often never fully recover from it.
>
> My wife, for example, was "put down" when she was in the school because of the strong anti-American sentiment there. She was the only American in her school. We're not talking about a child ten or twelve years old, but only six. All in all, it has made her a tremendously strong person, and I doubt if she would have been all that she is to me and to our children had she not had those tough experiences. But at the same time, were she not from strong English stock with tremendous gifts and graces, I don't know . . . maybe she would not have survived, because others haven't.
>
> I can't feel that this is a good policy at this point to make this the only answer for these families . . . to sepa-

rate tender little children from their parents. I know of one situation, for example, where the children have to take a long ride in a riverboat to see their parents; I'm talking about little children. It's a trip of several hours to their mission compound. Their mother says goodbye to them in the fall, and she does not see them for many months because of the expense of traveling. They could be taken by helicopter instead of the riverboat ride, but they don't have the money. We must do something to assist people like this, whatever the cost.

Dr. Cunningham and I agree that the true issue may actually be one of priorities. Meaningful family involvement outranks educational considerations by a wide margin, in my view. Furthermore, contact with parents during the early years is even more important than contact with peers. And finally, even missionaries (who have been called to a life of sacrifice and service) must reserve some of their resources for their own families. After all, a lifetime of successes on a foreign field will be rather pale and insignificant to those who lose their own children.

Question: Are you acquainted with a little booklet for parents entitled, *Children, Fun or Frenzy?* If so, would you comment on its recommendations for discipline of children?

Answer: Yes, I am familiar with that booklet, written by Pat Fabrizio. Many thousands of copies of this publication have been distributed or sold within the Christian community. In it (and in a similar publication entitled *Why Daddy Loves to Come Home*) Mrs. Fabrizio relates her own experiences as a permissive mother whose children were undisciplined and disrespectful. Through a process of struggle she and her husband discovered biblical principles of discipline which resulted in a turning point in their home.

Some valuable concepts are included in this booklet, and I would not condemn it. But I am concerned about Mrs. Fabrizio's undue emphasis on corporal punishment. While she was permissive and wishy-washy in the first instance, she seemed to become obsessed with the necessity of spanking in the second. Thus, it would appear to me that the author went from one extreme to another in her philosophy of child rearing. Let me quote her writings:

". . . *every time* (Fabrizio's italics) I ask my child to do anything, either, 'Come here,' 'Don't touch,' 'Hush,' 'Put that down,' or whatever it is, I must see that he obeys. When I have said it once in a normal tone, if he does not obey immediately, I *must* (italics mine) take up a switch and spank him (love demands this) enough to hurt so he will not want it repeated."

In another instance, she wrote of the necessity of spanking for the "slightest disobedience" and continued, "no matter the nature of the circumstance of the offense, the correction is always the same because the wrongdoing is always one of disobedience."

Likewise, Mrs. Fabrizio describes a spanking that she administered because her daughter, "intended to obey me, but she got busy playing and forgot." These are classic examples of overextending a healthy biblical principle to the point of danger. A spanking should come only in response to deliberate defiance, in my view. It should be the parental reaction to a child's "I will not!" But how unwise to spank a youngster for forgetting! I am even more distressed by an illustration describing an evening when Mr. and Mrs. Fabrizio failed to discipline their naughty toddler before sending him to bed.

> So Daddy went in and woke him. He sat him on his lap until he was thoroughly awake and then told him that Daddy did not have peace about the incident and confessed to him that we had not been obeying the Lord in being sure that he obeyed us. Daddy told him that he would have to spank him because he did not obey. So he spanked him and put him back to bed.[6]

Can you imagine what this was like from a child's perspective? He was awakened out of a sound sleep and spanked for something that happened hours before! A twenty-month-old child can hardly remember his actions from one moment to the next; the events of yesterday are a gray memory. His guilt-ridden father "confessed to him that (he) had not been obeying the Lord." How frightening! What better way is there to give a child nightmares than never to know when the Lord will send Daddy in to spank him for some behavior that was tolerated yesterday?

The reason this booklet frustrates me is that the central message is so badly needed. Children must be taught respect and responsibility. They must be brought under parental authority. And *most* of them need to be spanked now and then. But we are not limited to one disciplinary technique, nor will a single formula fit every situation or every human being. There will be times when a child should be required to spend ten minutes sitting on a chair, as suggested earlier. Or a privilege may be taken away or the child may be sent to bed an hour early. There are many measures which should be varied to fit the offense and the circumstances. And occasionally, I have found it useful to talk to a repentant child and grant him unexpected and undeserved mercy. My point is that children are infinitely complex, and their leadership requires tact, cunning, courage, skill, and knowledge.

Ultimately, the key to competent parenthood is in being able to get behind the eyes of your child, seeing what he sees and feeling what he feels. When he is lonely, he needs your company. When he is defiant, he needs your help in controlling his impulses. When he is afraid, he needs the security of your embrace. When he is curious, he needs your patient instruction. When he is happy, he needs to share his laughter and joy with those he loves.

Thus, the parent who intuitively comprehends his child's feelings is in a position to respond appropriately and meet the needs that are apparent. And at this point, raising healthy children becomes a highly developed art, requiring the greatest wisdom, patience, devotion and love that God has given to us. The Apostle Paul called the Christian life a "reasonable service." We parents would do well to apply that sane standard to the behavior of our children.

I don't want to be too critical of Mrs. Fabrizio's writings, for it is apparent that she seeks to implement biblical principles which we both love and trust. However, overzealousness with children can be a dangerous virtue. You see, it is extremely important that boys and girls understand the purpose of punishment and perceive it as reasonable and deserved. When spankings are given routinely for the "slightest disobedience," then lasting resentment can be generated which sets the stage for later adolescent explosions.

Question: You have discussed child abuse and the anger of parents. Would you comment further on the violence in our society at large, and the forces which are propelling it?

Answer: There are few subjects that cause me greater concern than the exposure being given to crime and violence in America today. Only yesterday, a squadron of Los Angeles police cornered a desperate gunman in a residential area of the community. The fugitive had barricaded himself in a small house, and held three juvenile hostages inside. Television crews were on hand to photograph one of the children, a teen-aged boy, as he was forced outside and then shot in the head by his abductor, who subsequently committed suicide. The pathetic young victim died on the sidewalk in a pool of his own blood. I sat stunned, literally sick to my stomach, while the drama was broadcast in full color last night.

A flood of emotions ran through my mind as I gazed into the immobile, unfocused eyes of the dying adolescent. Mixed with deep pity and remorse was a sudden outpouring of indignation—a revulsion which has been accumulating for years. I was angry at the profiteers who have nurtured violence in our society, and at those millions who seem to thrive on it; I was angry at movie producers like Sam Peckinpah, who have smeared blood and guts all over the silver screen; I was angry at theater patrons for demanding a dozen disembowelments per hour in their visual entertainment; I was angry at television networks for giving us continuous police stories, with their guns and silly automobile chases and karate chops and

SWAT teams. I was angry at the Supreme Court for legalizing 900,000 abortions by American women last year; I was angry at the Palestine Liberation Army for killing eight innocent athletes at the Olympic Games in Munich; I was angry at Truman Capote for writing *In Cold Blood,* and at his thrill-seeking readers for wanting to know how a peaceful family was mercilessly butchered on their farm; and I was particularly angry at the pathetic system of American justice which makes crime so profitable and punishment so improbable.

But my indignation will change nothing and the wave of violence and lawlessness will continue unabated. We have become so desensitized to human suffering and exploitation that even the most horrible events are accepted as part of our regular evening "entertainment" on the tube.

I think it is time that millions of decent, law-abiding citizens rise up with one voice to oppose the industries that are profiting from violence. A valiant campaign of this nature was waged in 1977 by the National Parent Teacher Association, directing their efforts at television networks and companies that support the most damaging programs. Of course, this pressure from the PTA brought an anguished cry of "foul play" from the greedy profiteers whose pockets were lined with bloodstained money. Nevertheless, Sears Roebuck, Union Oil, and other large companies pledged to sponsor no more violent programs on television. This form of economic sanction is the most powerful tool available to influence our free enterprise system, and we should use it incisively against those who would destroy us from within. We have sat on our hands long enough!

Question: How do you feel about the Equal Rights Amendment which is being supported by the women's movement?

Answer: I am in favor of constitutional rights for both women and men, but I am unalterably opposed to this amendment. Why? Because the wording is so nebulous that the ultimate interpretation of its meaning will be made by the nation's judicial system. And frankly, I don't trust the judges to whom the legal issues will be appealed. I've seen their handiwork during the past ten years, and shudder to think that the future of our families may depend on their decisions. America's homes are too important to risk annihilation in the Federal courts. Anything that threatens this foundation of democracy must be viewed with alarm. Mine is not a popular view, but I feel it strongly.

The Scourge of Sibling Rivalry

5

In a recent book I described an episode that best expresses the frustration of parenthood. It happened when our son, Ryan, was four months old and my wife put him on the dressing table to change his diapers. As soon as she removed his wet garments, he made like a fountain and sprayed the wall and the carpet and a picture of Little Boy Blue. Shirley had no sooner repaired the damage when the telephone rang; while she was gone, Ryan was struck by a sudden attack of projectile diarrhea, and he machine-gunned his crib and the rest of the nursery. By the time my patient wife bathed her son and scoured the room, she was near exhaustion. She dressed Ryan in clean, sweet-smelling clothes and put him over her shoulder affectionately. At that moment, he deposited his breakfast down her neck and into her undergarments. When I arrived home from work that evening, I found Shirley sitting in a darkened corner of the family room, muttering quietly to herself and slowly shaking her head from side to side.

Such is the price of procreation. (One father described his infant son as "a noise at one end and a mess at the other.") I think it is time for us to admit that being a mother or father is not only one of life's greatest joys, but it can also represent a personal sacrifice and challenge. Everything of value is expensive, and children are no exception to the rule. On the other hand, I am also convinced that many of the frustrations of raising children result from our failure to plan and organize and understand the issues. Few problems of parenthood are new or unique; we have all experienced similar difficulties. And there are better ways of coping. Let's take a fresh look, then, at two of these universal stress points in this chapter and the next.

Bitter Brothers and Surly Sisters

If American women were asked to indicate *the* most irritating feature of child rearing, I'm convinced that sibling rivalry would get their unanimous vote. Little children (and older ones too) are not content just to hate each other in private. They attack one another like miniature warriors, mobilizing their troops and probing for a weakness in the defensive line. They argue, hit, kick, scream, grab toys, taunt, tattle, and sabotage the opposing forces. I knew one child who deeply resented being sick with a cold while his older sibling was healthy, so he secretly blew his nose on the mouthpiece of his brother's musical instrument! The big loser from such combat, of course, is the harassed mother who must listen to the noise of the battlefield and then try to patch up the wounded. If her emotional nature requires peace and tranquillity (and most women do) she may stagger under the barrage of cannon fire.

Columnist Ann Landers recently asked her readers to respond to the question, "If you had known then what you know now, would you have had children?" Among ten thousand women who answered, 70 percent said No! A subsequent survey by *Good Housekeeping* posed the same question and 95 percent of the respondents answered Yes. It is impossible to explain the contradictory results from these two inquiries, although the accompanying comments were enlightening. One unidentified woman wrote, "Would I have children again? A thousand times, NO! My children have completely destroyed my life, my marriage, and my identity as a person. There are no joys. Prayers don't help—nothing stops a 'screaming kid.' "

It is my contention that something *will* stop a screaming kid, or even a dozen of them. It is not necessary or healthy to allow children to destroy each other and make life miserable for the adults around them. Sibling rivalry is difficult to "cure" but it can certainly be treated. Toward that objective, let me offer three suggestions which should be helpful in achieving a state of armistice at home.

1. *Don't Inflame the Natural Jealousy of Children.*

Sibling rivalry is not new, of course. It was responsible for the first murder on record (when Cain killed Abel), and has been represented in virtually every two-child family from that time to this. The underlying source of this conflict is old-fashioned jealousy and competition between children. Marguerite and Willard Beecher, writing in their book *Parents on the Run,* expressed the inevitability of this struggle as follows:

> It was once believed that if parents would explain to a child that he was having a little brother or sister, he would not resent it. He was told that his parents had enjoyed him so much that they wanted to increase their happiness. This was supposed to avoid jealous competition and rivalry. It did not work. Why should it? Needless to say, if a man tells his wife he has loved her so much that he now plans to bring another wife into the home to "increase his happiness," she would not be immune to jealousy. On the contrary, the fight would just begin—in exactly the same fashion as it does with children.[1]

If jealousy is so common, then how can parents minimize the natural antagonism which children feel for their siblings? The first step is to avoid circumstances which compare them unfavorably with each other. Lecturer Bill Gothard has stated that the root of all feelings of inferiority is *comparison.* I agree. The question is not "How am I doing?" It is "How am I doing compared with John or Steven or Marion?" The issue is not how fast can I run, but who crosses the finish line first. A boy does not care how tall he is; he is vitally interested in "who is tallest." Each child systematically measures himself against his peers, and is tremendously sensitive to failure within his own family.

Accordingly, parents should guard against comparative statements which routinely favor one child over another. This is particularly true in three areas. First, children are extremely sensitive about the matter of physical attractiveness and body characteristics. It is highly inflammatory to commend one child at the expense of the other. Suppose, for example, that Sharon is permitted to hear the casual remark about her sister, "Betty is sure going to be a gorgeous girl." The very fact that Sharon was not mentioned will probably establish the two girls as rivals. If there is a significant difference in beauty between the two, you can be assured that Sharon has already concluded, "Yeah, I'm the ugly one." When her fears are then confirmed by her parents, resentment and jealousy are generated.

Beauty is *the* most significant factor in the self-esteem of Western children, as I attempted to express in *Hide or Seek*. Anything that a parent utters on this subject within the hearing of children should be screened carefully. It has the power to make brothers and sisters hate one another.

Second, the matter of intelligence is another sensitive nerve to be handled with care. It is not uncommon to hear parents say in front of their children, "I think the younger boy is actually brighter than his brother." Adults find it difficult to comprehend how powerful that kind of assessment can be in a child's mind. Even when the comments are unplanned and are spoken routinely, they convey how a child is "seen" within his family. We are all vulnerable to that bit of evidence.

Third, children (and especially boys) are extremely competitive with regard to athletic abilities. Those who are slower, weaker, and less coordinated than their brothers are rarely able to accept "second best" with grace and dignity. Consider, for example, the following note given to me by the mother of two boys. It was written by her nine-year-old son to his eight-year-old brother, the evening after the younger child had beaten him in a race.

> Dear Jim:
> I am the greatest and your the badest. And I can beat everybody in a race and you can't beat anybody in a race. I'm the smartest and your the dumbest. I'm the best sport player and your the badest sport player. And your also a hog. I can beat anybody up. And that's the truth. And that's the end of this story.
>
> Yours truly,
Richard

This note is humorous to me, because Richard's motive was so poorly disguised. He had been badly stung by his humiliation on the field of honor, so he came home and raised the battle flags. He will probably spend the next eight weeks looking for opportunities to fire torpedos into Jim's soft underbelly. Such is the nature of mankind.

Am I suggesting, then, that parents eliminate all aspects of individuality within family life or that healthy competition should be discouraged? Definitely not. I am saying that in matters relative to beauty, brains, and athletic ability, each child should know that in his parents' eyes, he is respected and has equal worth with his siblings. Praise and criticism *at home* should be distributed as evenly as possible, although some children will inevitably be more successful in the outside world. And finally, we should remember that children do not build fortresses around strengths—they construct them to protect weakness. Thus, when a child like Richard begins to brag and boast and attack his siblings, he is revealing the threats he feels at that point. Our sensitivity to those signals will help minimize the potential for jealousy within our children.

2. *Establish a Workable System of Justice.*

Sibling rivalry is also at its worst when there is no reasonable system of justice in the home—where the "lawbreakers" do not get caught, or if apprehended are set free without standing trial. It is important to understand that laws in a society are established and enforced for the purpose of protecting people from each other. Likewise, a family is a mini-society with the same requirement for protection of human rights.

For purposes of illustration, suppose that I live in a community where there is no established law. Policemen do not exist and there are no courts to whom disagreements can be appealed. Under those circumstances, my neighbor and I can abuse each other with impunity. He can take my lawnmower and throw rocks through my windows, while I steal the peaches from his favorite tree and dump my leaves over his fence. This kind of mutual antagonism has a way of escalating day by day, becoming ever more violent with the passage of time. When permitted to run its natural course, as in early American history, the end result can be feudal hatred and murder.

As indicated, individual families are similar to societies in their need for law and order. In the absence of justice, "neighboring" siblings begin to assault one another. The older child is bigger and tougher, which allows him to oppress his younger brothers and sisters. But the junior member of the family is not without weapons of his own. He strikes back by breaking the toys and prized possessions of the older sibling and interferes when friends are visiting. Mutual hatred then erupts like an angry volcano, spewing its destructive contents on everyone in its path.

Nevertheless, when the children appeal to their parents for intervention, they are often left to fight it out among themselves. In many homes, the parents do not have sufficient disciplinary control to enforce their judgments. In others, they are so exasperated with constant bickering among siblings that they refuse to get involved. In still others, parents require an older child to live with an admitted injustice "because your brother is smaller than you." Thus, they tie his hands and render him utterly defenseless against the mischief of his bratty little brother or sister. Even more commonly today, mothers and fathers are both working while their children are at home busily disassembling each other.

I will say it again to parents: one of your most important responsibilities is to establish an equitable system of justice and a balance of power at home. There should be reasonable "laws" which are enforced fairly for each member of the family. For purposes of illustration, let me list the boundaries and rules which have evolved through the years in my own home.

1. Neither child is *ever* allowed to make fun of the other in a destructive way. Period! This is an inflexible rule with no exceptions.

2. Each child's room is his private territory. There are locks on both doors, and permission to enter is a revokable privilege. (Families with more than one child in each bedroom can allocate available living space for each youngster.)

3. The older child is not permitted to tease the younger child.

4. The younger child is forbidden to harass the older child.

5. The children are not required to play with each other when they prefer to be alone or with other friends.

6. We mediate any genuine conflict as quickly as possible, being careful to show impartiality and extreme fairness.

As with any plan of justice, this plan requires (1) respect for leadership of the parent, (2) willingness by the parent to mediate, (3) occasional enforcement or punishment. When this approach is accomplished with love, the emotional tone of the home can be changed from one of hatred to (at least) tolerance.

3. *Recognize That the Hidden "Target" of Sibling Rivalry Is You.*

It would be naive to miss the true meaning of sibling conflict: it often represents a form of manipulation of parents. Quarreling and fighting provide an opportunity for both children to "capture" adult attention. It has been written, "Some children had rather be wanted for murder than not wanted at all." Toward this end, a pair of obnoxious kids can tacitly agree to bug their parents until they get a response—even if it is an angry reaction.

One father told me recently that his son and his nephew began to argue and then beat each other with their fists. Both fathers were nearby and decided to let the fight run its natural course. During the first lull in the action one of the boys glanced sideways toward the passive men and said, "Isn't anybody going to stop us before we get hurt?!" The fight, you see, was something neither boy wanted. Their violent combat was directly related to the presence of the two adults and would have taken a different form if the boys had been alone. Children will often "hook" their parents' attention and intervention in this way.

Believe it or not, this form of sibling rivalry is easiest to control. The parent must simply render the behavior unprofitable to each participant. Instead of wringing their hands and crying and begging and screaming (which actually reinforces the disruptive behavior and makes it worse), a mother or father should approach the conflict with dignity and self-control.

I would recommend that a modified version of the following "speech" be given to quarreling children, depending on the age and circumstances: "Tommy and Chuck, I want you to sit in these chairs and give me your complete attention. Now you both know that you have been harassing and irritating each other all through the morning. Tommy, you knocked over the castle that Chuck was building, and Chuck, you messed up Tommy's hair.

So every few minutes I've found myself telling you to quit quarreling. Well, I'm not angry at you, because all brothers fight like that, but I am telling you that I'm tired of hearing it. I have important things to do, and I can't take the time to be separating a couple of scratching cats every few minutes.

"Now listen carefully. If the two of you want to pick on each other and make yourselves miserable, then be my guest [assuming there is a fairly equal balance of power between them]. Go outside and fight until you're exhausted. But it's not going to occur under my feet anymore. It's over! And you know that I mean business when I make that kind of statement. Do we understand each other?"

Would that implied warning end the conflict? Of course not—at least, not the first time. It would be necessary to deliver on the promise of "action." Having made the boundaries clear, I would act decisively the *instant* either boy returned to his bickering. If I had separate bedrooms, I would confine one child to each room for at least thirty minutes of complete boredom—without radio or television. Or I would assign one to clean the garage and the other to mow the lawn. Or I would make them take a nap. My avowed purpose would be to make them believe me the next time I offered a suggestion for peace and tranquillity.

It is simply not necessary to permit children to destroy the joy in living, as expressed by the frustrated mother to *Good Housekeeping*. And what is most surprising, children are the happiest when their parents enforce these reasonable limits with love and dignity.

Questions

Question: We are planning our family very carefully, and want to space the children properly. Is there an ideal age span that will bring greater harmony between them?

Answer: Children who are two years apart and of the same sex are more likely to be competitive with one another. On the other hand, they are also more likely to enjoy mutual companionship. If you produce your babies four or more years apart there will be less camaraderie between them but at least you'll have only one child in college at a time. My evasive reply to your question reflects my personal bias: There are many more important reasons for planning a baby at a particular time than the age of those already born. Of greater significance is the health of the mother, the desire for another child, financial considerations, and the stability of the marriage. The relative ages of siblings are not one of the major determiners, in my opinion.

Question: (The following excerpt was taken from an actual letter sent to me by a creative mother.) You recommended in *Dare to Discipline* and *Hide or Seek* that we use a monetary reward system to encourage our children to accept new responsibilities. This approach has helped a great deal and our family is functioning much smoother. However, I had an idea for improving the system which has worked beautifully with my two boys, ages six and eight. In order for them to earn a reward for brushing their teeth, making their bed, putting away their clothes, etc., they *both* must complete the jobs as assigned. In other words, I tax them both for one child's failure and reward them both for mutual successes. They got in the spirit of the game immediately, cooperating with one another and working together to achieve the goal. It has made them business partners, in a sense. I thought you would be interested in this approach.

Answer: This mother has done what I hope other parents will do: use my writings as a springboard to creative approaches of their own. My illustrations merely show that the most successful parents are those who find unique solutions to the routine problems of living. The writer of this letter has done that beautifully.

Question: You referred to siblings who manipulate their mothers and fathers. On the other hand, isn't the parent "manipulating" the child by the use of rewards and negative consequences?

Answer: No more than a factory supervisor is manipulating his employees by insisting that they arrive at work by 9 A.M. No more than a policeman manipulates the speeding driver by giving him a traffic ticket. No more than an insurance company manipulates that same driver by increasing his premium. The word "manipulation" implies a sinister or selfish motive. I prefer the term *leadership*, which is in the best interest of everyone concerned—even when it involves unpleasant consequences.

Question: Thank you for admitting that children can be terribly frustrating to parents. It helps just to hear that other mothers have felt the same desire to run—to escape to some quiet place. I think I can do a better job by knowing that I'm not the only woman in the world who occasionally feels inadequate for the task of raising children.

Answer: I receive many comments similar to yours from mothers who have trouble coping with domestic responsibilities. One woman wrote, "I finally got it all together but I can't remember where I left it!" We obviously live in a very hectic period of American history, where fatigue and time pressure are our worst enemies. But running away usually offers no lasting solutions because the problems are *within us* rather than being imposed from the outside. Whenever I hear someone talk simplistically about running from their problems, I'm reminded of the man who concluded during the 1930s that the world was about to disintegrate. Thus, he packed his belongings and moved to the loneliest spot he could find in the South Pacific—a forgotten little island called Guadalcanal. And, of course, he woke up a few years later to find World War II in his front yard. It is very difficult to avoid our problems on this shrinking earth.

I received some desperate mail from people who have fled in the night to escape intolerable frustration at home. Consider the words of the mother who recently wrote the following S.O.S. from an unidentified Holiday Inn.

August 20, 1976

Dear Dr. Dobson:

I am writing you from this motel because I have "run away" from my loving husband, my six-year-old daughter (Annie) and my five-month-old son (Paulie). My little girl is a beautiful blonde with blue eyes, but she throws temper tantrums and irritates me to the breaking point. My son seems to cry twenty-four hours a day. I need one uninterrupted night's sleep so badly.

I've tried so hard to be a good mother and wife . . . a good neighbor and Christian daughter. I've wanted to meet my responsibilities to my family, but I'm completely exhausted. I became a monster this past week. I hit my daughter across the face, bruised her arm from shaking her so hard, yelled and screamed and cried, then wanted to die from guilt.

I've come here to try to get a hold of what's left of me but I don't think I can. I feel my prayers take too long to be answered, or else I don't recognize the answers when they come. When I'm home, there's not enough time to even brush my teeth, let alone pray about Annie's behavior and my inferiority as a parent. If I spank her she retorts, "That didn't even hurt" or she scratches, kicks, and pulls my hair. Yet when I left last night she sobbed for me not to go, despite my reassuring her that I would come back.

We spent $100 last month to take four counseling sessions on parenting techniques. Well, some of it works but some of it is too far removed from my child's misbehavior to do any good. Annie was hostile and aggressive even before Paulie arrived. I can't help wanting to get away from her. She spent a week with Grandma and went to Disneyland recently. I really felt guilty because I hardly missed her.

I just talked with my husband by telephone and he said Annie was having a temper tantrum. She wants to go find me and I don't even want to go home! I adore my husband. I've had little chance to show him how much, and I've been blessed with a daughter and son, both of whom I always wanted to have. The problem now is that I can't handle the "routine panic" of our lives. Next Thursday will be my 28th birthday. Please help me.

Mrs. J. S.

Unfortunately, Mrs. J. S. did not include her return address in her letter and I had no way to contact her. I have often wondered if she received the help she was so desperately seeking in that distant motel.

Perhaps it would be constructive to include another letter which arrived the same week as the one above, expressing a very different kind of despair. It came from Oxford, England, and the writer gave me permission to quote her words of frustration:

Dear Dr. Dobson:

I have just read your book *What Wives Wish Their Husbands Knew About Women,* and was very helped by it. It is one of the best books I have ever read. But, please, why don't you authors ever write for people like me?

Why is nothing written for women who are barren; who desperately long for a child of their own but do not have one. Why don't you help us to live with the feeling of being an incomplete woman, to cope with relatives and friends having babies and rearing their families while you have nothing; to cope with the veiled pressure from family to provide grandchildren for your parents (which you would love to do if only you could); to beat the deep, terrible depressions when finally you become pregnant (twice) only to lose both in miscarriages. To exist around Christmas when *everything's* geared to children and it all just gets unbearable (so that last year I took an overdose of drugs to try and escape it). To look forward hopefully to the future, when there seems to be little to plan for or look forward to.

I know Christ can help; but why don't *people?* Why does society imply that a marriage isn't fulfilled without children, and so add to the guilt and unhappiness?

Why don't people like you ever write books to help people like us?

Yours,
Mrs. R. K.

Mrs. K. is absolutely right. The world seems designed for children and those who produce them. We who have been blessed by little ones should be sensitive to the feelings of those like this woman who value motherhood more than life itself. Human kindness would go a long way toward easing their distress, if we weren't so busy thinking of ourselves. I wish I could get the writer of the first letter together with the author of the second. A fascinating (and helpful?) conversation might develop between them.

Question: I am a single mother and am worried about my seven-year-old son. There are no male members of my family living nearby, so my boy is growing up in a world of women. I am also concerned about how to discipline him. What can I do?

Answer: Your question touches an increasingly important aspect of parenthood in America today. There are vast numbers of divorced or widowed mothers and fathers who struggle with the responsibilities of solitary parenthood. The U.S. Census Bureau reports that households headed by singles under thirty-four increased 55 percent between 1970 and 1973! The upward trend continues to this moment, and its depressing effects are difficult to overstate. I particularly empathize with the single mother, such as yourself, who must arise early each morning, take her children to a child care center, work eight or nine hours at a job, then try to meet the physical, emotional, and spiritual needs of her youngsters at the end of the day when others are resting. It can't be done! Something will be shortchanged. There is simply not enough energy in the human body to work eighteen hours a day, every day, year in and year out. And as your question acknowledges, mothers don't make very good fathers and fathers are often lousy mothers.

Do I have a magic solution for the problem? No. Parenthood was designed to be a two-person job, and when the task falls to a single adult, enormous pressures are inevitable. I can offer two suggestions, however, which may be helpful with regard to the more specific question of masculine identification.

The first will require a small amount of money, but I believe it will be well invested. I would suggest that you call the nearest high school guidance office and ask to speak to the counselor of third or fourth year students. Then explain your need to "rent" a mature, athletic boy who can take your son to a park and teach him to throw a ball, cast a fishing line, or build a playhouse. Request the counselor's recommendation of a stable young man who is likely to enjoy working with a seven-year-old boy. Then pay this fellow the going hourly rate (for high school students) to spend two or three hours with your son each Saturday.

Second, it is clearly the task of the *church* to assist you with your parenting responsibilities. This requirement is implicit in Jesus' commandment that we love and support the needy in all walks of life. He said, "Inasmuch as ye do it unto the least of these, ye do it unto me." If Jesus meant these words, and He obviously did, then our effort on behalf of a fatherless or motherless child is seen by the Master of the universe as a direct service to Himself!

But the commandment to Christians is more explicitly stated in James 1:27: "The Christian who is pure and without fault, from God the Father's point of view, is the one who takes care of orphans and widows, and who remains true to the Lord." (TLB)

Perhaps you could xerox a copy of this page of my book and send it to the pastor of your church, asking if he knows a responsible father within his congregation who might take these scriptural commandments literally.

As to the larger question of discipline by a single parent, let me emphasize that the principles I have outlined remain the same even when the family constellation changes. Children still need discipline and love and stability and opportunity, just as they did when both parents were available to lead them. The only thing unique for the single parent is that the task becomes much more difficult and demanding. (I seriously doubt if any single parents really need me to tell them that!)

Let me recommend a book which may provide additional assistance. It is entitled *The Single Parent,* by Virginia Watts, and is published by Fleming H. Revell (1977). This Christian book provides an overview of the unique problems faced by a single mother or father, and offers some practical suggestions and insights.

Question: Would you comment on the views of Dr. Haim Ginott, who wrote *Between Parent and Child,* and *Between Parent and Teenager?*

Answer: The popular Dr. Ginott was very eloquent in teaching parents to understand and communicate with their children. No one has written more effectively on that subject than he. However, I don't believe he had any significant grasp of the principles of discipline. If you go through his books and lift out his statements relating to teaching respect and responsibility, all of his recommendations leaned in the direction of permissiveness. Consider the four paraphrased examples that follow.

Concerning Homework:

Dr. Ginott recommended that parents not assume *any* responsibility for overseeing children's homework. They were advised to remain uninvolved, even if a child blatantly chose to disregard his assignments and accept unnecessary failure. The only occasion when they should check or supervise the homework would be at the specific invitation of the student.

Concerning Routine Chores and Responsibilities:

It was Ginott's opinion that the assignment of routine chores at home could have a detrimental influence on the development of a child's character. Whereas daily obligations might produce cleaner houses and yards and contribute to obedience, Ginott felt the emotional consequences of these tasks were on the negative side of the ledger. Even when pets were adopted by the child, the parents were to retain responsibility for their care and maintenance.

Concerning Spankings:

As might be predicted, Ginott viewed spankings as an act of violence on the part of the parent. He felt this form of punishment gave children a taste of the jungle, and taught them to hit and abuse others. Instead of spankings, Ginott hoped that parents could find some civilized outlets for their *own* uncivilized emotions.

Concerning Public Rowdiness:

Ginott gave an example of a child who jumped on the sofa while he and his mother were visiting Aunt Mary. Incredibly, Ginott recommended that the mother ignore her bouncing son, leaving the discipline exclusively in the hands of Aunt Mary. His point was that children obey outsiders more readily than mothers and fathers who should be relieved of disciplinary responsibilities while in the homes of others.

Regarding this final example, can't you visualize the scene? Donnie is turning cartwheels on Auntie Mary's new sofa, while Mother sits passively as though she doesn't notice. Auntie's blood pressure is zinging up near 220 but she's too civilized to do what she's thinking. When she finally blows, she's liable to throw Donnie and his stoic momma right through the front door. Ginott didn't see it that way. He stated that the host has the responsibility to establish rules and enforce them in his own home. Let's suppose, as Ginott suggests, that Aunt Mary quietly takes the bouncing Donaldo by the neck and crams him into a chair in the corner. Then we would see some dramatic changes in Mom's blood pressure. The only one remaining cool in both instances is the little brat who was using the furniture as a trampoline.

No, Dr. Ginott had little understanding of the principles of discipline, from my point of view. His books do have other value, however.

The Problem of Hyperactivity

or Jiggle, Jump, Climb, and Roll on the Floor

We should turn our attention now to the common problem of hyperactivity, which parents also find particularly distressing. A mother complained to me recently that her preschooler was like a human jet engine, flying at top velocity during every waking hour. She said trying to get him to hold still was like trying to sew a button on a poached egg. My deepest sympathies are with her. I have seen similar children in my practice who threatened to destroy my office during the course of a brief visit.

One such youngster was a seven-year-old boy named Kurt who was afflicted with Downs Syndrome (a form of mental retardation which was originally called mongolism). This little fellow was frantically active, and literally "attacked" my furniture when he entered the room. He

161

scrambled over the top of my desk, knocking over pictures and files and paper weights. Then this lad grabbed for the telephone and held it in the direction of my ear. I humored him by faking a conversation with a mythical caller, but Kurt had other purposes in mind. He jumped from my desk and scurried into the office of a psychologist next door, insisting that my colleague play the same game. As it happened, our two phones were on the same extension, and this little seven-year-old boy had succeeded in outsmarting the two child development "experts." There we were, talking to each other on the phone without anything relevant to say. It was a humbling experience.

A truly hyperactive child can humble any adult, particularly if the disorder is not understood by his parent. His problem is certainly relevant to the theme of this book, since there are no more "strong-willed" children than those whose defiance and disobedience have an organic or emotional origin. Let's discuss the nature of this behavioral difficulty, then, and offer some suggestions for discipline and management of affected youngsters. Perhaps a question and answer format will allow us to present the topic most expeditiously.

What Is Hyperactivity?

Hyperactivity (also called hyperkinesis, minimal brain dysfunction, impulse disorder, and at least thirty other terms) is defined as excessive and *uncontrollable* movement. It usually involves distractibility, restlessness, and a short attention span. I italicized the word uncontrollable, because the severely affected child is absolutely incapable of sitting quietly in a chair or slowing down his level of activity. He is propelled from within by forces he can neither explain or ameliorate.

What Causes the Phenomenon?

Hyperactivity often appears related to damage to the central nervous system, although it can also be caused by emotional stress and fatigue. Some authorities believe that virtually all children born through the birth canal (that is, not by cesarean section) are likely to sustain damage to brain tissue during the birth process. The difference between patients who are severely affected (and are called cerebral palsied) and those who have no obvious symptoms may reflect three variables: (1) Where the damage is located; (2) How massive the lesion is; and (3) How quickly it occurred. Thus, it is possible that some hyperactive children were afflicted by an unidentified brain interference very early which caused no other symptoms or problems. I must emphasize, however, that this explanation is merely speculative and that the medical understanding of this disorder is far from complete.

How Can Damage to Brain Tissue Cause Frantic Activity in a Child?

Relatively little is known about the human brain and its malfunctions. I knew one neurologically impaired child, for example, who could read the words, "Go shut the door," with no understanding of the written command. However, if a tape recording was made while he read, "Go shut the door," this child could hear the replay of his own voice and understand the words perfectly. Another patient in a mental hospital could completely disassemble and repair complex television sets, yet did not have the common sense to handle the routine responsibilities of living outside a hospital setting. Another man, wounded in combat, had the sad characteristic of being unable to keep any thought to himself. He mumbled his innermost ideas, to the embarrassment and shock of everyone nearby.

Brain disorders are expressed in many strange ways, including the frenzy of hyperactivity. No one can explain exactly why it happens, other than the obvious fact that the electrochemical mechanisms which control body movement have been altered, resulting in excessive stimulation to the muscles.

How Can Anxiety or Emotional Problems Cause Hyperactivity?

When adults are under severe stress or anxiety, their inner tension is typically expressed in the form of physical activity. An expectant father "paces the floor," or smokes one cigarette after another, or his hands may tremble. A basketball coach will race up and down the sidelines while the outcome of the game is in doubt. Another anxious person may sit quietly in a chair, but his fingernails will be chewed into the quick or he will move his lower jaw slowly from side to side. My point is that tension increases the amount of bodily movement observed in adults.

How much more true that is of an immature child. He doesn't merely drum his fingers on a table when he is anxious; he tries to climb the curtains and walk on the ceiling.

How Early Can the Problem Be Identified?

The severely hyperactive child can be recognized during early toddlerhood. In fact, he can't be ignored. By the time he is thirty months of age he may have exhausted his mother, irritated his siblings, and caused the grandparents to retire from babysitting duties. No family member is "uninvolved" with his problem. Instead of growing out of it, as the physician may promise, he continues to attack his world with the objective of disassembling it. Dr. Domeena Renshaw described one such child in her excellent book *The Hyperactive Child:*

> The youngest patient brought to the author was a 1½-year-old boy, youngest in a sibship of six. The father was a civil engineer. The mother cheerful and sensible. She reported a normal labor but a very rapid delivery. The child developed slowly till age fifteen months when he began to run, not having crawled. He had then begun to speak in sentences, not having babbled at all. From then on, "it was like having a hurricane in the house, everything up for grabs." He would climb out of his crib (by fifteen months) early in the morning and not fall asleep till midnight. Daytime naps had ceased by fifteen months. His activity was ceaseless. He was extremely distractible, never watched TV, never finished a meal without needing to be brought back to his highchair at the table a dozen times. He had no concept of danger, had two greenstick arm fractures from two falls from the same tree (three similar falls resulted in abrasions only). He was consid-

ered a "bully" by his sibs and older peers. He did not respond to rewards or punishments.[1]

We will see what happened to this child later in this chapter.

Is There a "Normal" Hyperactivity?

Certainly. Not every child who squirms, churns, and bounces is technically "hyperactive." Most toddlers are "on the move" from dawn to dark (as are their mothers).

Then How Can I Tell Whether My Child Is Just Normally Active or Genuinely Hyperactive? And How Can I Decipher Whether His Problem Is the Result of Emotional or a Physical Impairment?

These questions are difficult to answer, and few parents have the training to resolve them. Your best resource in evaluating your child's problem is your pediatrician or family physician. Even he may have to guess at a diagnosis and its cause. He can, however, make a complete medical evaluation and then refer you, if necessary, to other professionals for specific assistance. Your child may require the services of a remedial reading teacher or a speech and hearing therapist or a psychologist who can assess intellectual and perceptual abilities and offer management advice. You should not try alone to cope with an excessively active child if this additional support and consultation is available.

What Role Does Nutrition Play?

The role of nutrition in hyperactivity is a very controversial issue which I am not qualified to resolve; I can only offer my opinion on the subject. The American people have been told that hyperactivity is a product of red food coloring, too much sugar intake, inadequate vitamins, and many related causes resulting from poor nutrition. I don't doubt for a moment that improper eating habits have the capacity to destroy us physically and could easily be related to the phenomenon of hyperactivity. However, I am of the opinion that the writers of many faddish books on this subject are trying to make their guesses sound like proven facts. Many of the answers are not yet available, which explains why so many "authorities" disagree violently among themselves.

The nutritionists whom I respect most highly are those who take a cautious, scientific approach to these complex questions. I am suspicious of the self-appointed experts who bypass their own professional publications and come directly to the lay public with unsupported conclusions which even their colleagues reject.

The above paragraph may irritate some parents who are following the advice of a lone-wolf nutritional writer. To those readers I can only say, "Do what succeeds." If your child is more calm and sedate when avoiding certain foods, then use your judgment as you continue the successful dietary regimen. Your opinion is probably as valid as mine.

How Common Is Hyperactivity?

Authorities disagree on the incidence of hyperactivity, but this disorder apparently affects between 6 and 10 percent of all children under ten years of age. Males outnumber females four to one.

How Do Parents React?

The mother of a hyperactive child typically experiences a distressing tug of war in her mind. On the one side, she understands her child's problem and feels a deep empathy and love for her little fellow. There is nothing that she wouldn't do to help him. But on the other side, she resents the chaos he has brought into her life. Speedy Gonzales spills his milk and breaks vases and teeters on the brink of disaster throughout the day. He embarrasses his mother in public and shows little appreciation for the sacrifices she is making on his behalf. By the time bedtime arrives, she often feels as if she has spent the entire day in a foxhole.

What happens, then, when genuine love and strong resentment collide in the mind of a mother or father? The inevitable result is parental guilt in sizeable proportions—guilt that is terribly destructive to a woman's peace of mind and even to her health.

What Other Problems Does the Hyperactive Child Face?

The child with exaggerated activity usually experiences three specific difficulties in addition to his frantic motion. First, he is likely to develop psychological problems resulting from rejection by his peers. His nervous energy is not only irritating to adults, but tends to drive away friends as well. He may be branded as a troublemaker and a goof-off in the classroom. Furthermore, his emotional response is often unstable, swinging unpredictably from laughter to tears in a matter of moments, and causing his peers to think him strange. In short, the hyperactive child can easily fall victim to feelings of inferiority and the emotional upheaval which is inevitably generated by rejection and low self-esteem.

Second, the active child frequently experiences severe learning problems during the school years. He finds it difficult, if not impossible, to remain in his seat and concentrate on his lessons. His attention span is miniscule throughout elementary school, which leads to mischievousness and distractibility while his teachers are speaking. He never seems to know what the educational program is all about, and his frustrated teachers often describe him as being "in a fog."

But there is another academic difficulty which is also extremely common among hyperactive children: visual perceptual problems. A child may have perfectly normal vision, yet not "perceive" symbols and printed material accurately. In other words, his eyes may be perfect but his brain does not process the signal properly. Such a child may "see" letters and numbers reversed or distorted. It is particularly difficult for him to learn to read or write.

Reading is a highly complex neurological skill. It requires the recognition of symbols and their transmittal to the brain, where they must be interpreted, remembered, and (perhaps) spoken as language. Any break in this functional chain will inhibit the final product. Furthermore, this process must occur rapidly enough to permit a steady flow of ideas from the written materials. Many hyperactive children simply do not have the neurological apparatus to develop these skills and are destined to experience failure during the primary grades in school.

What Are the Solutions?

There are dozens of medications which have been shown to be effective in calming the hyperactive child. Since every child's chemistry is unique, it may be necessary for a physician to "fish" for the right substance and dosage. Let me stress that I am opposed to the administration of such drugs to children who do not require them. In some instances these substances have been given indiscriminately to children simply because their parents or teachers preferred them sedated, which is inexcusable. Every medication has an undesirable side effect (even aspirin) and should be administered only after careful evaluation and study. However, if your child displays the symptoms I have described in the preceding section and has been evaluated by a neurologist or other knowledgeable physician, you should not hesitate to accept his prescription of an appropriate medication. Some dramatic behavioral changes can occur when the proper substance is identified for a particular child.

The frantic young patient described earlier by Dr. Renshaw was placed on dextroamphetamine, with the following results:

By the third day of treatment he was asleep at 8 P.M. and eating with the family was possible with only two trips away from the table. He is now six years old, doing exceptionally well in regular first grade, and is being seen at the clinic at three-month intervals. (p. 81)

But Won't the Long-term Use of Medication Increase the Possibility of My Child Becoming a Drug User During Adolescence?

Most authorities feel that the use of medication in childhood does not necessarily lead to drug abuse later in life. In fact, a federal task force was appointed in 1971 to consider that possibility. The conclusion from their investigation emphasized the appropriateness of medications in treatment of hyperactive children. Some children need, and should get, the proper calming agent.

Do Medications Solve All the Problems?

Usually not. Let's consider the three primary symptoms as related to medications:

1. *Hyperactivity.* The proper prescription can be very effective in "normalizing" a child's motor activity. Treatment is most successful in controlling this symptom.

2. *Psychological difficulties.* Medication is less effective in eliminating emotional problems. Once a child has been "slowed down," the process of building his self-image and social acceptance must begin in earnest. The administration of drugs may make that objective possible, but it does not, in itself, eradicate the problem.

3. *Visual-perceptual problems.* Drug usage is of no value in resolving neurological malfunctions which interfere with perception. There are training materials available which have been shown to be helpful, including those provided by the Marianne Frostig Center for Educational Therapy. Dr. Frostig is a pioneer in the field of learning disabilities, and has provided books, films, and evaluative tests for use by teachers and trained professionals. Your local school district can obtain a list of available resources by contacting this organization at 5981 Venice Boulevard, Los Angeles, California 90034. Many school districts also provide special classes for children with unique learning disabilities, which can be of inestimable value to a handicapped student.

It is obvious that drug therapy cannot provide the total remedy. A pharmaceutical approach must be combined with parental adaptations and educational alternatives, among others.

How Does the Parent "Discipline" a Hyperactive Child?

It is often assumed that an excessively active child should be indulged, simply because he has a physical problem. I couldn't disagree more. Every youngster needs the security of defined limits, and the hyperactive boy or girl is no exception. Such a child should be held responsible for his behavior, like the rest of the family. Of course, your level of expectation must be adjusted to fit his limitations. For example, most children can be required to sit in a chair for disciplinary reasons, whereas the hyperactive child would not be able to remain there. Similarly, spankings are sometimes ineffective with a highly excitable little bundle of electricity. As with every aspect of parenthood, disciplinary measures for the hyperactive child must be suited to his unique characteristics and needs.

How, then, is the child to be controlled? What advice is available for the parents of a child with this problem? Listed below are eighteen helpful suggestions quoted from the previously mentioned text by Dr. Renshaw.[2]

1. Be carefully consistent in rules and disciplines.
2. Keep your own voice quiet and slow. Anger is normal. Anger can be controlled. Anger does not mean you do not love a child.
3. Try hard to keep your emotions cool by bracing for expectable turmoil. Recognize and respond to any positive behavior, however small. If you search for good things, you will find a few.
4. Avoid a ceaselessly negative approach: "Stop"—"Don't"—"No"—
5. Separate behavior which you may not like, from the child's person, which you like, e.g., "I like you. I don't like your tracking mud through the house."
6. Have a very clear routine for this child. Construct a timetable for waking, eating, play, TV, study, chores, and bedtime. Follow it flexibly although he disrupts it. Slowly your structure will reassure him until he develops his own.
7. Demonstrate new or difficult tasks, using action accompanied by short, clear, quiet, explanations. Repeat the demonstration until learned. This uses audio-visual-sensory perceptions to reinforce the learning. The memory traces of a hyperkinetic child take longer to form. Be patient and repeat.
8. Try a separate room or a part of a room which is his own special area. Avoid brilliant colors or complex patterns in

decor. Simplicity, solid colors, minimal clutter, and a worktable facing a blank wall away from distractions assist concentration. A hyperkinetic child cannot "filter" out overstimulation himself yet.

9. Do one thing at a time: give him one toy from a closed box; clear the table of everything else when coloring; turn off the radio/TV when he is doing homework. Multiple stimuli prevent his concentration from focusing on his primary task.

10. Give him responsibility, which is essential for growth. The task should be within his capacity, although the assignment may need much supervision. Acceptance and recognition of his efforts (even when imperfect) should not be forgotten.

11. Read his pre-explosive warning signals. Quietly intervene to avoid explosions by distracting him or discussing the conflict calmly. Removal from the battle zone to the sanctuary of his room for a few minutes is useful.

12. Restrict playmates to one or at most two at one time, because he is so excitable. Your home is more suitable, so you can provide structure and supervision. Explain your rules to the playmate and briefly tell the other parent your reasons.

13. Do not pity, tease, be frightened by, or overindulge this child. He has a special condition of the nervous system which is manageable.

14. Know the name and dose of his medications. Give these regularly. Watch and remember the effects to report back to your physician.

15. Openly discuss any fears you have about the use of medications with your physician.

16. Lock up all medications, including these, to avoid accidental misuse.

17. Always supervise the taking of medication, even if it is routine over a long period of years. Responsibility remains with the parents! One day's supply at a time can be put in a regular place and checked routinely as he becomes older and more self-reliant.
18. Share your successful "helps" with his teacher. The outlined ways to help your hyperkinetic child are as important to him as diet and insulin are to a diabetic child.

How Should the Parent Respond to School Failure?

Let's talk about the child with a learning deficit. What should be the attitude of his parent in response to poor classroom performance? Obviously, tutorial assistance and special instruction should be provided if possible. Beyond that, however, I would *strongly* suggest that academic achievement be de-emphasized at home.

Requiring a visually handicapped child to compete academically is like forcing a polio victim to run the hundred yard dash. Imagine a mother and father standing disapprovingly at the end of the track, berating their crippled child as he hobbles across the finish line in last place.

"Why don't you run faster, son?" his mother asks with obvious displeasure.

"I don't think you really care whether you win or lose," says his embarrassed father.

How can this lad explain, if they don't already understand, that his legs will not carry him as fast as those of his peers? All he knows is that the other sprinters run past him to the cheering of the crowd. But who would expect a crippled child to win a race against healthy peers? No one, simply because his handicap is obvious. Everyone can see it.

Unfortunately, the child with a learning deficit is not so well understood. His academic failure is more difficult to understand and may be attributed to laziness, mischievousness or deliberate defiance. Consequently, he experiences pressures to do the impossible. And one of the most serious threats to emotional health occurs when a child faces demands that he *cannot* satisfy.

Let me restate the preceding viewpoint in its most concise terms: I believe in academic excellence. I want to maximize every ounce of intellectual potential which a child possesses. I don't believe in letting him behave irresponsibly simply because he doesn't choose to work. Without question, there is lasting benefit to be derived from educational discipline.

But, on the other hand, some things in life are more important than academic excellence, and self-esteem is one of them. A child can survive, if he must, without knowing a noun from a verb. But if he doesn't have some measure of self-confidence and personal respect, he won't have a chance in life.

I want to assert my conviction that the child who is unequipped to prosper in the traditional educational setting is *not* inferior to his peers. He possesses the same degree of human worth and dignity as the intellectual young superstar. It is a foolish cultural distortion that causes us to evaluate the worth of children according to the abilities and physical features they may (or may not) possess.

Every child is of equal worth in the sight of God, and that is good enough for me. Thus, if my little boy or girl can't be successful in one environment, we'll just look for another. Any loving parent would do the same.

What Does the Future Hold?

In case you haven't heard, help is on the way. The maturation and glandular changes associated with puberty often calm the hyperactive youngster between twelve and eighteen years of age. This explains why we seldom see adults jumping from the backs of chairs and rolling on the floor. But for harassed parents who spend their days chasing a nonstop toddler around the house, there may be little consolation in knowing that the crisis will last only nine more years.

Note: For parents who want to learn more about children with hyperactivity, I would refer them to Dr. Renshaw's excellent book. While the writing style is somewhat technical, it is certainly readable and contains helpful insights. See note 1 for publication details.

Questions

Question: What do you think of the phrase "Children should be seen and not heard"?

Answer: That statement reveals a profound ignorance of children and their needs. I can't imagine how any loving adult could raise a vulnerable little boy or girl by that philosophy. Children are like clocks, they must be allowed to run!

Question: My six-year-old son has always been an energetic child with some of the other symptoms you described. He has a short attention span and flits from one activity to another. I took him to his pediatrician who said he was not actually hyperactive, in the medical sense, and should not be given medication for this mild problem. However, he's beginning to have learning problems in school because he can't stay in his seat and concentrate on his lessons. What should I do?

Answer: It is likely that your son is immature in comparison with his peers, and could profit from being retained in the first grade next year. If his birthday is between December 1 and July 1, I would definitely ask the school guidance office to advise you on this possibility. Retaining an immature boy during his early school career (kindergarten or first grade) can give him a great social and academic advantage throughout the remaining years of elementary school. However, it is very important to help him "save face" with his peers. If possible, he should change schools for at least a year to avoid embarrassing questions and ridicule from his former classmates.

Question: He wets the bed, too. Can you offer any advice for dealing with that recurring problem?

Answer: The fact that your child has enuresis (is a bedwetter) is further confirmation that you have a boy who is developmentally immature. Bed-wetting is often part of the pattern you described above. There is no reason to worry about his babyishness. Each child has his own timetable of maturation, and some are in no great hurry. However, enuresis can produce emotional and social distress for the older child. His peers may call him a "midnight sailor" and less complimentary names. Thus, it is wise to help him conquer the problem as soon as possible. I would recommend that you make use of a buzzer device that emits a loud noise when your boy urinates at night. Sears, Roebuck and Co. sells a unit called a Wee Alert, which I have found effective *when used properly* for children four years of age and older.

Bed-wetting occurs in most cases as a result of very sound sleep, which makes it difficult, if not impossible, for the child to learn nighttime control on his own. His mind does not respond to the signal or reflex action that ordinarily awakens a lighter sleeper. Fortunately, that reflex action can be trained or conditioned to awaken even a deep sleeper in most instances.

The Wee Alert system produces a very irritating sound when urination occurs at night. The child has been instructed to awaken one parent (determining which one can create some interesting marital arguments) who must place him in a tub of cool water or splash cold water on his face. Both alternatives are unpleasant, of course, but are essential to success of the program. The child is told that this is *not* a form of punishment for wetting the bed. It is necessary to help him break the habit so he can invite friends to spend the night and he can go to other homes, as well. The cold water awakens the child fully and gives him a reason not to want to repeat the experience. It is a form of aversive conditioning, such as is used to help break the habit of smoking. Later, the relaxation immediately prior to urination is associated with the unpleasantness of the bell and the cold water. When that connection is made, urinary control is mastered.

This procedure may take from four to eight weeks to conquer bed-wetting, but success can occur much more quickly in some cases. My own son remained dry the third night we used the equipment. As indicated in the Wee

180

Alert instructions, it is unnecessary to restrict liquids, get the child up at night, use punishment, etc. None of these standard procedures communicate with the unconscious mind during periods of deep, dreamy sleep. The Wee Alert system apparently does.

(Please note that I did not invent the Wee Alert system and receive no compensation from Sears for recommending this product. I merely suggest the device because it usually works.)

Question: How do you get children to behave politely and responsibly, especially when they pay no attention to your repeated instructions?

Answer: Kids love games of all sorts, especially if adults will get involved with them. It is often possible to turn a teaching situation into a fun activity which "sensitizes" the entire family to the issue you're trying to teach. If you'll pardon yet another personal example, let me tell you how we taught our children to put their napkins in their laps before eating. We tried reminding them for two or three years, but simply weren't getting through. Then we turned it into a family game.

Now, if one of the Dobsons takes a single bite of food before putting his napkin in his lap, he is required to go to his bedroom and count to twenty-five in a loud voice. This game is highly effective, although it has some definite disadvantages. You can't imagine how foolish Shirley and I feel when we're standing in an empty section of the house, counting to twenty-five while our kids giggle. Ryan, particularly, *never* forgets his napkin and he loves to catch the rest of us in a moment of preoccupation. He will sit perfectly still, looking straight ahead until the first bite of food goes in. Then he wheels toward the offender, points his finger, and says, "Gotcha!!"

For all of those many teaching objectives that involve teaching responsibility (rather than conquering willful defiance), game-playing should be considered as the method of choice.

An Evaluation of Parent Effectiveness Training (P.E.T.)

The recommendations offered to this point have clearly reflected my conviction that loving parental authority is healthy for children and their families. This concept has been accepted *prima facie* for thousands of years, but is now being challenged vigorously in some professional circles. In fact, the entire Judeo-Christian heritage relating to family life has been contradicted during the past decade. Consequently, the American people have recently been exposed to some of the most foolish ideas in the history of mankind, including open marriage and the "God is dead" theory and the new morality and unisex, to name a few. But at the top of the list of "dumb thinking" is the notion that children are somehow endangered by the conscientious leadership of their loving parents.

The first book on this subject to get wide publicity was written by the well known educator John Holt. Mr. Holt became famous by authoring *How Children Fail,* which was a runaway best seller. Then in 1974, he produced what I consider to be a literary disaster entitled *Escape from Childhood.* The Los Angeles *Times* reviewed his book as follows:

> In the latest (book), he plainly advocates the overthrow of parental authority in just about every area. He sets forth that children, *age whatever,* should have the right to: experience sex, drink and use drugs, drive, vote, work, own property, travel, have a guaranteed income, choose their guardians, control their learning, and have legal and financial responsibility.
>
> In short, Holt is proposing that parents discard the protectorate position they have held over their children in this and other countries over the past several hundred years and thrust them, or rather let them thrust themselves—when they feel like they want to—into the real-life world.[1]

Does that sound foolish to anyone but me? Can you imagine a six-year-old girl driving her own car to an escrow office, where she and her preschool male friend will discuss the purchase of a new home over a martini or two? Can you visualize a teary-eyed mother and father standing in the doorway, saying "goodbye" to their five-year-old son who had decided to pack his teddy bear and go live with someone else? Have we gone completely mad? Discard the protectorate position, indeed!

Let me repeat that these recommendations were not written by an unknown crank from somewhere out in never-never land. They are the philosophical offerings of one of America's best known educators. And what may be more startling is the reaction Mr. Holt has received to many of his revolutionary ideas. The *Times* quoted him directly in regard to that public response:

> "Oddly enough, the chapter on the matter of drinking and drugs, letting young people do whatever older people do, as well as manage their own sex lives, hasn't brought as much flak as I would have expected. . . . The understanding, sympathetic responses (from readers) have clearly outweighed the negative or hostile ones," he said.[2]

John Holt's views are shared by others who "advocate the overthrow of parental authority in just about every area." A psychologist named Richard Farson has written a similar and equally outrageous book entitled *Birthrights: A Bill of Rights for Children*. These men are at the forefront of a movement which the Los Angeles *Times* called, "The Mounting March for Children's Rights." Their writings have inspired an aggressive campaign in Washington and in various state legislatures to implement the objectives of this vigorous movement.

A more reasonable (and less extreme) example of this antiauthority philosophy is incorporated into a program entitled Parent Effectiveness Training. Its creator, Dr. Thomas Gordon, is perhaps the most influential advisor of parents in America today. There are more than 8000 P.E.T. classes in operation throughout the country, each marketing Dr. Gordon's parenting techniques with missionary zeal. More than a quarter of a million parents have taken his course, prompting the New York *Times* to call it "a national movement." Furthermore, many Christians have participated in the P.E.T. courses, and some churches have sponsored the training sessions for their laymen.

In view of the impact of Dr. Gordon's program, it might be helpful to examine his philosophy and recommendations in the light of traditional Christian values.

No Win, No Lose

The most effective aspect of the P.E.T. program involves the teaching of listening skills. Dr. Gordon accurately recognizes the failure of many parents to comprehend what their children are actually saying. They hear the words, of course, but do not discern the true meaning which the child is conveying. The ability to engage in active listening, as it is called, is a valuable skill which should be learned by every parent. I can enthusiastically recommend this feature of Gordon's program.

The essence of the P.E.T. philosophy, however, is expressed in a "no-win—no-lose" approach to parent-child relationships. According to this system, solutions are sought to conflicts which are acceptable to both parties. Let me explain by paraphrasing an example from Gordon's writings which describes a five-year-old girl named Bonnie who doesn't like to get dressed in the morning. Even when her mother awakens her sufficiently early, the kindergartner dawdles and plays, eventually making the family late for its various activities. Mother could yell at Bonnie or she could punish the child for being late or reward her for being on time. Instead, however, Mother discusses the problem with Bonnie, seeking a solution upon which they can mutually agree. During the conversation Bonnie reveals that she doesn't like school anyway, and she would "rather stay home and play with Mommie." Eventually, Mother and Bonnie agree that if the youngster will hurry each morning, the two of them will spend a fun-filled hour together after school instead of Bonnie's taking her usual nap. In this manner, they developed a plan of action which theoretically resulted in the child's hurrying to get dressed each morning (which Mom wanted) and a fun-and-games session each afternoon, (which Bonnie coveted). Therefore, neither party "won" at the expense of the other, nor did they really "lose."

I would certainly agree that on many occasions compromise and negotiation are appropriate between parent and child. Six-year-old Johnny may voluntarily rest or nap in the afternoon so that he can watch a late evening children's program on television. Mom may offer to drive her ten-year-old son to baseball practice, provided he agrees to keep his room clean and neat. Obviously, there is time and place for negotiation in human affairs, whether it be between father and son, husband and wife, or Henry Kissinger and the Arabs. And when it occurs, the objective is a "no-win—no-lose" consequence for each negotiator.

My concern about P.E.T., then, is not in its use of the conference table when the situation warrants. Rather, it is Gordon's rejection of parental authority in any form. Consider the following quotations from his book:

> The stubborn persistence of the idea that parents must and should use authority in dealing with children has, in my opinion, prevented for centuries any significant

change or improvement in the way children are raised by parents and treated by adults. (p. 164)

Children resent those who have power over them. (p. 177) . . . children do not want the parent to try to limit or modify their behavior by using or threatening to use their authority. In short, children want to limit their behavior *themselves*, if it becomes apparent *to them* that their behavior must be limited or modified. Children, like adults, prefer to be their own authority over their behavior. (p. 188)

My own conviction is that as more people begin to understand power and authority more completely and accept its use as unethical, more parents . . . will be forced to search for creative new non-power methods that all adults can use with children and youth. (p. 191)[3]

These condemnations of authority are also apparent in the books Gordon personally recommends. Two of the authors represented in his "Suggested Reading for Parents" are John Holt and Richard Farson, mentioned earlier. Of Farson's *Birthrights*, Gordon wrote, "This book will help parents construct a new way of looking at their role that frees them from the guilt of total responsibility for their children's values and behavior."

It is my belief that these antiauthority views are directly contradictory to the teachings of Scripture. As mentioned earlier, 1 Timothy 3:4, 5 states, "He [speaking of the father] must have the proper *authority* in his own household, and be able to control and command the respect of his children" (Phillips). Colossians 3:20 expresses this divine principle to the younger generation, "Children, obey your parents in all things, for this is well pleasing unto the Lord" (KJV). I find no place in the Bible where

our little ones are installed as co-discussants at a conference table, deciding what they will and will not accept
from the older generation.

Why is parental authority so vigorously supported
throughout the Bible? Is it simply catering to the whims
of oppressive, power-hungry adults, as Gordon would
surmise? No, the leadership of parents plays a significant
role in the development of a child! By learning to yield to
the loving authority (leadership) of his parents, a child
learns to submit to other forms of authority which will
confront him later in life. The way he sees his parents'
leadership sets the tone for his eventual relationships with
his teachers, school principal, police, neighbors, and employers. Despite P.E.T.'s disregard for these forms of authority, they are necessary to healthy human relationships.
Without respect for leadership, there is anarchy, chaos,
and confusion for everyone concerned.

There is an even more important reason for the pres-
ervation of authority in the home: while yielding to the
loving leadership of their parents, children are also learning to yield to the benevolent leadership of God Himself.
It is a well known fact that a child identifies his parents
with God, whether the adults want that role or not. Most
children "see" God the way they perceive their earthly
fathers (and, to a lesser degree, their mothers). This fact
was illustrated in our home when little Ryan was just two
years old. Since the time of his babyhood, he had seen his
sister, mother, and father say "grace" before eating our
meals, for we always thank God for our food in that way.
But because of his age, the little toddler had never been
asked to lead the prayer. On one occasion when I was
gone, Shirley put the lunch on the table and spontane-

ously turned to Ryan saying, "Would you like to pray for our food, today?" Her unexpected request apparently startled him and he glanced around nervously, then clasped his little hands together and said, "I love you, Daddy. Amen."

When I returned home and heard about Ryan's prayer, it was immediately apparent that my son had actually confused me with God. And I'll confess, I wish he hadn't! I appreciated the thought, but I was uncomfortable with its implications. It's too big a job for an ordinary dad to handle. There will be times when I will disappoint my son—times when I will be too tired to be what he needs of me—times when my human frailties will be all too apparent. There have already been occasions when I have fallen short of his expectation, and the older he gets, the greater will be the gap between who I am and who he thought I was. No, I don't want to represent God to my son and daughter. But whether I like it or not, they have given me this position, and your children have done the same to you! The Creator has given to us parents the awesome responsibility of representing Him to our children. As such, we must reflect the two aspects of Divine nature to the next generation. First, our Heavenly Father is a God of unlimited love, and our children must become acquainted with His mercy and tenderness through our own love toward them. But make no mistake about it, our Lord is also the possessor of majestic authority! The universe is ordered by a supreme Lord who requires obedience from His children and has warned them that "the wages of sin is death." To show our little ones love without authority is as serious a distortion of God's nature as to reveal an ironfisted authority without love.

From this perspective, then, it is unreasonable to think that a child who has only "negotiated" with his parents and teachers has been learning to submit to the authority of the Almighty. And I find this fact to be absolutely irrefutable; if a little child is taught to disrespect the authority of his parents, systematically from the tender years of childhood—to mock their leadership, to "sass" them and disobey their instructions, to exercise extreme self-will from the earliest moments of awareness—then it is most unlikely that this same child will turn his face up to God, about twenty years later, and say humbly, "Here am I, Lord; send me!" To repeat, a child learns to yield to the authority of God by first learning to submit (rather than bargain) to the leadership of his parents. And the literal application of P.E.T. sacrifices that experience!

But what does the apostle Paul mean in the letter to Timothy when he sanctions the "proper authority?" Does he give parents the right to be mean and harsh with their children, disregarding their feelings and instilling fearful anxiety? Certainly not! Let me refer again to Ephesians 6:4 which spells out the approach: "And now a word to you parents. Don't keep on scolding and nagging your children, making them angry and resentful. Rather, bring them up with the loving discipline the Lord himself approves, with suggestions and godly advice" (TLB). Whereas Gordon and his allies write derogatorily about the uses of parental "power," the Bible strongly and consistently supports the role of loving, parental *leadership* in raising a child. Forced to choose between two alternatives, I'll cast my lot with the immutable, everlasting Word of God!

Not only is Gordon's view of authority of concern to me but I am also bothered by two other aspects of his philosophy which are widely echoed in non-Christian circles:

1. *"Children Are Basically 'Good,' But They Are Corrupted by Bad Relationships with Parents and Others in Their Society."*

Gordon expressed this optimistic concept when appearing on Mike Douglas's television show in January, 1976. He also revealed that perspective throughout his book. Concerning the tendency to lie, for example, he wrote:

> While children lie a lot because so many parents rely heavily on rewards and punishment, I firmly believe that the tendency to lie is not natural in youngsters. It is a learned response. . . .[4]

I wish that Gordon's assessment of human nature were accurate. But again, it contradicts Scriptural understandings. Jeremiah wrote, "The heart is deceitful above all things, and desperately wicked: who can know it?" (Jer. 17:9 KJV). Jeremiah's inspired insight into human nature is validated by the sordid history of mankind. The record of civilization is blotted by murder, war, rape, and plundering from the time of Adam forward. Surely, during those thousands of years, there must have been at least *one* generation for whom parents did things right. Yet greed, lust, and selfishness have characterized us all. Is this nature also evident in children? King David thought so, for he confessed, ". . . in sin did my mother conceive me" (Ps. 51:5 KJV).

What meaningful difference, then, is made by the distinction between the two views of children? Practically everything, in fact. Parents who believe all toddlers are infused with goodness and sunshine are urged to get out of the way and let their pleasant nature unfold. On the other hand, parents who recognize the inevitable internal war between good and evil will do their best to influence the child's choices—to shape his will and provide a solid spiritual foundation. They recognize the dangers of willful defiance as expressed in 1 Samuel 15:23—"For rebellion is as bad as the sin of witchcraft, and stubbornness is as bad as worshiping idols." (TLB)

My entire book, you see, is a product of the biblical orientation to human nature. We are not typically kind and loving and generous and yielded to God. Our tendency is toward selfishness and stubbornness and sin. We are all, in effect, "strong-willed children" as we stand before God. Jesus, who represents the only sinless human being, expressed the opposite nature when He said in the Garden of Gethsemane, "Not my will but Thine be done." Thus, the Christian parent hopes to lead his child to this Jesus Christ, who alone can "cleanse" him of rebellion. It's a very old explanation of human nature and it sounds terribly unscientific. But the Bible teaches it, and I believe it. That leads us to the second area of concern in Gordon's writings.

2. *"We Have No Rights or Obligation As Parents to Instill Our Values, Attitudes, and Beliefs in Our Children."*

This foolish notion would have brought universal scorn and contempt if uttered a few years ago, yet Gordon assaults the wisdom of the ages without a flinch. He wrote in P.E.T.,

> The problem is *who is to decide* what is in the best interest of society. The child? The parent? Who knows best? These are difficult questions, and there are dangers in leaving the determination of "best interest" with the parent. He may not be wise enough to make this determination.[5]

I sympathize with Dr. Gordon in his suspiciousness of human wisdom. I would lack confidence, too, if I had no standard or guide upon which to base my parental judgments and determinations. However, the Christian mother and father need not "lean on their own understanding," for they have access to the wisdom of God Himself. The Creator of heaven and earth and little children has shared His knowledge with us in the form of eternal truths. Furthermore, he inspired Solomon to write the book of Proverbs in which we are urged to "train up a child in the way he should go: and when he is old, he will not depart from it."

It is apparent to me as I consider the fundamentals of Parent Effectiveness Training that Tom Gordon does not draw his precepts and inspiration from the same interpretation of biblical principles on which I depend. In fact,

I'm inclined to see his system as only one of many recent offerings in the field of psychology which blatantly contradict the Judeo-Christian ethic. Traditions which have been honored for several thousand years are suddenly vilified. Not even the flag, motherhood, and apple pie are safe; we burned the flag in the sixties, we are mocking motherhood in the seventies, and the way I've got it figured, apple pie is living on borrowed time!

A Final Comment

Portions of the preceding discussion were first published by the editors of *Moody Monthly*,[6] who asked me to write this article. Having considered my earlier views, however, I may have underemphasized the beneficial aspects of the P.E.T. classes. No successful program is completely devoid of useful information, and it would be unfair to mention only P.E.T.'s shortcomings. These sessions offer some worthwhile suggestions in the area of listening skills, in the use of parent-child negotiation, and in the cultivation of parental tolerance. Furthermore, there are few alternatives available for parents who seek to understand their children and keep them healthy.

Nevertheless, it is my view that the great flaws in Tom Gordon's philosophy far outweigh the benefits. They are, again: (1) his failure to understand the proper role of authority in the home; (2) his humanistic viewpoint which teaches that children are born innately "good," and then learn to do wrong; (3) his tendency to weaken parental resolve to *instill* spiritual principles systematically during a child's "teachable" years. All things considered, therefore, I would not recommend that Christian parents attend the

P.E.T. program unless they are braced for the contradictions and deficiencies I have outlined.

Questions

Question: Dr. Gordon often cites an illustration of a child who puts his feet on an expensive item of living room furniture. His parents become irritated at this gesture and order him to take his dirty shoes from the chair or table. Gordon then shows how much more politely those parents would have handled the same indiscretion if the offender had been an adult guest. They might have cautiously asked him to remove his shoes, but would certainly not have felt it necessary to discipline or criticize the visitor. Dr. Gordon then asks, "Aren't children people, too? Why don't we treat them with the same respect that we do our adult friends?" Would you comment on this example?

Answer: I have heard Dr. Gordon relate the same illustration and feel that it contains both truth and distortion. If his point is that we need to exercise greater kindness and respect in dealing with our children, then I certainly agree. However, to equate children with adult visitors in the home is an error in reasoning. I do not bear *any* responsibility for teaching proper manners and courtesy to my guests; I certainly do have that obligation on behalf of my children. Furthermore, the illustration implies that children and adults think and act identically, and have the same needs. They don't. As described previously, a child often behaves offensively for the precise purpose of testing the courage of his parents. He wants them to establish firm boundaries. By contrast, a guest who puts his feet on a coffee table is more likely to be acting through ignorance or insensitivity.

More important, this illustration cleverly redefines the traditional parental relationship with children. Instead of bearing direct responsibility for training and teaching and leading them, Mom and Dad have become cautious co-equals who can only hope their independent little "guests" will gradually get the message.

No, our children are not casual guests in our home. They have been loaned to us temporarily for the purpose of loving them and instilling a foundation of values on which their future lives will be built. And we will be accountable through eternity for the way we discharge that responsibility.

Question: You referred to the "proper" use of authority as opposed to raw parental power. Dr. Gordon uses these concepts interchangeably throughout his book. Is there a distinction, and if so, what is it?

Answer: You are right in saying that Tom Gordon uses these terms synonymously in Parent Effectiveness Training. Consider the following quotations to that effect:

1. Probably the most frequent attitude about *power and authority* expressed by parents in the P.E.T. classes is that it (a singular pronoun referring to a singular subject) is justified because of parents' responsibility. . . . (p. 190)
2. My own conviction is that as more people begin to understand *power and authority* more completely and accept its use (singular pronoun and verb) as unethical. . . . (p. 191)

3. Children do not want the parent to try to limit or modify their behavior by using or threatening to use *authority*. [He did not say power; he was opposing the use of authority, which he perceives as synonymous with power.] (p. 188)

4. [NOTE THIS ONE:] The use of parental *authority* (or *power*), seemingly effective under certain conditions, is quite ineffective under other conditions. [THE PARENTHESES ARE HIS, NOT MINE.](p. 169)[7]

There are at least twenty other references in which Dr. Gordon blurs the distinction between power and authority. I can only assume that he views all authority as a form of unethical oppression. In fact, he stated that viewpoint very plainly in the second quotation, above.

In my opinion, the two concepts are as different as love and hate. Parental power can be defined as a hostile form of manipulation in order to satisfy selfish adult purposes. As such, it disregards the best interests of the little child on whom it tramples, and produces a relationship of fear and intimidation. Drill instructors in the Marine Corps have been known to depend on this form of power to indoctrinate their beleaguered recruits.

Proper authority, by contrast, is defined as loving *leadership*. Without decision-makers and others who agree to follow, there is inevitable chaos and confusion and disorder in human relationships. Loving authority is the glue that holds social orders together, and it is absolutely necessary for the healthy functioning of a family.

There are times when I say to my child, "Ryan, you are tired because you were up too late last night. I want you to brush your teeth right now and put on your paja-mas." My words may sound like a suggestion, but Ryan would be wise to remember who's making it. If that is parental power, according to Dr. Gordon's definition, then so be it. I do not always have time to negotiate, nor do I feel obligated in every instance to struggle for com-promises. I have the *authority* to do what I think is in Ryan's best interest, and there are times when I expect him not to negotiate, but to *obey*. And as I said, his learn-ing to yield to my loving leadership is excellent training for his later submission to the loving authority of God. This is very different from the use of vicious and hostile power, resulting from the fact that I outweigh him.

Question: How about Gordon's suggested use of "I" messages, versus "you" messages?

Answer: There is substantial truth in the basic idea. "I" messages can request change or improvement without being offensive: "Diane, it embarrasses me when our neighbors see your messy room. I wish you would straighten it." By contrast, "You" messages often attack the personhood of the recipient and put him on the de-fensive: "Why don't you keep your stuff picked up?! So help me, Diane, you get sloppier and more irresponsible every day." I agree with Dr. Gordon that the first method of communicating is usually superior to the second, and there is wisdom in his recommendation.

However, let's suppose I have taken my four-year-old son, Dale, to the market where he breaks all known rules. He throws a temper tantrum because I won't buy him a balloon, and he hits the daughter of another customer, and grabs a handful of gum at the checkout stand. When I get darlin' Dale outside the store there is little doubt that he is going to hear a few "you" messages—such as, "When *you* get home, young man, *you* are going to have *your* bottom tanned!"

From my perspective, again, there are a few occasions in the life of a parent when he speaks not as an equal or a comrade or a pal, but as an *authority*. And in those circumstances, an occasional "you" message will fit the circumstance better than an expression of personal frustration by the parent.

Question: Dr. Gordon said parents cannot know what is in the best interest of their children. Do you claim to make weighty decisions on behalf of your kids with unshakable confidence? How do you know that what you're doing will ultimately be healthy for them?

Answer: It is certain that I will make mistakes and errors. My human frailties are impossible to hide and my children occasionally fall victim to those imperfections. But I cannot abandon my responsibilities to provide leadership, simply because I lack infinite wisdom and insight. Besides, I do have more experience and a better perspective on which to base those decisions than my children possess at this time. I've been where they're going.

Perhaps a crude example would be illustrative. My daughter has a pet hamster (uncreatively named Hammy) who has a passion for freedom. He spends a portion of every night gnawing on the metal bars of his cage and forcing his head through the trap door. Recently I sat watching Hammy busily trying to escape. But I was not the only one observing the furry little creature. Sitting in the shadows a few feet away was old Sigmund, our dachshund. His erect ears, squinted eyes, and panting tongue betrayed his sinister thoughts. Siggie was thinking, "Come on baby, break through to freedom! Bite those bars, Ham-bone, and I'll give you a thrill like you've never experienced!"

How interesting, I thought, that the hamster's greatest desire would bring him instant and violent death if he should be so unfortunate to achieve it. Hammy simply lacked the perspective to realize the folly of his wishes. The application to human experience was too striking to be missed and I shook my head silently as the animal drama spoke to me. There are occasions when the longings and desires of our children would be harmful or disastrous if granted. They would choose midnight bedtime hours and no schoolwork and endless cartoons on television and chocolate sundaes by the dozen. And in later years, they might not see the harm of drug abuse and premarital sex and a life of uninterrupted fun and games. Like Hammy, they lack the "perspective" to observe the dangers which lurk in the shadows. Alas, many young people are "devoured" before they even know that they have made a fatal mistake.

Then my thoughts meandered a bit farther to my own relationship with God and the requests I submit to Him in personal prayer. I wondered how many times I had asked Him to open the door on my "cage," not appreciating the security it was providing. I resolved to accept His negative answers with greater submission in the future.

Returning to the question, let me repeat that my decisions on behalf of my children do not reflect infinite wisdom. They do, however, emanate from love and an intense desire to do the best I can. Beyond that, the ultimate outcome is committed to God virtually every day of my life.

Question: You implied earlier that children find it difficult to accept love before they have tested the courage and strength of their leaders. Why do you think this is true?

Answer: I don't know. But every school teacher will verify the fact that respect for authority must *precede* the acceptance of love. Those teachers who try to spread love in September and discipline next January are destined for trouble. It won't work. (That's why I recommended—half seriously—that teachers not smile 'til Thanksgiving!)

Perhaps the most frustrating experience of my professional career occurred when I was asked to speak to a group of college students who were majoring in education. Most of these men and women were in their final year of preparation, and would soon be teaching in their own classrooms. The distress that I felt came from my inability to convince these idealistic young people of the principle described above. They really believed that they could pour out love and gain instant respect from these rebels who had been at war with everyone. I felt empathy for the new teachers who would soon find themselves in the jungles of inner city schools, alone and afraid. They were bound to get their "love" thrown back in their startled faces. *Students simply cannot accept a teacher's love until they know that the giver is worthy of their respect.*

It should come as no shock to the reader by this point that I believe in the value of authority in the classroom, as well as in the home. In its absence, we have the situation where teachers are afraid of the principal, the principal is afraid of the superintendent, the superintendent is afraid of the school board, the school board is afraid of the parents, the parents are afraid of the kids, and, would you believe, the kids aren't afraid of anybody!

Though I am technically unqualified to extend this principle into the area of theology, I will share my personal views. It is my deep conviction that man's relationship with God is a reflection of the same phenomenon.

We had to understand the scope of His majesty and authority—and even His wrath—before we could comprehend the depth of His love expressed through the life and death of Jesus! Thus, it is logical that He gave us the content of the Old Testament before the New.

Few things concern me more as a Christian layman than for ministers to focus on one of these divine messages of love and justice to the exclusion of the other. Those who concentrate *only* on judgment and wrath are presenting an image of God that is distorted. He is also a God of infinite love. But the more common distortion in this permissive day is to go to the opposite extreme, depicting God as a doting grandfather who winks at sin and ignores the disobedience of His children. Nowhere in the Bible is this description found.

Though it seems contradictory, those ministers who focus only on the love of God make it impossible for their listeners to comprehend that love. You see, without an understanding of the justice of our Creator and of our obligations to serve Him—and of His promise to punish wickedness—Jesus' death on the cross is of no consequence. He died to provide a remedy for the curse of sin! Unless one understands the curse—the disease—then there is no need for a cure.

Similarly, penicillin is nothing more than a sticky, gooey substance until we understand the meaning of bacterial infection. It is only when one comprehends the way bacteria can destroy the human body that antibiotics assume the significance of "miracle cures." It seems to me that many ministers have told their congregations that Jesus loves them, but deprived them of any true understanding of His most miraculous redemptive gift.

Thus, I feel that the ministers who "edit out" the unpopular themes of the Bible are doing a great disservice to their congregations and may even be yielding to cowardice. Someone wrote, "Silence is not always golden; sometimes it's just yellow." I'm inclined to agree.

Question: Would you comment on methods of discipline that are typical in various churches. Our program tends to be rather wild, and we need to tighten it down. What would you suggest?

Answer: You have touched one of my "sensitive nerves." Perhaps I can best reply by quoting from the manuscript of a recent family life seminar in which the comments of several participants were recorded word for word by a court reporter.[8]

Rev. Dobson: I have heard you express some criticism of the Christian church generally with regard to discipline and behavior in Sunday schools. It ought to be restated here.

Dr. Dobson: Well, it has been my strong conviction that the church should support the family in its attempt to implement biblical principles in the home. This is especially true with reference to the teaching of respect for authority. This isn't an easy time to be a parent because authority has eroded drastically in our society. Therefore, mothers and fathers who are trying to teach respect and responsibility to their children, as the Bible prescribes, need all the help they can get, particularly from the church.

But in my opinion, the church fails miserably at this point. There is no aspect of the church mission that I feel is weaker or more ineffective than discipline in the Sunday school. Parents who have struggled to maintain order and respect all week send their kids off to church on Sunday morning and what happens? They are permitted to throw erasers and shoot paper wads and swing on the light fixtures. This is particularly distressing to me. I am not referring to one denomination. I've seen it happen in almost all of them. In fact, I think I was one of those eraser throwers in my day.

Rev. Dobson: Why do you think our Sunday schools are so lax and permissive?

Dr. Dobson: Teachers are volunteers who may not know how to handle kids. But more important, they are afraid of irritating sensitive parents. They don't feel they have a right to teach children to respect God's house. If they try, they might anger Mama Bear and lose the entire family.

Dr. Cunningham: And they well could. That's the problem. People are so sensitive about their kids. I came through a permissive atmosphere in the Chicago public school system where a teacher was forbidden by law to touch a child—and the same restriction was put on the police department. I've seen kids in that city just stand and taunt policemen and dare them to do anything to them by threatening to sue. Everybody is so scared of lawsuits, you know, and is afraid to reprimand or punish someone else's child.

Dr. Dobson: I'm not recommending that we spank children in the Sunday school, of course. But there are ways to maintain order among children, once we decide that it is important to us. Training sessions can help teachers to do a better job. Pastors can back up Sunday school workers, etc. My concern is that we can't seem to agree that discipline has a place on Sunday morning. In its absence, the chaos that results is an insult to God and to the meaning of worship. You can't accomplish anything in an atmosphere of confusion. You can't teach students when they don't even hear you.

Dr. Cunningham: I couldn't agree with you more. We are trying to insist on discipline and obedience in our church Sunday program. I don't think we have to lose families by doing so. We are just obligated to deal with some children in more creative, meaningful ways—just like they have to do in the public school. We may remove a child from the setting or perhaps have a teacher assigned to him alone until he cools down. I would not want to say, "You can't come back to Sunday school," to any child. Instead, we will try to adapt. We will say, "We care so much about this child that we're going to go to whatever lengths are necessary to try to communicate God's Word to him. And so, parents, we wanted you to know how we are having to approach instruction of your child. We hope we have your support. We love this child and we care about him and we want him to make it. So when this kind of experience is no longer necessary, we'll reintroduce him to the classroom."

Dr. Dobson: I like that, Paul.

The Strong-willed Adolescent
(Is There Any Other Kind?)

Alas, we arrive now at the door of adolescence: that dynamic time of life which comes in with a pimple and goes out with a beard—those flirtatious years when girls begin to powder and boys begin to puff. It's an exciting phase of childhood, I suppose, but to be honest, I wouldn't want to stumble through it again. I doubt that the reader would either. We adults remember all too clearly the fears and jeers and tears that represented our own tumultuous youth. Perhaps that is why parents begin to quake and tremble when their children approach the adolescent years. (By the way, have you heard of the new wristwatch created exclusively for the anxious parents of teen-agers? After 11 P.M. it wrings its hands every fifteen minutes.)

It would be a great mistake to imply that I have immediate answers to every problem faced by the perplexed parents of adolescents. I recognize my own limitations and willingly admit that it is often easier to write about teen-age turmoil than it is to cope with it in real life. Whenever I'm tempted to become self-important and authoritative on this or any other subject, I'm reminded of what the mother whale told her baby: "When you get to the top and start to 'blow,' that's when you get harpooned!" With that admonition in mind, let me humbly offer several suggestions which may be helpful in coping with the strong-willed adolescent.

1. A Teen-ager Is Often Desperately in Need of Respect and Dignity. Give Him These Gifts!

The period of *early* adolescence is typically a painful time of life, marked by rapid physical and emotional changes. This characteristic difficulty was expressed by a seventh-grade boy who had been asked to recite Patrick Henry's historic speech at a Bicentennial program in 1976. But when the young man stood nervously before an audience of parents, he became confused and blurted out, "Give me puberty or give me death!" His statement is not as ridiculous as it sounds. Many teens sincerely believe they must choose between these dubious alternatives.

The thirteenth and fourteenth years commonly are the most difficult twenty-four months in life. It is during this time that self-doubt and feelings of inferiority reach an all-time high, amidst the greatest social pressures yet experienced. An adolescent's worth as a human being hangs precariously on peer group acceptance, which is notoriously fickle. Thus, relatively minor evidences of rejection or ridicule are of major significance to those who already see themselves as fools and failures. It is difficult to over-estimate the impact of having no one to sit with on the school-sponsored bus trip, or of not being invited to an important event, or of being laughed at by the "in" group, or of waking up in the morning to find seven shiny new pimples on your bumpy forehead, or of being slapped by the girl you thought had liked you as much as you liked her. Some boys and girls consistently face this kind of social catastrophe throughout their teen years. They will never forget the experience.

The self-esteem of an early adolescent is also assaulted in the Western culture by his youthful status. All of the highly advertised adult privileges and vices are forbidden to him because he is "too young." He can't drive or marry or enlist or drink or smoke or work or leave home. And his sexual desires are denied gratification at a time when they scream for release. The only thing he is permitted to do, it seems, is stay in school and read his dreary textbooks. This is an overstatement, of course, but it is expressed from the viewpoint of the young man or woman who feels disenfranchised and insulted by society. Much of the anger of today's youth is generated by their perception of this "injustice."

Dr. Urie Bronfenbrenner, eminent authority on child development at Cornell University, has also identified the period of early adolescence as the most destructive years of life. He expressed these concerns in a taped interview with Susan Byrne, subsequently published in *Psychology Today*, May 1977.

In that article, Bronfenbrenner recalled being asked during a U.S. Senate hearing to indicate the most critical years in a child's development. He knew that the Senators expected him to emphasize the importance of preschool experience, reflecting the popular notion that all significant learning takes place during the first six years of life. However, Bronfenbrenner said he had never been able to validate that assumption. He agreed that the preschool years are vital, but so is every other phase of childhood. In fact, he told the Senate committee that the junior high years are probably the most critical to the development of a child's mental health. It is during this period of self-doubt that the personality is often assaulted and damaged beyond repair. Consequently, said Bronfenbrenner, it is not unusual for healthy, happy children to enter junior high school, but then emerge two years later as broken, discouraged teen-agers.

I couldn't agree more emphatically with Bronfenbrenner's opinion at this point. Junior high school students are typically brutal to one another, attacking and slashing a weak victim in much the same way a pack of northern wolves kill and devour a deformed caribou. Few events stir my righteous indignation more than seeing a vulnerable child—fresh from the hand of the Creator in the morning of his life—being taught to hate himself and despise his physical body and wish he had never been born. I am determined to give my assistance to those boys and girls who desperately need a friend during this period of intensive self-doubt.

Not only do I remember the emotional conflicts of my own early adolescence, but I have had ample opportunity since then to observe this troubled time of life in others. I was privileged to teach in public schools from 1960 to 1963, and two of those profitable years were spent at the junior high level. I taught science and math to 225 rambunctious troops each day, although I learned much more from them than they did from me. There on the firing line is where my concepts of discipline began to solidify. The workable solutions were validated and took their place in a system I know to be practical. But the lofty theories dreamed up by grandmotherly educators exploded like so much TNT when tested on the battlefield each day.

One of the most important lessons of those years related to the matter of low self-esteem, which we have been discussing. It became clear to me very early that I could impose all manner of discipline and strict behavioral requirements on my students, *provided* I treated each young person with genuine dignity and respect. I earned their friendship before and after school, during lunch, and through classroom encounters. I was tough, especially when challenged, but never discourteous, mean, or insulting. I defended the underdog and tenaciously tried to build each child's confidence and self-respect. However, I never compromised my standards of deportment. Students entered my classroom without talking each day. They did not chew gum, or behave disrespectfully, or curse or stab one another with ball point pens. I was clearly the captain of the ship and I directed it with military zeal.

The result of this combination of kindness and firm discipline stands as one of the most pleasant memories of my professional life. I *loved* my students and had every reason to believe that I was loved in return. I actually missed them on weekends (a fact my wife never quite understood). At the end of the final year when I was packing my books and saying goodbye, there were twenty-five or thirty teary-eyed kids who hung around my gloomy room for several hours and finally stood sobbing in the parking lot as I drove away. And yes, I shed a few tears of my own that day. (Please forgive this self-congratulatory paragraph. I haven't bothered to tell you about my failures, which are far less interesting.)

One young lady to whom I said "goodbye" in the school parking lot in 1963 called me on the telephone during 1975. I hadn't seen Julie for more than a decade, and she had become a grown woman in the ensuing years. I remembered her as a seventh-grader whose crisis of confidence was revealed in her sad brown eyes. She seemed embarrassed by her Latin heritage and the fact that she was slightly overweight. She had only one friend, who moved away the following year.

Julie and I talked amiably on the phone about old times at Cedarlane Junior High School, and then she asked me a pointed question: "Where do you go to church?"

I told her where we attended, and she replied, "I wonder if you'd mind my visiting there some Sunday morning?"

I said, "Julie, I'd be delighted."

The next week, my wife and I met Julie in the vestibule of the sanctuary, and she sat with us during the service. Through a process of growth and guidance in subsequent months, this young woman became a vibrant Christian. She now participates in the choir, and many members of the congregation have commented on the radiant glow she seems to transmit when singing.

I stopped her as we were leaving the church a few months later and said, "Julie, I want to ask you a question. Will you tell me why you went to so much trouble to obtain my unlisted phone number and call me last fall. Why did you want to talk to me after all those years, and why did you ask what church I attended?"

Julie thought for a moment and then paid me the highest compliment anyone has ever sent my way. She said, "Because when I was a seventh-grade student in junior high school, you were the *only* person in my life who acted like you respected and believed in me . . . and I wanted to know your God."

If you can communicate that kind of dignity to your oppressed and harassed teen-agers, then many of the characteristic dicipline problems of adolescence can be circumvented. That is, after all, the best way to deal with people of *any* age.

Let's look now at the second suggestion which can be, in effect, a means of implementing the first.

2. Verbalize Conflicts and Re-establish the Boundaries

There is often an *irrationality* associated with adolescence which can be terribly frustrating to parents. Let me offer an illustration which may explain the problem.

A student graduated from medical school in Los Angeles a few years ago and was required as part of his internship to spend a few weeks working in a psychiatric hospital. However, he was given little orientation to the nature of mental illness and he mistakenly thought he could "reason" his patients back to a world of reality. One schizophrenic inmate was particularly interesting to him, because the man believed himself to be dead.

"Yeah, it's true," the patient would tell anyone who asked. "I'm dead. Been dead for years."

The intern couldn't resist trying to "talk" the schizophrenic out of his fantasy. Therefore, he sat down with the patient and said, "I understand you think you're dead. Is that right?"

"Sure is," replied the inmate. "I'm deader than a doornail."

The intern continued, "Well, tell me this, do dead people bleed?"

"No, of course not," answered the schizophrenic, sounding perfectly sane. The intern then took the patient's hand in his own and stuck a needle into the fleshy part of his thumb. As the blood oozed from the puncture, the schizophrenic gasped and exclaimed, "Well, what do you know! Dead people *do* bleed!"

There may be times when the reader will find himself holding similar "conversations" with his uncomprehending adolescent. These moments usually occur while trying to explain why he must be home by a certain hour—or why he should keep his room straight—or why he can't have the car on Friday night—or why it doesn't *really* matter that he wasn't invited to the smashing party given by the senior sweetheart, Helen Highschool. These issues defy reason, responding instead to the dynamic emotional, social, and chemical forces which propel them.

On the other hand, we can't afford to abandon our communicative efforts just because parents and teens have difficulty understanding one another. We simply must remain "in touch" during these turbulent years. This is especially true for the pleasant and happy child who seemingly degenerates overnight into a sour and critical fourteen-year-old anarchist (a common phenomenon). Not only are parents distressed by this radical change but the child is often worried about it too. He may be confused by the resentment and hostility which has become so much a part of his personality. He clearly needs the patient reassurance of a loving parent who can explain the "normality" of this agitation and help him ventilate the accumulated tension.

But how can this be accomplished? 'Tis a difficult question to answer. The task of prying open the door of communication with an angry adolescent can require more tact and skill than any other assignment in parenthood. The typical reaction by mothers and fathers is to be drawn into endless verbal battles that leave them exhausted but without strategic advantage. There has to be a better way of communicating than shouting at one another. Let me propose an alternative that might be workable in this situation.

For purposes of illustration, suppose that Brian is now fourteen years old and has entered a period of rebelliousness and defiance as described above. He is breaking rules right and left, and seems to hate the entire family. He becomes angry when his parents discipline him, of course, but even during tranquil times he seems to resent them for merely being there. Last Friday night he arrived home an hour beyond his deadline, but refused to explain why he was late or make apologetic noises. What course of action would be best for his parents to take?

Let's assume that you are Brian's father. I would recommend that you invite him out to breakfast on a Saturday morning, leaving the rest of the family at home. It would be best if this event could occur during a relatively tranquil time, certainly not in the midst of a hassle or intergenerational battle. Admit that you have some important matters to discuss with him which can't be communicated adequately at home, but don't "tip your hand" before Saturday morning. Then at the appropriate moment during breakfast, convey the following messages (or an adaptation thereof):

A. Brian, I wanted to talk to you this morning because of the changes that are taking place in you and in our home. We both know that the past few weeks have not been very pleasant. You have been angry most of the time and have become disobedient and rude. And your mother and I haven't done so well either. We've become irritable and we've said things that we've regretted later. This is not what God wants of us as parents, or of you as our son. There has to be a more creative way of solving our problems. That's why we're all here.

B. As a place to begin, Brian, I want you to understand what is happening. You have gone into a new period of life known as adolescence. This is the final phase of childhood, and it is often a very stormy and difficult few years. Nearly everyone on earth goes through these rough years during their early teens, and you are right on schedule at this moment. Many of the problems you face today were predictable from the day you were born, simply because growing up has never been an easy thing to do. There are even greater pressures on kids today than when we were young. I've said that to tell you this: we understand you and love you as much as we ever did, even though the past few months have been difficult in our home.

C. What is actually taking place, you see, is that you have had a taste of freedom. You are tired of being a little boy who was told what to wear and when to go to bed and what to eat. That is a healthy attitude which will help you grow up. However, now you want to be your own boss and make your own decisions without interference from anyone. *Brian, you will get what you want in a very short time.* You are fourteen now, and you'll soon be fifteen and seventeen and nineteen. You will be grown in a twinkling of an eye, and we will no longer have any responsibility for you. The day is coming when you will marry whomever you wish, go to whatever school you choose, select the profession or job that suits you. Your mother and I will not try to make those decisions for you. We will respect your adulthood. Furthermore, Brian, the closer you get to those days, the more freedom we plan to give you. You have more privileges now than you had last year, and that trend will continue. We will soon set you free, and you will be accountable only to God and yourself.

D. But, Brian, you must understand this message: *you are not grown yet.* During the past few weeks, you have wanted your mother and me to leave you alone—to let you stay out half the night if you chose—to fail in school—to carry no responsibility at home. And you have "blown up" whenever we have denied even your most extreme demands. The truth of the matter is, you have wanted us to grant you twenty-year-old freedom during the fourteenth year, although you still expect to have your shirts ironed and your meals fixed and your bills paid. You have wanted the best of both worlds with none of the responsibilities. So what are we to do? The easiest thing would be for us to let you have your way. There would be no hassles and no conflict and no more frustration. Many parents of fourteen-year-old sons and daughters have done just that. But we *must not* yield to this temptation. You are not ready for that complete independence, and we would be showing hatred for you (instead of love) if we surrendered at this time. We would regret our mistake for the rest of our lives, and you would soon blame us, too. And as you know, you have two younger sisters who are watching you very closely, and must be protected from the things you are teaching them.

E. Besides, Brian, God has given us a responsibility as parents to do what is right for you, and He is holding us accountable for the way we do that job. I want to read you an important passage from the Bible which describes a father named Eli who did not discipline and correct his two unruly teen-age sons. (Read the dramatic story from the Living Bible, 1 Samuel 2:12–17, 22–25, 27–34; 3:11–14; 4:1–3 and 10–22.) It is very clear that God was angry at Eli for permitting his sons to be disrespectful and disobedient. Not only did He allow the sons to be killed in battle, but He also punished their father for not accepting his parental responsibilities. This assignment to parents can be found throughout the Bible: mothers and fathers are expected to train their children and discipline them when required. What I'm saying is that God will not hold us blameless if we let you behave in ways that are harmful to yourself and others.

F. That brings us to the question of where we go from this moment. I want to make a pledge to you, here and now: your mother and I intend to be more sensitive to your needs and feelings than we've been in the past. We're not perfect, as you well know, and it is possible that you will feel we have been unfair at one time or another. If that occurs, you can express your views and we will listen to

you. We want to keep the door of communication standing wide open between us. When you seek a new privilege, I'm going to ask myself this question, "Is there any
way I can grant this request without harming Brian or
other people?" If I can permit what you want in good
conscience, I will do so. I will compromise and bend as far
as my best judgment will let me.

G. But hear this, Brian. There will be a few matters that
cannot be compromised. There will be occasions when I
will have to say "no." And when those times come, you
can expect me to stand like the Rock of Gibraltar. No
amount of violence and temper tantrums and door slam-
ming will change a thing. In fact, if you choose to fight me
in those remaining rules, then I promise that you will lose
dramatically. Admittedly you're too big and grown to
spank, but I can still make you uncomfortable. And that
will be my goal. Believe me, Brian, I'll lie awake nights
figuring how to make you miserable. I have the courage
and the determination to do my job during these last few
years you are at home, and I intend to use all of my
resources for this purpose, if necessary. So it's up to you.
We can have a peaceful time of cooperation at home, or
we can spend this last part of your childhood in unpleasantness and struggle. Either way, you *will* arrive home
when you are told, and you *will* carry your share of responsibility in the family and you *will* continue to respect
your mother and me.

H. Finally, Brian, let me emphasize the message I gave you
in the beginning. We love you more than you can imagine,
and we're going to remain friends during this difficult
time. There is so much pain in the world today. Life involves disappointment and loss and rejection and aging
and sickness and ultimately death. You haven't felt much
of that discomfort yet, but you'll taste it soon enough. So

with all that heartache outside our door, let's not bring more of it on ourselves. We need each other. We need you, and believe it or not, you still need us occasionally. And that, I suppose, is what we wanted to convey to you this morning. Let's make it better from now on.

I. Do you have things that need to be said to us?

The content of this message should be modified to fit individual circumstances and the needs of particular adolescents. Furthermore, the responses of children will vary tremendously from person to person. An "open" boy or girl may reveal his deepest feelings at such a moment of communication, permitting a priceless time of catharsis and ventilation. On the other hand, a stubborn, defiant, proud adolescent may sit immobile with head downward. But even if your teen-ager remains stoic or hostile, at least the cards have been laid on the table and parental intentions explained.

We must deal now with the child who listens to these parental messages but then defiantly chooses to fight it out, anyway.

3. Link Behavior with Desirable and Undesirable Consequences

As stated in the preceding section (and in an earlier chapter) one of the most common mistakes of parenthood is to be drawn into verbal battles with our children which leave us exhausted but without strategic advantage. Let me say it again: don't yield to this impulse. Don't argue with your teen. Don't subject him to perpetual threats and finger-wagging accusations and insulting indictments.

And most important, don't *nag* him endlessly. Adolescents hate to be nagged by "Mommie" and "Daddy"! When that occurs, they typically "protect" themselves by appearing deaf. Thus, the quickest way to terminate all communication between generations is to follow a young person around the house, repeating the same monotonous messages of disapproval with the regularity of a cuckoo clock.

During the 1950s a popular rock and roll song cleverly expressed this kind of harassment of a teen-ager by his nagging parents. It was entitled, appropriately, "Yakety Yak (Don't Talk Back)" and was recorded initially by the Coasters.[1]

Take out the papers and the trash
   or you don't get no spending cash;
If you don't scrub that kitchen floor
   you ain't gonna rock and roll no more.
Yakety Yak (Don't talk back)!

Just finish cleaning up your room
   let's see that dust fly with that broom.
Get all that garbage out of sight
   or you don't go out Friday night.
Yakety Yak (Don't talk back)!

You just put on your coat and hat
   and walk yourself to the laundry mat.
And when you finish doing that
   Bring in the dog and put out the cat.
Yakety Yak (Don't talk back)!

Don't give me no dirty looks;
  Your father's hip, he knows what cooks.
Just tell your hoodlum friends outside
  You ain't got time to take a ride.
Yakety Yak (Don't talk back)! Yakety Yak Yakety Yak

If Yakety-yaking is not the answer, then what is the proper response to slovenliness, disobedience, defiance, and irresponsibility? That question takes us back to the threat, implied to Brian, that his father would make him "miserable" if he did not cooperate. Don't let the news leak out, but the tools available to implement that promise are relatively weak. Since it is unwise (and unproductive) to spank a teen-ager, parents can only manipulate environmental circumstances when discipline is required. They have the keys to the family automobile and can allow their son or daughter to use it (or be chauffered in it). They may grant or withhold privileges, including permission to go to the beach or to the mountains or to a friend's house or to a party. They control the family purse and can choose to share it or loan it or dole it or close it. They can "ground" their adolescent or deny him the use of the telephone or television for awhile.

Now obviously, these are not very influential "motivators," and are at times totally inadequate for the situation at hand. After we have appealed to reason and cooperation and family loyalty, all that remains are relatively weak methods of "punishment." We can only link behavior of our kids with desirable and undesirable consequences and hope the connection will be of sufficient influence to elicit their cooperation.

If that sounds pretty wobbly-legged, let me admit what I am implying: a willful, angry, sixteen-year-old boy or girl *CAN* win a confrontation with his parents today, if worst comes to worst. The law leans ever more in the direction of emancipation of the teen-ager. He can leave home in many areas and avoid being returned. He can drink and smoke pot and break many other civil laws before he is punished by society. His girlfriend can obtain birth control pills in many states without her parents' knowledge or permission, and if that fails, she can slip into a clinic for an unannounced abortion. Very few "adult" privileges and vices can be denied a teen-ager who has the passion for independence and a will to fight.

How different was the situation when Billy-Joe was raised on the farm in days of old, living perhaps eight or ten miles by horseback from the home of his nearest contemporary. His dad, Farmer Brown, impressed by his own authority, could "talk sense" to his rebellious boy without the interference of outside pressures. There is no doubt that it was much easier for father and son to come to terms while sitting on a plow at the far end of Forgotten Field.

But today, every spark of adolescent discontent is fanned into a smoldering flame. The grab for the teen dollar has become big business, enticing magazines, record companies, radio, television, and concert entrepreneurs to cater to each youthful whim. And, of course, masses of high school students congregate idly in the city and patronize those obliging companies. They have become a force to be considered. Only last week, 2500 teens "crashed" a party given in my neighborhood, strewing beer cans and broken glass up and down the block. When the Chief of Police was asked why he didn't break up the disturbance, he replied, (to my recollection):

"What were we to do? There were twenty-four policemen against 2500 kids. We made a few arrests, but each student seized had to be escorted to the station by two men. It was just not feasible to control the entire mob. Furthermore, it is not illegal to stand in a crowd of young people. Before taking any action, we had to witness a specific offense being committed there in the dark, and then catch the particular person responsible. The rest of the crowd considered policemen to be enemies, of course, and interfered with the apprehensions. All in all, it was an impossible assignment."

If policemen are unable to control teens today, then parents are in an even more delicate position. Unless their sons and daughters have an inner tug toward cooperation and responsibility, the situation can get bloody very quickly. But where does that voice of restraint originate? It has been my contention that the early years of childhood are vital to the establishment of respect between generations. This book, in effect, is devoted to helping parents of strong-willed children create a relationship of love and control during the preteen years that will contribute toward adolescent sanity. Without that foundation—without a touch of awe in the child's perception of his parent—then the balance of power and control is definitely shifted toward the younger combatant. I would be doing a disservice to my readers if I implied otherwise.

On the other hand, we must do the best job we can during the teen years, even if that foundation has not been laid. Our avowed purpose in that situation is to prevent the emerging adult from making costly errors with lifetime implications, including drug addictions, disastrous early marriage, pregnancy, school failure, alcoholism, etc. There may be occasions when these serious threats require a radical response by mothers and fathers.

My parents were once in that position. When I was sixteen years old, I began to play some "games" which they viewed with alarm. I had not yet crossed the line into all out rebellion, but I was definitely leaning in that direction. My father was a minister who was traveling consistently during that time, and when my mother informed him of my sudden defiance, he reacted decisively. He cancelled his three-year speaking schedule and accepted a pastoral assignment which permitted him to be home with me for my last two years in high school. He sold our home and moved the family seven hundred miles south to give me a fresh environment, new friends, and the opportunity to hunt and fish. I didn't know that I had motivated this relocation, but now I understand my parents' reasoning and appreciate their caring enough to sacrifice their home, job, friends, and personal desires, just for my welfare. This was one way they revealed their love for me at a critical stage of my development.

The story does not end there, of course. It was difficult making new friends in a strange high school at the beginning of my junior year. I was lonely and felt out of place in a town that failed to acknowledge my arrival. My mother sensed this feeling of friendlessness and in her characteristic way, was "hurting" with me. One day after we had been in the new community for about two weeks, she took my hand and pressed a piece of paper into the palm. She looked in my eyes and said, "This is for you. Don't tell anybody. Just take it and use it for anything you want. It isn't much, but I want you to get something that looks good to you."

I unfolded the "paper," which turned out to be a twenty-dollar bill. It was money that my mother and father didn't have, considering the cost of the move and the small salary my dad was to be paid. But no matter. I stood at the top of their list of priorities during those stormy days. We all know that money won't buy friends and twenty dollars (even then) did not change my life significantly. Nevertheless, my mother used that method of saying to me, "I feel what you feel; I know it's difficult right now, but I'm your friend and I want to help." Every troubled teen should be so fortunate as to have parents who are still pulling for him and praying for him and feeling for him, even when he has become most unlovable.

In summary, I have been suggesting that parents be willing to take whatever corrective action is required, but to avoid nagging, moaning, groaning, and growling when possible. Anger does not motivate teen-agers! How foolish it is, for example, for the vice principal of Kamakaze High School to stand screaming in the parking lot as students roar past in their cars. He can solve the speeding problem once and for all by placing a bump in the road which will tear the wheels off their love-buggies if they ignore its sinister presence. In Russia, by the way, students who are convicted of taking drugs are placed at the end of a waiting list to obtain cars. This policy has had a remarkable impact on the unpopularity of narcotics there, I'm told. These two illustrations contain the key to adolescent discipline, if in fact one exists. It involves the manipulation of circumstances, whatever they may be, to influence the behavior of youngsters, combined with an appeal to love and reason and cooperation and compromise. It ain't much, as they say, but it's all we've got.

4. Prepare for Adolescence

At the risk of being redundant, I feel I must repeat a word of advice offered in my book *Hide or Seek*. I stressed there the importance of preparing the preteen-ager for adolescence. We know, as parents, that the teen years can be extremely distressing and tense, yet we typically keep that information to ourselves. We fail to brace our children properly for the social pressures and physical changes that await their arrival at puberty. Instead, we send them skipping unsuspectingly into this hazardous terrain, like Little Red Riding Hood dancing merrily down the path with a basket of goodies. If that sweet child's parents had warned her about the Big Bad Wolf, she might have noticed that Grandmummie had grown hairier and produced a tail since they last met. (I've often wondered what that old woman must have looked like, considering she could have been confused with a wolf by a member of her own family.) Instead, naive Little Red practically climbed into Lobo's mouth to examine the size of his (her) fangs and was saved by the woodsman at the last second. In real life, unfortunately, the story does not usually end with a dramatic rescue and a "happy ever after" conclusion.

It should be our purpose to help our kids avoid the adolescent "wolves" which threaten to devour them. Great strides can be made in that direction by taking the preteen-ager away from home for at least one day for the purpose of discussing the experiences and events that are approaching. These conversations are most productive when scheduled immediately prior to puberty and should be planned carefully to expose the major "stress points" of adolescence. To assist with this task, I have prepared a six-cassette tape album entitled "Preparing for Adolescence," which deals with topics to be presented. It is my understanding that this series, published by One Way Library, is one of the best selling tape albums in America today. Why? Simply because the preadolescent is in such a delicate period of life; nevertheless, very few Christian materials have been directed to his specific needs or expressed in language he can comprehend.

The subjects discussed on the six tapes are listed below, which will also provide suggested topics for parents who want to handle the assignment without recorded assistance.

Tape #1   *The Canyon of Inferiority.* This tape discusses the widespread feelings of inferiority among adolescents, and why this low self-esteem occurs. It also suggests how to overcome a lack of confidence. Older teen-agers should hear this tape, as well.

Tape #2   *Conformity in Adolescence.* This second tape reveals the enormous peer pressure experienced during the teen-age years. The dangers of group pressure, including drug abuse and alcoholism, are discussed.

Tape #3   *Explanation of Puberty.* This tape is devoted to an in-depth presentation of the physical changes which often frighten the uninformed child. Fears of abnormality, disease and freakishness (such as very early or late development) are pacified and relieved. Sexual development is also discussed openly and confidently, including an explanation of menstruation, nocturnal emissions, masturbation, size of breasts and reproductive organs, etc. This understanding can prevent years of suffering and unnecessary worry if presented at the proper time.

Tape #4   *The Meaning of Love.* This tape is designed to clarify the ten most common misconceptions about romantic love. Many adults will enjoy this discussion.

Tape #5   *The Search for Identity.* This tape serves as a wrap-up presentation, discussing the other emotions that so frequently accompany adolescence.

Tape #6   *Rap Session.* This final tape is perhaps the most interesting presentation in the album. Four teenagers gathered for a rap session in my home, discussing their early experiences as an adolescent. Their previous fears, embarrassment and anxieties are exposed in an open and lively interaction.

I have not wanted this section to sound like an advertisement for my own creative effort, although I suppose that is what it is. However, I have offered this recommendation simply because the preteen-ager needs more attention than he is getting. The tranquility of his next six or eight years may depend on the orientation he is given at the gateway to adolescence. Thus, whether my tapes are used or not, an effort should be made by parents, teachers, and churches to pacify the fears and doubts and pressures of the teen experiences. (The "Preparing for Adolescence" album can be obtained at many Christian bookstores.)

This brings us to the concluding recommendation of *The Strong-willed Child*, which also deals with the concluding responsibility of parenthood.

5. "Hold On" with an Open Hand

The most common mistake made by parents of "older" teen-agers (sixteen to nineteen years of age) is in refusing to grant them the independence and maturity they require. Our inclination as loving guardians is to hold our kids too tightly, despite their attempts to squirm free. We try to make all their decisions and keep them snugly beneath our wings and prevent even the possibility of failure. And in so doing, we force our young adults into one of two destructive patterns: either they passively accept our overprotection and remain dependent "children" into adult life, or else they rise up in great wrath to reject our bondage and interference. They lose on both counts. On the one hand they become emotional cripples who are incapable of independent thought, and on the other they grow into angry and guilt-ridden adults who have severed ties with the families they need. Indeed, parents who refuse to grant appropriate independence to their older adolescents are courting disaster not only for their children, but also for themselves.

Let me state it more strongly: I believe American parents are the world's worst when it comes to letting go of their children. This observation was powerfully illustrated in a popular book entitled *What Really Happened to the Class of '65?* The narrative began in the mid-sixties when *Time* Magazine selected the senior class of Palisades High School in Southern California as the focus for its cover story on "Today's Teen-ager." The editors had clearly chosen the cream of the crop for their report. These graduating young men and women lived in one of the wealthiest school districts in America, with an average income of $42,000 per family in 1965 (which would exceed $100,000 today). Listed among the members of their class were the children of many famous people, including James Arness, Henry Miller, Karl Malden, Betty Hutton, Sterling Hayden, and Irving Wallace. These students were part of the most beautiful, healthiest, best educated, and most affluent generation in the history of the world, and they knew it. Little wonder that *Time* perceived them to be standing "on the fringe of a golden era" as they left high school and headed for college. Their future sparkled like the sunrise on a summer day.

But that was in 1965. Now we can ask, what *really* happened to the golden young graduates of that year? Two members of their class, Michael Medved and David Wallechinsky, have sought to answer that precise question. Their book presents a follow-up report on thirty of their fellow graduates, ten years after leaving Palisades High School. The result is a fascinating (although profane and vulgar) commentary on a generation of overindulged kids, not only from Pacific Palisades but from all across the United States. It focuses on the major stereotypes which populate every American secondary school, including the gorgeous cheerleader, the cool quarterback, the Jewish intellectual, the goof-off, the dreamboat, the flirt, the underachiever and the wild girl (who made love to 425 boys before losing count). One by one, their private lives and personal histories are revealed.

The outcome of this investigation is striking. This class of 1965, far from entering a "golden era," has been plagued by personal tragedy and emotional unrest. In fact, the students who graduated from American high schools in that year may be the most unstable and "lost" group of young men and women ever produced in our country. A few weeks after this group received their diplomas, our cities began to burn during the long hot summer of racial strife. That signaled the start of the chaos to come. They entered college at a time when drug abuse was not only prevalent but became almost universal for students and teachers alike. Intellectual deterioration was inevitable in this narcotic climate. The Viet Nam war soon heated campus passions to an incendiary level, generating anger and disdain for the government, the President, the military, both political parties, and indeed, the American way of life. That hostility gave rise to bombings and riotings and burning of "establishment" edifices. This generation of college students had already witnessed the brutal assassination of their romantic idol, John F. Kennedy, when they were barely sixteen years old. Then at a critical point in their season of passion, they lost two more beloved heroes, Robert Kennedy and Martin Luther King. Those murders were followed by the killing of students at Kent State University and the street wars that punctuated the 1968 Democratic Convention. These violent convulsions reached their overt culmination in the wake of President Nixon's military foray into Cambodia, which virtually closed down American campuses.

Accompanying this social upheaval was a sudden disintegration of moral and ethical principles, such as has never occurred in the history of mankind. All at once, there were no definite values. There were no standards. No absolutes. No rules. No traditional beliefs on which to lean. Nor could anyone over thirty even be trusted. And as will be recalled, some bright-eyed theologians chose that moment of confusion to announce the death of God. It was a distressing time to be young—to be groping aimlessly in search of personal identity and a place in the sun.

That's what really happened to the class of '65. And their personal lives reflect the turmoil of the times. In case after case, they have tasted the sordid and seamy offerings of a valueless society. They have been hooked on heroin, LSD, barbiturates, and alcohol. They represent broken marriages and sexual extravaganzas and experimental life styles. They produced unwanted children who hadn't the slightest chance of being raised properly. Eleven percent of the class has served time in jail, and one individual (the school's most popular "dreamboat") committed suicide in 1971. Eighteen members admit to having been hospitalized for psychiatric treatment. Thus, a former teacher at Palisades High School characterized the decade from 1965–1975 as "the saddest years of the century." I certainly agree.

My reason for describing this depressing era in such detail is to help us learn from the mistakes of that period. Unfortunately the conditions that produced it are still evident today! You see, the problem was not only powered by disruptive social forces, but was also caused by parental failure to allow the class of 1965 to grow up. Although the older generation exercised very little influence over their sons and daughters after graduation, they nevertheless failed to emancipate them. An amazingly consistent pattern is evident throughout the book, with Moms and Dads bailing their kids out of jail, paying their bills, making it unnecessary to work, and encouraging them to live at home again. They offered volumes of unsolicited advice to accompany their undeserved and unappreciated material gifts. Consider the following quotations from five individuals which reveal parental overindulgence and interference:

1. During the final moments of our conversation, Lisa's mother came into the house carrying a bag of groceries for her (twenty-five-year-old) daughter. . . . Despite her hammer blows against convention, (Lisa) had always been dependent on her parents . . . to get her out of jail, to shelter her in times of stress, to support her habits, and nurture her ambitions. For all Lisa's rebellion, she had won little independence. She said, "I will say that my mother has been very helpful financially. My parents understand. Like I told you before: I've never held a job for more than three months. I'm an artist."

2. "Actually I think a lot of my problems had to do with the Palisades. There is no doubt in my mind that if I hadn't grown up in such a protected background, I would have been better off. I would have chosen something like Neil's background. His family is a little more ordinary, a little more middleclass. They have this feeling that at seventeen or eighteen you're grown up. You make your own

decisions. With me, I was just a "nice" girl who never got into trouble and was never allowed to make any mistakes. So when I started making decisions for myself . . . I went haywire."

3. "I paid no attention to school. My parents had given me fourteen hundred dollars so I would learn how to take care of money. During the six months I was supposed to be going to school, mostly what I did was . . . spend money. It was the most lovely and free and learningful time of my life. Consequently, I did not achieve too much scholastically. As a matter of fact, all of my teachers gave me F's."

4. "Because I could rely on my parents to give me concrete financial support, I early on developed an aversion to working in a structured situation where I had to be some place at a certain time. I didn't like being asked to sell my life in order to buy back my life from the patriarchs who have turned the economy into a munitions plant."

5. "For six months it was cool [referring to drug abuse]. There was no thievery or crashing cars or falling down stairs. But after that I was really hooked. I finally crashed my parents' Pegueot. A nice car. No one was hurt in the accident. I remember bouncing around inside the car as it rolled over. I also remember finding myself out on the street before the police came and remembering that I had a marijuana joint in my pocket and not wanting to get busted for possession. I threw the joint away and did not get busted, but I could not walk a straight line at the police station. They put me in a tank overnight. My father came down and he was so exasperated and horrified at what I had become that he said through the jail grille that I could just stay there. *This was quite a blow to me, because they had always rescued me in the past.*"

One of the class members, Jamie Kelso, accurately summarized the circumstances that kept his age-mates in a state of perpetual dependency:

> "For two reasons it was certain that many members of the class of '65 would become parasites living off their parents or the tax-payers. First, their parents prevented the children from understanding the problem of survival by always solving their problems for them. By age eighteen, a man or woman's character is largely set. *If, up to this age, the parents have freely provided cars, tuition, allowances, vacations, clothes, apartments, and entertainment, then they shouldn't be too surprised when they discover that their son or daughter is a moral cripple.* The second reason to expect parasites is the unreality of what was taught at Pali. Bearing with us from high school no philosophical substance, and irrationality as method, we were easy prey for the sharpies in the university, and sitting ducks for the spiritual con men of our time."[2]

Jamie Kelso is a very perceptive young man. He has observed the necessity for parents to set their children free—to allow them to make mistakes and to learn from their failures even when they are very young. This experience is vital because, in a sense, all of childhood is a preparation for adolescence and beyond. Thus, parents would be wise to remember that the day is fast approaching when the child they have raised will pack his suitcase and leave home, never to return. And as he walks through the door to confront the outside world, he will no longer be accountable to parental authority and supervision. He can do what he chooses. No one can require him to eat properly, or get his needed rest, or find a job, or live responsibly, or serve God. He will sink or swim on his own. This sudden independence can be devastating for some individuals who have not been properly prepared for it. But how can a mother and father train an individual so that he won't go wild in the first dizzying months of freedom? How can they equip him for that moment of emancipation?

The best time to begin preparing a child for the ultimate release is during toddlerhood, before a relationship of dependence is established. However, the natural inclination of parents is to do the opposite. As Renshaw wrote,

> It may be easier for the child to feed himself; more untidy for him to dress himself; less clean when he attempts to bathe himself; less perfect for him to comb his hair; but unless his mother learns to sit on her hands and allow the child to cry and to try, she will overdo for the child, and independence will be delayed.[3]

This process of granting appropriate independence must continue through the elementary school years. Parents should permit their kids to go to summer camp even though it might be "safer" to keep them at home. Likewise, boys and girls ought to be allowed to spend the night with their friends when invited. They should make their own beds, take care of their animals, and do their homework. In short, the parental purpose should be to grant increasing freedom and responsibility year by year, so that when the child gets beyond adult control, he will no longer need it.

When this assignment is handled properly, a high school senior should be virtually emancipated, even though he still lives with his parents. This was the case during my last year at home. When I was seventeen years of age, my parents tested my independence by going on a two-week trip, and leaving me behind. They loaned me the family car, and gave me permission to invite my (male) friends to spend the fourteen nights at our home. I remember being surprised by this move and the obvious risks they were taking. I could have thrown fourteen wild parties and wrecked the car and destroyed our residence. Frankly, I wondered if they were wise to give me that much latitude. I did behave responsibly (although our house suffered the effects of some typical adolescent horseplay).

After I was grown and married, I asked my mother why she took those risks—why she left me unsupervised for two weeks. She smiled and replied, "Because I knew in approximately one year you would be leaving for college, where you would have complete freedom with no one to tell you how to behave. And I wanted to expose you to that independence while you were still under my influence." Her intuitive wisdom was apparent, once more. She was preparing me for the ultimate release, which often causes an overprotected young man or woman to behave foolishly the moment they escape the heavy hand of authority.

Our objective as parents, then, is to do *nothing* for boys and girls which they can profit from doing for themselves. I admit the difficulty of implementing this policy. Our deep love for our children makes us tremendously vulnerable to their needs. Life inevitably brings pain and sorrow to little people, and we hurt when they hurt. When others ridicule them or laugh at them, when they feel lonely and rejected, when they fail at something important, when they cry in the midnight hours, when physical harm threatens their existence—these are the trials which seem unbearable to those of us who watch from the sidelines. We want to rise like a mighty shield to protect them from life's sting—to hold them snugly within the safety of our embrace. Yet there are times when we must let them struggle. Children can't grow without taking risks. Toddlers can't walk initially without falling down. Students can't learn without facing some hardships. And ultimately, an adolescent can't enter young adulthood until we release him from our protective custody. But as I have indicated, parents in the Western world find it difficult to let their offspring face and conquer the routine challenges of everyday living. As Jamie Kelso said of the class of 1965, "Their parents prevented the children from understanding the problem of survival by always solving their problems for them." They also failed to provide a moral and spiritual foundation—a reason for living—which Jamie referred to as having "no philosophical substance."

Let me offer three phrases which will guide our parenting efforts during the final era of childhood. The first is simply, "Hold on with an open hand." This implies that we still care about the outcome during early adulthood, but we must not clutch our children too tightly. Our grip must be relaxed. We should pray for them, love them, and even offer advice to them when it is sought. But the responsibility to make personal decisions must be borne by the next generation and they must also accept the consequences of those choices.

Another phrase expressing a similar concept is, "Hold them close and let them go." This seven-word suggestion could almost represent the theme of my book. Parents should be deeply involved in the lives of their young children, providing love and protection and authority. But when those children reach their late teens and early twenties, the cage door must be opened to the world outside. That is the most frightening time of parenthood, particularly for Christian mothers and fathers who care so deeply about the spiritual welfare of their families. How difficult it is to await an answer to the question, "Did I train them properly?" The tendency is to retain control in order to avoid hearing the wrong reply to that all-important question. Nevertheless, our sons and daughters are more likely to make proper choices when they do not have to rebel against our meddling interference.

The third phrase could easily have been one of King Solomon's Proverbs, although it does not appear in the Bible. It states, "If you love something, set it free. If it comes back to you, then it's yours. If it doesn't return, then it never was yours in the first place." This little statement contains great wisdom. It reminds me of a day last year when a wild coyote pup trotted in front of my house. He had strayed into our residential area from the nearby mountains. I managed to chase him into our backyard where I trapped him in a corner. After fifteen or twenty minutes of effort, I succeeded in placing a collar and leash around his neck. He fought the noose with all his strength, jumping, diving, gnawing, and straining at the tether. Finally, in exhaustion, he submitted to his servitude. He was my captive, to the delight of the neighborhood children. I kept the little rascal for an entire day and considered trying to make a pet of him. However, I contacted an authority on coyotes, who told me the chances were very slim that I could tame his wild streak. Obviously, I could have kept him chained or caged, but he would never really have belonged to me. Thus, I asked a game warden to return the lop-eared creature to his native territory in the canyons above Los Angeles. You see, his "friendship" meant nothing to me unless I could set him free and retain him by his own choice.

My point is that love demands freedom. It is true not only of relationships between animals and man, but also in all human interactions. For example, the quickest way to destroy a romantic love between a husband and wife is for one partner to clamp a steel cage around the other. I've seen hundreds of women trying unsuccessfully to demand love and fidelity from their husbands. It won't work. Think back to your dating experiences before marriage. Do you recall that any romantic relationship was doomed the moment one partner began to worry about losing the other, phoning six or eight times a day and hiding behind trees to see who was competing for the lover's attention? That hand wringing performance will devastate a perfectly good love affair in a matter of days. To repeat, *love demands freedom.*

Why else did God give us the choice of either serving Him or rejecting His companionship? Why did He give Adam and Eve the option of eating forbidden fruit in the Garden of Eden, instead of forcing their obedience? Why didn't He just make men and women His slaves who were programmed to worship at His feet? The answers are found in the meaning of love. God gave us a free choice because there is no significance to love that knows no alternative. It is only when we come to Him because we hungrily seek His fellowship and communion that the relationship has any validity. Isn't this the meaning of Proverbs 8:17, whereby He says, "I love them that love me; and those that seek me early shall find me"? That is the love that only freedom can produce. It cannot be demanded or coerced or required or programmed against our will. It can only be the product of a free choice which is honored even by the Almighty.

The application of this perspective to older adolescents (especially those in their early twenties) should be obvious. There comes a point where our record as parents is in the books, our training has been completed, and the moment of release has arrived. As I did with the young coyote, we must unsnap the leash and remove the collar. If our "child" runs, he runs. If he marries the wrong person, he marries the wrong person. If he takes drugs, he takes drugs. If he goes to the wrong school, or rejects his faith, or refuses to work, or squanders his inheritance on liquor and prostitutes, then he must be permitted to make these destructive choices. *But it is not our task to pay the bills, ameliorate the consequences, or support his folly.*

A lesson can be learned from the prodigal son of whom Jesus spoke. He became so desperately hungry when he ran out of money that even the pigs' food began to look good to him. Nevertheless, "no one gave him anything." There were no food stamps or welfare checks or unemployment programs to support his life as a swinger, and he was systematically starving. It was in that state of utter need that "he came to his senses." Deprivation has a way of bringing us back to the basics, or in the case of the prodigal son, back to Daddy. We parents would be wise to follow the example of the loving father in this story, who symbolizes God Himself. First, he set the boy free with no strings attached. Second, he allowed him to suffer the consequences of his own foolishness even though he could, as a wealthy farmer, have sent his servants to bail him out. And third, he revealed his immeasurable love by welcoming home his repentant son without insults or accusations, saying joyfully, "He was lost and is found!"

In summary, let me say that adolescence is not an easy time of life for either generation; in fact, it can be downright terrifying. But the key to surviving this emotional experience is to lay the proper foundation and then face it with courage. Even the inevitable rebellion of the teen years can be a healthy factor. This conflict contributes to the process by which an individual changes from a dependent child to a mature adult, taking his place as a co-equal with his parents. Without that friction, the relationship could continue to be an unhealthy "mommie-daddy-child" triad, late into adult life, with serious implications for future marital harmony. If the strain between generations were not part of the divine plan of human development, it would not be so universally prevalent, even in homes where love and authority have been maintained in proper balance.

Questions

Question: I have a fourteen-year-old daughter, Margretta, who wants to date a seventeen-year-old boy. I don't feel good about letting her go, but I'm not sure just how to respond. What should we say to her?

Answer: Rather than stamping your foot and screaming "No! And that's semi-final!" I would suggest that you sit down with your daughter and work out a reasonable plan for the years ahead and a rationale to support it. You might say, "Margretta, you are fourteen years old and I understand your new interest in boys. That's the way it's supposed to be. However, you are not ready to handle the pressures that an older boy can put on a girl your age." (Explain what you mean if she asks.)

"Your dad and I want to help you get ready for dating in the future, but there are some in-between steps you need to take. You have to learn how to be 'friends' with boys before you become a 'lover' with one. To do this, you should get acquainted in groups of boys or girls your age. We'll invite them to our house or you can go to the homes of others. Then when you are between fifteen and sixteen, you can begin double-dating to places that are chaperoned by adults. And finally, you can go on single dates sometime during your sixteenth year.

"Your dad and I want you to date and have fun with boys, and we intend to be reasonable about this. But you're not ready to plunge into single dating with a high school senior, and we'll just have to find other ways to satisfy your social needs."

Question: We have been concerned by the lack of discipline evident at the junior high and high school level today. What suggestion do you have to reinstate reasonable authority in public education?

Answer: I intend to write another book soon dealing with practical methods of school discipline (which explains the absence of that topic in *The Strong-willed Child*). I will only say here that black activist Jesse Jackson makes more sense than anyone writing on this subject, particularly with reference to discipline in inner-city, "ghetto" schools. Quoted below is a sampling of Rev. Jackson's views as reported by Donald Cole in a recent *Moody Monthly* editorial:

"Violence and vandalism in the nation's public schools are approaching epidemic proportions," said an article in *U.S. News and World Report* early this year. "And nobody," it added, "knows what to do about it."

Nobody? Not quite. These days Chicago based black activist Jesse Jackson is talking about decadence in the schools, and what he says makes sense, perhaps because it is also biblical.

What is he saying? In a recent speech he recounted his visit to a Los Angeles high school. There he saw students "walking down the halls with their eyes red from marijuana, minds empty and foggy. No self-respect, no bounds. And the debate," he went on, "was not whether they should smoke it, but where!"

When the principal told him how wonderful the students were, Jackson cut her off. "I told her they were little gangsters," he recalls; "that her students weren't wonderful, but that they could be. We've got to change them. Our challenge is to make flowers bloom in the desert!"

Jackson is calling for fundamental changes in people. It's a tall order. He believes that 7 to 9 P.M. or 8 to 10 P.M. should be mandatory citywide study hours "with no radio and TV to interfere." Parents should be required to call at the school for their children's report cards, and if they refuse, committees of parents should visit them to find out why, and, of course, apply a little pressure.

He would ban outlandish clothing: no superfly suits, no platform shoes. "I'm convinced," he says, "that if we begin to instill discipline and responsibility and self-respect, there will be better conduct." Then the learning can begin, and learning is what school is all about.

Jackson scoffs at those who complain that achievement tests are rigged against blacks. "We can't read or write," he says, "because of one of two reasons. Either we are retarded or we don't practice. We do well what we do most—dance, talk, jive, be deceptive. We're not so inferior that we can't learn to read and write, but we're not so superior that we can do it without practicing."

What he wants is new values. "Maybe we should begin to define men by their ability to heal," he declares, "not their ability to kill. Maybe we will say that a man is not a man if he can make a baby; that he is a man if he can provide for a baby, take care of a baby, love the mother."

The heart of his program is parental responsibility. "Care and discipline and chastisement do not cost money," he adds, "they cost new priorities." And that, of course, is just the problem.

If parents in every community were willing to pay the price, a little order could be imposed upon the chaotic schools. But in many families it is the parents who are spiritually bankrupt.

For parents who have some notion of decency and purpose, however, now is the time to respond and seek to exert a holy influence on the local school boards. Those who are Christians should let their lights shine, insisting before school boards and others on a return to first principles. Let the salt of the earth penetrate the public schools; let its tang check the violence and end the vandalism in our schools. Otherwise the system is doomed and all the fine speeches in the world will never save it.[4]

Question: You recommended in *Dare to Discipline* that pre-adolescents be taught the fundamentals of reproduction by watching the birth process in a cat or hamster. Your intentions were honorable, but this suggestion could result in the proliferation of unwanted animals and their starvation and cruel abuse. Those strays that survive in the streets are killed in pounds and vets' offices. I feel you should reconsider this unfortunate position.

Answer: To my complete surprise, that seemingly innocuous recommendation in *Dare to Discipline* has drawn more flak and criticism than all other aspects of the book combined. One dedicated crusader from Denver (she'll know who I mean) selected me as her "project" for the year and badgered me regularly to delete that section of my book. When I resisted, she gave my name to a veterinarian who adopted the cause. Finally, I wrote the woman a letter containing this statement: "Dear Mrs. _____, You win! I surrender! I'll change my recommendation in future publications; you are a credit to bulldogs the world over, and I congratulate you for your tenacity." (I am fulfilling my pledge to her, now.)

Actually, I capitulated because this lady and the others who have written me are absolutely right. There are millions of animals (notably dogs and cats) who roam the streets—hungry, disease-ridden and miserable. Many others will be destroyed in pounds and veterinarians' offices. I don't want to contribute to that unnecessary suffering, and hereby caution parents not to permit animal births unless they intend to care for the little creatures they have produced.

There, Mrs. X, my conscience is clean. Best wishes on your new project.

Question: You mentioned the fact that girls can obtain abortions without parental knowledge or consent in many states. This method of terminating a pregnancy is obviously very controversial now, and I would like to have your *opinion* on the moral issues involved.

Answer: My viewpoint on this extremely important matter has been in a state of evolution during the past ten years. When the controversy initially surfaced, I deliberately withheld judgment until I could consider the issue objectively from every vantage point. I have now completed that examination and find myself absolutely and unequivocally opposed to "abortion on demand," referring to the concept that a woman has the legal authority to kill her unborn child.

There were many considerations which led to this position, including the impact of abortions on our perception of human life. It is interesting to note, for example, that a woman who plans to terminate her pregnancy usually refers to the life within her as "the fetus." But if she intends to deliver and love and care for the little child, she affectionately calls him "my baby." The need for this distinction is obvious: If we are going to kill a human being without experiencing guilt, we must first strip it of worth and dignity. We must give it a clinical name that denies its personhood. That has been so effectively accomplished in our society that an unborn child during his first six months in gestation can now be sacrificed with no sense of loss on anyone's part. There would be a far greater public outcry if we were destroying puppies or kittens than there is for the million abortions that occur in America each year. Psychiatrist Thomas Szasz reflects the casualness with which we have accepted these deaths by writing, "[abortions]should be available in the same way as, say, an operation for beautification of the nose."[5]

I agree with Francis Schaeffer that the changing legal attitudes toward abortions carry major implications for human life at all levels. If the rights of the unborn child can be sacrificed by reinterpretation by the Supreme Court, why could not other unnecessary people be legislated out of existence? For example, the expense and inconvenience of caring for the severely retarded could easily lead to the same social justification that has encouraged us to kill the unborn (i.e., they will be an expensive nuisance if permitted to live). And how about getting rid of the very old members of our population who contribute nothing to society? And why should we allow deformed infants to live, etc? Perhaps the reader feels those chilling possibilities would never materialize, but I'm not so sure. We already live in a society where some parents will kill an unborn child if they determine through amniocentesis that its sex is not the one they desired.

There are many other aspects of the abortion issue that underscore its inherent evil, but the most important evidence for me came from the Scripture. Of course the Bible does not address itself directly to the practice of abortions. However, I was amazed to observe how many references are made in both the Old and New Testaments to God's personal acquaintance with children *prior* to birth. Not only was He aware of their gestations but He was specifically knowledgeable of them as unique individuals and personalities.

Consider the following examples:

1. The angel Gabriel said of John the Baptist, "and he shall be filled with the Holy Ghost *even from his mother's womb.*" (Luke 1:15)
2. The prophet Jeremiah wrote about himself, "The Lord said to me, 'I knew you *before* you were formed within your mother's womb; *before you were born* I sanctified you and appointed you as my spokesman to the world'" Jeremiah 1:4, 5 TLB.

These two individuals were hardly inhuman embryos before their birth. They were already known to the Creator, who had assigned them a life's work by divine decree.

3. In the book of Genesis we are told that Isaac "pleaded with Jehovah to give Rebekah a child, for even after many years of marriage she had no children. Then at last she became pregnant. And it seemed as though children were fighting each other inside her.

   "'I can't endure this,' she exclaimed. So she asked the Lord about it.

   "And he told her, 'The sons in your womb shall become two rival nations. One will be stronger than the other; and the older shall be the servant of the younger!'" (Genesis 25:21–23)TLB.

Again, God was aware of the developing personalities in these unborn twins and foretold their future conflicts. The mutual hatred of their descendants is still evident in the Middle East today.

4. Jesus Himself was *conceived* by the Holy Spirit, which fixes God's involvement with Christ from the time He was a single cell inside Mary's uterus (Matthew 1:18).

The most dramatic example, however, is found in the 139th Psalm. King David describes his own prenatal relationship with God, which is stunning in its impact.

> You made all the delicate, inner parts of my body, and knit them together in my mother's womb. Thank you for making me so wonderfully complex! It is amazing to think about. Your workmanship is marvelous—and how well I know it. You were there while I was being formed in utter seclusion! You saw me before I was born and scheduled each day of my life before I began to breathe. Every day was recorded in your book! (Psalm 139:13–16) TLB

That passage is thrilling to me, because it implies that God not only scheduled each day of David's life, but He did the same for *me*. He was there when *I* was being formed in utter seclusion, and He personally made all the delicate inner parts of *my* body. Imagine that! The Great Creator of the universe lovingly supervised my development during those preconscious days *in utero*, as He did for every human being on earth. Surely, anyone who can grasp that concept without sensing an exhilaration is stone-cold dead!

From my point of view, these scriptural references absolutely refute the notion that unborn children do not have a soul or personhood until they are born at full term. I can't believe it! No rationalization can justify detaching a healthy little human being from his place of safety and leaving him to suffocate on a porcelain table. No social or financial considerations can counter-balance our collective guilt for destroying those lives which were being fashioned in the image of God Himself. Throughout the Gospels, Jesus revealed a tenderness toward boys and girls ("suffer little children to come unto me"), and some of his most frightening warnings were addressed to those who would hurt them. It is my deepest conviction that He will not hold us blameless for our wanton infanticide. As He said to Cain, who had killed Abel, "Your brother's blood calls to me from the ground!"

Surely, other Christians have drawn the same conclusion. I must ask, where are those moral leaders who agree with me? Why have pastors and ministers been so timid and mute on this vital matter? It is time that the Christian church found its tongue and spoke in defense of the unborn children who are unable to plead for their own lives.

The Eternal Source

When a child was born during the 1800s or before, his inexperienced mother was assisted by many friends and relatives who hovered around to offer their advice and support. Very few of these aunts and grandmothers and neighbors had ever read a book on child-rearing, but that was no handicap. They possessed a certain folk wisdom which gave them confidence in handling babies and children. They had a prescribed answer for every situation, whether it proved to be right or wrong. Thus, a young woman was systematically taught how to "mother" by older women who had many years' experience in caring for little people.

With the disappearance of this "extended family," however, the job of motherhood became more frightening. Many young couples today do not have access to such supportive relatives and friends. They live in a mobile society wherein the next-door neighbors are often total strangers. Furthermore, their own mothers and fathers may live in far-away Detroit or Dallas or Portland (and might not be trusted even if they were available to help). Consequently, young parents often experience great anxieties over their lack of preparation for raising children. Dr. Benjamin Spock described their fears in this way: "I can remember mothers who cried on the morning they were to take their baby home. 'I won't know what to do,' they wailed."

This anxiety has brought parents rushing to the "experts" for information and advice. They have turned to pediatricians, psychologists, psychiatrists and educators for answers to their questions about the complexities of parenthood. Therefore, increasing numbers of American children have been reared according to this professional consultation during the past forty years. In fact, no country on earth has embraced the teachings of child psychology and the offerings of family specialists more than has the United States.

It is now appropriate that we ask, "What has been the effect of this professional influence?" One would expect that the mental health of our children would exceed that of individuals raised in nations not having this technical assistance. Such has not been the case. Juvenile delinquency, drug abuse, alcoholism, unwanted pregnancies, mental illness, and suicide are rampant among the young, and continue their steady rise. In many ways, we have made a mess of parenthood! Of course, I would not be so naive as to blame all these woes on the bad advice of the "experts," but I believe they have played a role in creating the problem. Why? *Because in general, behavioral scientists have lacked confidence in the Judeo-Christian ethic and have disregarded the wisdom of this priceless tradition!*

It appears to me that the twentieth century has spawned a generation of professionals who felt qualified to ignore the parental attitudes and practices of more than 2000 years, substituting instead their own wobbly-legged insights of the moment. Each authority, writing from his own limited experience and reflecting his own unique biases, has sold us his guesses and suppositions as though they represented Truth itself. One anthropologist, for example, wrote an incredibly gallish article in *The Saturday Evening Post*, November 1968, entitled "We Scientists Have a Right to Play God." Dr. Edmund Leach stated,

> There can be no source for these moral judgments except the scientist himself. In traditional religion, morality was held to derive from God, but God was only credited with the authority to establish and enforce moral rules because He was also credited with supernatural powers of creation and destruction. Those powers have now been usurped by man, and he must take on the moral responsibility that goes with them.[1]

That paragraph summarizes the many ills of our day. Arrogant men like Edmund Leach have argued God out of existence and put themselves in His exalted place. Armed with that authority, they have issued their ridiculous opinions to the public with unflinching confidence. In turn, desperate families grabbed their porous recommendations like life preservers, which often sank to the bottom, taking their passengers down with them.

These false teachings have included the notions that loving discipline is damaging, and irresponsibility is healthy, and religious instruction is hazardous, and defiance is a valuable ventilator of anger, and all authority is dangerous, and on and on it goes. In more recent years, this humanistic perspective has become even more extreme and anti-Christian. For example, one mother told me recently that she works in a youth project which has obtained the consultative services of a certain psychologist. He has been teaching the parents of kids in the program that in order for young girls to grow up with more healthy attitudes toward sexuality, their fathers should have intercourse with them when they are twelve years of age. If you gasped at that suggestion, be assured that it shocked me also. Yet this is where moral relativism leads—this is the ultimate product of a human endeavor which accepts no standards, honors no cultural values, acknowledges no absolutes, and serves no "god" except the human mind. King Solomon wrote about such foolish efforts in Proverbs 14:12: "There is a way that *seemeth* right unto a man, but the end thereof are the ways of death."

Now admittedly, the book you have been reading about the strong-willed child also contains many suggestions and perspectives which I have not attempted to validate or prove. How do my writings differ from the unsupported recommendations of those whom I have criticized? The distinction lies in the *source* of the views being presented. The underlying principles expressed herein are not my own innovative insights which would be forgotten in a brief season or two. Instead, they originated with the inspired biblical writers who gave us the foundation for all relationships in the home. As such, these principles have been handed down generation after generation to this very day. Our ancestors taught it to their children who taught it to their children, keeping the knowledge alive for posterity. Now, unfortunately, that understanding is being vigorously challenged in some circles and altogether forgotten in others.

If I have had a primary mission in writing this book, therefore, it has not been to earn royalty or propagate the name of James Dobson or demonstrate my professional skills. My purpose has been nothing more ambitious than to verbalize the Judeo-Christian tradition regarding discipline of children and to apply those concepts to today's families. This approach has been deeply ingrained in the Western culture but has never been expressly written, to my knowledge. It involves control with love, and a reasonable introduction to self-discipline and responsibility, and parental *leadership* which seeks the best interest of the child, and respect for the dignity and worth of every member of the family, and realistic boundaries that are enforced with confident firmness, and finally, a judicious use of rewards and punishment when required for training. It is a system that has existed for more than twenty centuries of parenthood. I did not invent it, nor can I change it. My task has been merely to report what I believe to be the prescription of the Creator Himself. And I am convinced that this understanding will remain viable for as long as mothers and fathers and children cohabit the face of the earth. It will certainly outlive humanism and the puny efforts of mankind to find an alternative.

A Final Comment

We began this discussion 245 pages ago with the story of my dog, Siggie, and his earlier revolutionary tendencies. Perhaps it would be appropriate to close the book with a look at the aging Sigmund today. He is now twelve years old and no longer has the fire of youthful exuberance. In fact, he has developed a progressive "heart leak" and will probably not live more than one more year. So he takes life easy these days, yawning and stretching and going back to sleep in the sun. (We have nicknamed him "Hal" because of his constant halitosis in these declining years.)

It is difficult to explain how a worthless old hound could be so loved by his family, but we're all going to miss little Siggie. (Dog lovers will understand our sentiment, but others will think it foolish.) He is a year older than our eldest child and has been her pal throughout childhood. So we have begun to prepare both children for his inevitable demise.

One day last month the moment of crisis came without warning. I was brushing my teeth in the early morning when I heard Siggie's sharp cry. He can scream like a baby, and my wife rushed to his assistance.

"Jim, come quickly!" she said. "Siggie is having a heart attack!"

I joined her in the family room with toothbrush still in my hand. Siggie was lying just outside his bed and he appeared to be in great pain. He was hunched down on his paws and his eyes were unfocused and glassy. I bent down and petted him gently and agreed that he was probably experiencing heart failure. I was not sure what to do for a dog in the midst of a coronary thrombosis, since the local paramedics are rather sensitive about offering their services to animals. I picked him up and laid him carefully on his bed, and he rolled on one side and remained completely motionless. His feet were held rigidly together, and it did, indeed, look as though the end had come.

I returned to my study to telephone the veterinarian, but Shirley again called me. She had taken a closer look at the immobile dog and discovered the nature of his problem. (Are you ready for this?) There are little claws or toenails on the sides of a dog's legs, and Siggie had somehow managed to get them hooked! That is why he couldn't move, and why he experienced pain when he tried to walk. There is not another dog anywhere in the world who could handcuff (pawcuff?) himself, but with Siggie, anything can happen. Shirley unhooked his toenails and the senile dog celebrated his release by acting like a puppy again.

When I am an old man and I think back on the joys of parenthood—the Christmas seasons and the camping trips and the high-pitched voices of two bubbly children in our home—I will remember a stubborn little dachshund named Sigmund Freud who played such an important role throughout those happy days.

Notes

CHAPTER 1

1. Raymond Corsini and Genevieve Painter, *Family Circle*, April 1975, p. 26.
2. Dr. Herbert Birch, Dr. Stella Chess, and Dr. Alexander Thomas, *Parent and Child* (New York: Redbook Publishing Company, 1976), "The Individuality Factor," pp. 4, 5, 97).

CHAPTER 2

1. John Valusek, *Parade Magazine*, February 6, 1977, n.p.
2. Dr. James C. Dobson, *Hide or Seek* (Old Tappan, N.J.: Fleming H. Revell Company, 1974), n.p. Used by permission.
3. T. Berry Brazelton, *Toddlers and Parents: A Declaration of Independence* (New York: Delacorte Press, 1974), pp. 101–110.
4. From the *APA Monitor* (published by the American Psychological Association, Washington, D.C.), Vol. 7, No. 4, 1976, n.p.
5. Dr. Luther Woodward, in *Your Child from 2 to 5*, Morton Edwards, editor (New York: Permabooks, 1955), pp. 95, 96.
6. Dr. James Dobson, *Dare to Discipline* (Wheaton, Ill.: Tyndale House Publishers, 1970), p. 20.
7. Reprinted by permission of United Press International.

CHAPTER 3

1. Marguerite and Willard Beecher, *Parents on the Run: A Common-sense Book for Today's Parents* (New York: Crown Publishers, Inc., © 1955 by Marguerite and Willard Beecher), pp. 6–8. Used by permission of Crown Publishers, Inc.
2. Philip Yancey, "Benedict Arnold Seagull," *Campus Life,* © 1975 Youth for Christ International, Wheaton, Illinois. Reprinted by permission.
3. Dr. Milton I. Levine, in *Your Child from 2 to 5,* Morton Edwards, editor, pp. 182–184.

CHAPTER 4

1. Dr. Benjamin Spock, "How Not to Bring up a Bratty Child," *Redbook,* February 1974, pp. 29–31.
2. *Ibid.*
3. *Ibid.*
4. Dobson, *Dare to Discipline,* pp. 37–40.
5. Fitzhugh Dodson, *How to Father* (New York: Nash Publishing Corp., 1974), p. 59. Reprinted by permission.
6. Pat Fabrizio, *Children—Fun or Frenzy?* (Palo Alto, Calif., published by author, 1969).

CHAPTER 5

1. Beecher, n.p.

CHAPTER 6

1. Domeena C. Renshaw, M.D., *The Hyperactive Child* (Chicago: Nelson-Hall Publishers, 1974), pp. 80, 81. Reprinted by permission.
2. *Ibid.,* pp. 118–120.

CHAPTER 7

1. Jim Stingley, "Advocating Children's Liberation," *Los Angeles Times,* July 28, 1974.
2. *Ibid.*
3. Dr. Thomas Gordon, *Parent Effectiveness Training* (New York: David McKay Company, Inc., 1970), pp. 164, 188, 191.
4. *Ibid.,* p. 179.

5. *Ibid.*, n.p.
6. Dr. James Dobson, *Moody Monthly,* reprinted by permission from the October 1976 issue. Copyright 1976, Moody Bible Institute of Chicago.
7. Gordon, pp. 190, 191, 188, 169.
8. Quoted from *Family under Fire,* a conference book by Dr. James Dobson. Other participants quoted were Rev. James Dobson, father of the author, and Dr. Paul Cunningham, pastor, both of whom have given permission for these quotations.

CHAPTER 8

1. "Yakety Yak (Don't Talk Back)," by Jerry Leiber and Mike Stoller. Copyright © 1958 by Tiger Music, Inc. All rights controlled by Unichappell Music, Inc., Quintet Music, Inc., and Freddy Bienstock. International copyright secured. All rights reserved. Used by permission.
2. Michael Medved and David Wallechinsky, *What Really Happened to the Class of '65?* (New York: Random House, Inc., 1976). Quotations used are taken from pp. 30, 55, 155, 160, 283.
3. Renshaw, p. 63.
4. This editorial by C. Donald Cole is reprinted by permission from the September 1976 issue of *Moody Monthly.* Copyright 1976, Moody Bible Institute of Chicago.
5. *Time,* August 22, 1977, p. 49.

CHAPTER 9

1. Dr. Edmund Leach, "We Scientists Have a Right to Play God," *The Saturday Evening Post,* November 1968. © 1968 The Curtis Publishing Company, Indianapolis, Ind.

PARENTING ISN'T FOR COWARDS

This book is affectionately dedicated to the mothers of the world, especially the one to whom I am married, who have dedicated themselves to the care and training of the next generation. They have been maligned, goaded, blamed and ridiculed in recent years, but most have stood their ground. Quietly and confidently they have continued to love and nourish their children and prepared them for a life of service to God and to mankind. There is no more important assignment on the face of the earth, and I hope this book will make their task a bit less difficult.

JAMES DOBSON

Contents

269

List of Tables

The Challenge

Have you noticed? Being a good parent seems to have become more difficult in recent years. It never has been all that easy, of course. For one thing, babies come into the world with no instructions and you pretty much have to assemble them on your own. They are also maddeningly complex and there are no guaranteed formulas that work in every instance. The techniques that succeed magnificently with one child can fail bewilderingly with another.

Many parents do not understand this frustrating aspect of child-rearing because they have never experienced it. Through no great achievement of their own, they managed to produce a house full of "easy" children. My wife and I are acquainted with a family like that. They were blessed with three of the most perfect children you are likely to find. All three made straight A's in school, kept their rooms perpetually clean, were musically talented, ate with one hand in their laps, were first-team athletes, spoke politely and correctly to adults, and even had teeth that didn't need straightening! It was almost disgusting to see how well they turned out.

Predictably, our friends awarded themselves complete credit for the successes of their children. They were also inclined, at the drop of a hat, to tell you how to raise yours. Overconfidence oozed from their fingertips.

But then an interesting thing happened. The Lord, who must have a sense of humor, gift-wrapped a little tornado and sent it as a surprise package on the mother's fortieth birthday. That family has been stumbling backward ever since. Their little caboose, who is now six years old, is as tough as nails and twice as sharp. He *loves* to fight with his parents and already knows considerably more than they. Just ask him. He'll tell you. The funny thing about his parents is that they quit giving child-rearing advice shortly after his birth. Their job suddenly got tougher!

When I think of these parents today, I'm reminded of a photograph in my files of an elegantly dressed woman who is holding a cup of coffee. Her little finger is cocked ever so daintily to the side and her face reveals utter self-assurance. Unfortunately, this woman does not yet know that her slip has collapsed around her feet. The caption reads, "Confidence is what you have before you understand the situation." Indeed!

More than one tough-minded youngster has sand-blasted the confidence of his parents. That's how he gets his kicks. If you have raised only compliant children who smiled regularly and then hustled off to do your bidding, then beware. You may not yet understand the situation. And the Lord could send *you* a surprise package too. Of this fact I'm certain: if you produce enough babies, you will discover sooner or later that there is nothing simple about human beings . . . of *any* age.

From the mail I receive from parents it is clear to me that many are struggling with their responsibilities at home. To learn why, I asked 1,000 mothers and fathers to describe the frustrations they were experiencing in child-rearing. Their answers were fascinating. Some talked of sticky telephones, wet toilet seats and knotted shoestrings. Others told the most delightful stories.

I'll never forget the mother who had been cooped up with her toddler for several weeks. In a desperate effort to get out of the house, she decided to take her son to a Muppet movie . . . his first. As soon as they arrived in the theater, the mother discovered a minor technical problem. The child didn't weigh enough to keep the spring seat down. There was nothing left to do but hold this churning, squirming two-year-old on her lap throughout the movie.

It was a mistake. Sometime during the next two hours, they lost control of a large Pepsi and a king-sized box of buttered popcorn! That gooey mixture flowed over the child onto the mother's lap and down her legs. She decided to sit it out since the movie was almost over. What she didn't know, unfortunately, was that she and her son were being systematically cemented together. When the movie was over, they stood up and the mother's wraparound skirt came unraveled. It stuck to the bottom of the toddler and followed him up the aisle! She stood there clutching her slip and thanking the Lord she had taken time to put one on!

Can't you see this mother desperately begging the child to drag her skirt back within reach? Parenthood can certainly be humiliating at times. It also seems specifically designed to irritate us. Tell me why it is that a toddler never throws up in the bathroom? Never! To do so would violate some great unwritten law in the universe. It is even more difficult to understand why he will gag violently at the sight of a perfectly wonderful breakfast of oatmeal, eggs, bacon and orange juice . . . and then go out and drink the dog's water. I have no idea what makes him do that. I only know that it drives his mother crazy!

Obviously, the parents who participated in our "Frustrations of Parenthood" poll did not just share their humorous experiences. They also provided some surprising and distressing answers. Rather than criticizing their children, as one might have expected, the most common response focused on their own inadequacies as mothers and fathers! Specific answers revealed the great self-doubt so prevalent among parents today:

- "not knowing how to cope with children's problems"
- "not being able to make the kids feel secure and loved"
- "I've lost confidence in my ability to parent"
- "I've failed my children"
- "I'm not the example I should be"
- "seeing my own bad habits and character-traits in my children"
- "inability to relate to my children"
- "dealing with guilt when it seems that I have failed my sons"
- "inability to cope"
- "it's too late to go back and do it right"
- "I'm overwhelmed by the responsibility of it all."

Isn't it incredible to observe just how tentative we have become about this task of raising children?

Parenting is hardly a new technology. Since Adam and Eve graced the Garden, 77 billion people have lived on this earth, yet we're still nervous about bringing up the baby. It is a sign of the times.

I'm quite certain that parents in past decades spent less energy worrying about their children. They had other things on their minds. I remember talking to my dad about this subject a few years before his death. Our children were young at the time and I was feeling the heavy responsibility of raising them properly.

I turned to my father and asked, "Do you remember worrying about me when I was a kid? Did you think about all the things that could go wrong as I came through the adolescent years? How did you feel about these pressures associated with being a father?"

Dad was rather embarrassed by the line of questioning. He smiled sheepishly and said, "Honestly, Bo," (his pet name for me) "I never really gave that a thought."

How do we explain his lack of concern? Was it because he didn't love me or because he was an uninvolved parent? No. He prayed for me until the day he died. And as I have said on many occasions, he was a wonderful father to me. Instead, his answer reflected the time in which I grew up. People worried about the depression that was just ending, and the war with Germany, and later the cold war with Russia. They did not invest much effort in hand-wringing over their children . . . at least not until a major problem developed. Trouble was not anticipated.

And why not? Because it was easier to raise kids in that era. I attended high school during the "Happy Days" of the 1950s, and I never saw or even heard of anyone taking an illegal drug. It happened, I suppose, but it was certainly no threat to me. Some of the other students liked to get drunk, but alcohol was not a big deal in my social environment. Others played around with sex, but the girls who did were considered "loose" and were not respected. Virginity was still in style for males *and* females. Occasionally a girl came up pregnant, but she was packed off in a hurry and I never knew where she went. Homosexuals were very weird and unusual people. I heard there were a few around but I didn't know them personally. Most of my friends respected their parents, went to church on Sunday, studied hard enough to get by and lived a fairly clean life. There were exceptions, of course, but this was the norm. It's no wonder my parents were concentrating on other anxieties.

It is also no wonder that parents are more concerned in the present era. Their children are walking through the Valley of the Shadow! Drugs, sex, alcohol, rebellion and deviant lifestyles are everywhere. Those dangers have never been so evident to me as they are today.

I'm writing this book in the heart of London, where my family has joined me for a couple of months. This wonderful and historic city is also the home of some of the most pitiful young people I've ever seen. Rockers and punkers and druggies are on the streets in search of something. Who knows what? Girls with green and orange hair walk by with strange-looking boyfriends. At least I *think* they're boys. They wear earrings and have blue "Mohawk" haircuts that stick four inches in the air. While gazing at that sight, a clang! clang! clang! sound is heard from the rear. The Hare Krishnas are coming. They dance by with their shaved heads and monk-like robes. Gays parade arm in arm and prostitutes advertise their services. I stand there thinking, *What in heaven's name have we allowed to happen to our kids?*

The same phenomenon is occurring in the United States and Canada. It is sometimes overwhelming to see what has happened to a value system that served us so well. When my daughter was eighteen, I attended a program put on by the music department at her high school. Sitting in front of me was one of Danae's girlfriends. At intermission we chatted about her plans, and she told me she would soon enroll at the University of California, Berkeley. She had just returned from a visit to the school and mentioned casually that something had bothered her about the dormitory in which she would reside. She had learned that the men and women lived side by side and they also shared the same bathrooms. What concerned this pretty young lady was that there was no curtain on the shower stall!

This is the world in which our children are growing up. Obviously, conservative communities still exist where traditional values are honored. Millions of kids still want to do what is right. But dangerous enticements are there, too, and parents know it. Some live in fear that the dragon of adolescence will consume their sons and daughters before they have even started out in life. That anxiety can take the pleasure out of raising children.

There is, however, another reason for the crisis of confidence that many parents are experiencing today. Mothers, especially, have been placed in an impossible bind. They have been blamed for everything that can conceivably go wrong with children. Even when their love and commitment are incalculable, the experts accuse them of making grievous errors in toilet training, disciplining, feeding, medicating and educating their youngsters. They are either overpossessive or undernourishing.

One psychiatrist even wrote an entire book on the dangers of religious training of all types. Thus, no matter how diligently "Mom" approaches her parenting responsibilities, she seems destined to be accused of twisting and warping her children.

Not only have mothers been blamed by the experts for things beyond their control, but they have also been quite willing to criticize themselves. Consider again the list of statements cited from our poll of parents. Eighty percent of the respondents were women, and their most frequent comment was, "I'm a failure as a mother!" What nonsense! Women have been *taught* to blame themselves in this way and it is time to set the record straight.

I don't believe that the task of procreation was intended to be so burdensome. Of course it is demanding. But parents in the twentieth century have saddled themselves with unnecessary guilt, fear and self-doubt. That is not the divine plan. Throughout the Scriptures, it is quite clear that the raising of children was viewed as a wonderful blessing from God—a welcome, joyful experience. And today, it remains one of the greatest privileges in living to bring a baby into the world . . . a vulnerable little human being who looks to us for all his needs. What a wonderful opportunity it is to teach these little ones to love God with all their hearts and to serve their fellowman throughout their lives. There is no higher calling than that!

The book you are reading, then, is intended as a celebration of parenthood. We've had enough of groveling and self-condemnation. What we need now is a double dose of confidence in our ability to raise our children properly. We also need to consider the specific frustrations that prevent us from enjoying our kids while they are young. Toward this end, the chapters that follow will deal with the contest of wills between generations, with the perils of adolescence, with parental burnout and its causes and with the other stress points that irritate and depress us. There is a more satisfying way to raise children, as I believe the reader will see. And there is no better time than now to apply it. Our sons and daughters will be grown so quickly and these days at home together will be nothing but a distant memory. Let's make the most of every moment.

The Tough and the Gentle

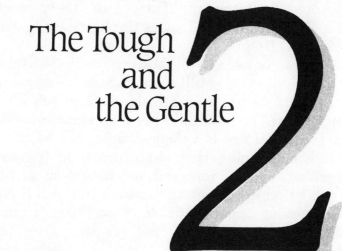

In the days of the wild and woolly West, a lone cowboy went riding through a valley and came unexpectedly upon an Indian lying motionless on the road. His right ear was pressed to the ground, and he was muttering soberly to himself. "Ummm," he said. "Stagecoach! Three people inside. Two men, one woman. Four horses. Three dapple gray, one black. Stagecoach moving west. Ummmmm." The cowboy was amazed and said, "That's incredible, pardner! You can tell all that just by listening to the ground?" The Indian replied, "Ummmmmm. No! Stagecoach run over me thirty minutes ago!"

When I first heard that story I was reminded of the mothers, bless them all, who are raising one or more rambunctious preschoolers simultaneously. If you are one of them, haven't you had moments like that Indian when you found yourself lying flat on the floor and muttering to yourself, "Mmmmm. Three kids. Dirty hands. Wet diapers. Mud on feet. Tearing through the house. Making me crazy! Help!"?

If you've been in this posture lately, then take heart. You are not alone. Millions of parents, past and present, can identify with the particular stresses you are experiencing right now. A child between eighteen and thirty-six months of age is a sheer delight, but he can also be utterly maddening. He is inquisitive, short-tempered, demanding, cuddly, innocent and dangerous at the same time. I find it fascinating to watch him run through his day, seeking opportunities to crush things, flush things, kill things, spill things, fall off things, eat horrible things—and think up ways to rattle his mother. Someone said it best: The Lord made Adam from the dust of the earth, but when the first toddler came along, He added *electricity*!

Adolescents are interesting too, and we'll discuss them at length in later chapters. But toddlers are a breed apart. Bill Cosby said he could conquer the world if he could somehow manage to mobilize about 200 aggressive two-year-olds. It wouldn't surprise me. His army should definitely include an energetic lad named Frankie who belongs, more or less, to some friends of ours.

Little Frankie is a classic toddler. One day recently he pulled a chair over to the front window and carefully placed it inside the drapes. He was standing there staring out at the world when his mother came looking for him. She spied his little white legs protruding beneath the drapes and quietly slipped in behind him. Then she heard him speaking to himself in very somber terms. He was saying, "I've *got* to get out of here!"

I could fill a book with wonderful pronouncements from the mouths of preschool children. They are among the most delightful little people on the face of the earth. But returning to our thesis, they (and all children) bring a special kind of stress into the lives of their parents. Humorist Erma Bombeck said in one of her books that she was frustrated by her children from the moment they were born. She remembered *how* she got three kids, but she couldn't recall *why*. She decided maybe they were a 4-H project that got out of hand.

For some parents, the overwhelming responsibility associated with child-rearing is not so funny. As indicated in the preceding chapter, there appears to be a growing number of husbands and wives today who are not coping well with parenthood. They've reached the end of the rope and it is frazzled. The letters they send to me are replete with self-condemnation, guilt and anger. Many seem to have experienced a kind of physical exhaustion that leaves them confused and depressed.

High on the list of irritants which keeps them off balance and agitated is the tendency of some children to test, challenge, resist and blatantly defy authority. These rebellious youngsters can create more stress in a single afternoon than their mothers can handle in a week. I wrote about them in an earlier book entitled *The Strong-Willed Child*, but they continue to fascinate me. For fifteen years I have watched them operate and wondered what makes them tick. I have interviewed adults who had been rebellious teenagers, and asked them what they were thinking during their season of anger. Even they do not fully understand themselves. I resolved to investigate further.

On behalf of those readers who have never encountered him, let me describe the tough-minded child. At birth he looks deceptively like his more compliant sibling. He weighs seven pounds and is totally dependent on those who care for him. Indeed, he would not survive for more than a day or two without their attention. Ineffectual little arms and legs dangle aimlessly in four directions, appearing to be God's afterthoughts. What a picture of vulnerability and innocence he is!

Isn't it amazing, given this beginning, what happens in twenty short months? Junior then weighs twenty-five pounds and he's itching for action. Would you believe this kid who couldn't even hold his own bottle less than two years ago now has the gall to look his two-hundred-pound father straight in the eye and tell him where to get off? What audacity! Obviously, there is something deep within his soul that longs for control. He will work at achieving it for the rest of his life.

In the early 1970s I had the privilege of living near one of these little spitfires. He was thirty-six months old at the time and had already bewildered and overwhelmed his mother. The contest of wills was over. He had won it. His sassy talk was legendary in the neighborhood, not only to his mother but to anyone who got in his way. Then one day my wife saw him ride his tricycle down the driveway and into the street, which panicked his mother. We lived on a curve and the cars came around that bend at high speed. Mom rushed out of the house and caught up with her son as he pedaled down the street. She took hold of his handlebars to redirect him, and he came unglued.

"Get your dirty hands off my tricycle!" he screamed. His eyes were squinted in fury. As Shirley watched in disbelief, this woman did as she was told. The life of her child was in danger, and yet this mother did not have the courage to confront him. He continued to ride down the street and she could only stand and watch.

How could it be that a tiny little boy at three years of

age was able to buffalo his thirty-year-old mother in this way? Well, it was clear to any observer that she had no idea how to manage him. But also, he was simply tougher than she—and they both knew it. This mild-mannered woman had produced an iron-willed kid who was giving her fits, and you can be sure that her physical and emotional resources were continually drained by his antics.

Contrast this independent youngster with his easy-going counterpart at the other end of the continuum. The compliant child approaches people from an entirely different direction. He wants to please them because he needs their approval. A word of displeasure or even the slightest frown from his parents can be disturbing to him. He is a lover, not a fighter.

A few years ago I talked with the mother of one of these easy-going kids. She was concerned about the difficulties her son was having in nursery school. He was regularly being bullied by more aggressive children, but it was not within him to defend himself. Thus, every afternoon when his mother came to get him, he had been whacked and harassed by these other boys. Even the girls were joining in the fun.

"You must defend yourself!" his mother said again and again. "Those other children will keep hitting you until you make them stop!"

Each day she urged her little lover to be more assertive, but it contradicted his nature to do so. Finally, his frustration became so great that he began trying to follow his mother's advice. As they were on the way to school one morning he said, "Mom! If those kids pick on me again today . . . I'm . . . I'm . . . I'm going to beat them up! Slightly."

How does one beat up an opponent *slightly*? I don't know, but it made perfect sense to this compliant child.

He didn't want to use any more force than was absolutely necessary to survive. Why? Because he had a peace-loving nature. His parents didn't teach it to him. It simply *was*.

As most mothers know, this kind of compliant child and his strong-willed sibling are so distinct that they could almost be from different planets. One cuddles to your embrace and the other kicks you in the navel. One is a natural sweetheart and the other goes through life like hot lava. One follows orders and the other gives them. Quite obviously, they are marching to a different set of drums.

I must make it clear that the compliant child is not necessarily wimpy or spineless. That fact is very important to our understanding of his nature and how he differs from his strong-willed sibling. The distinction between them is *not* a matter of confidence, willingness to take a risk, sparkling personality or other desirable characteristics. Rather, the issue under consideration is focused on the strength of the will—the inclination of some children to resist authority and determine their own course, as compared with those who are willing to be led. It is my supposition that these temperaments are pre-packaged before birth and do not have to be cultivated or encouraged. They will make themselves known soon enough.

Not everyone concurs. Many psychologists and psychiatrists of the past would have disagreed violently with this understanding. Sigmund Freud, the father of psychoanalysis, and J. B. Watson, the creator of behaviorism, believed that newborns come into the world as "blank slates" on which the environment would later write. For them, a baby had no inborn characteristics of personality that distinguished him from other infants. Everything he would become, both good and evil, would result from the experiences to be provided by the world around him. He could make no independent decisions because he had no real freedom of choice . . . no ability to consider his circumstances and act rationally on them. Watson even rejected the existence of a mind, viewing the brain as a simple switchboard that responded automatically to external stimuli. Hence, his system of thinking has been called, "Psychology out of its mind."

Watson bragged during the 1920s that he could train any infant "to become any type of specialist I might select . . . doctor, lawyer, artist, merchant, chief and, yes, even beggarman and thief." He thought children were simply "raw material" for parents "to fashion in ways to suit themselves."

In short, this belief that all behavior is caused is called *determinism*, and it will have significance for us in later discussions. I first heard the concept when I was in graduate school. I didn't accept it then, and I certainly don't believe it now. As a Christian psychologist, I have always filtered man-made theories through the screen of Scripture, and in this instance, determinism hangs up in the wire. If it were true, we would be unable to worship and serve God as a voluntary expression of our love. We would be mere puppets on a string, responding to the stimuli around us.

It is becoming clear today just how far off base these classical psychologists have been in their interpretation of human behavior. There is no doubt, as they said, that the environment is enormously influential in molding and shaping our personalities, but they failed to recognize our ability to think, to choose and to respond according to our own temperaments. We are rational human beings who can override our experience and external influences. Furthermore, at birth, except for identical twins, no two of us are alike. And how foolish it was to have thought otherwise. If God makes every grain of sand and every snowflake like no other on earth, how simplistic it was to have believed He mass-produced little human robots. We are, after all, made in *His* image.

A blob of tissue? A blank slate? A mass of protoplasm? Hardly! Individual differences in temperament can be discerned at birth or shortly thereafter. In one remarkable scriptural reference we even see references to a strong-willed temperament before the child was born. Genesis 16:11 reports a striking conversation between an angel of the Lord and Abraham's pregnant servant girl, Hagar. He said, "You are now with child and you will have a son, you shall name him Ishmael, for the Lord has heard of your misery. He will be a wild donkey of a man; his hand will be against everyone and everyone's hand against him, and he will live in hostility toward all his brothers."

Does that sound like anyone you know? I've met a few wild donkeys in my time, to be sure. In another example from the book of Genesis, we are told of the prenatal development of the twins, Jacob and Esau. One was rebellious and tough while the other was something of a mama's boy. They were also enemies before they were born and continued in conflict through much of their lives (see Genesis 25:22–27). Then later, in one of the most mysterious and disturbing chapters in the Bible, the Lord said, "Jacob have I loved and Esau have I hated" (Romans 9:13). Apparently, God discerned a rebellious nature in Esau before he was born and knew that he would not be receptive to the divine Spirit.*

Behavioral scientists are now observing and documenting the subtle understandings that have been evident in the Scriptures for thousands of years. One of the most ambitious of these efforts to study the temperaments of babies has been in progress for more than three decades. It is known as the New York Longitudinal Study. The findings from this investigation, led by psychiatrists Stella Chess and Alexander Thomas, are now reported in their excellent book for parents entitled, *Know Your Child*. I recommend it enthusiastically to anyone interested in child development.

To my delight, Chess and Thomas found that babies not only differ significantly from one another at the moment of birth, but those differences tend to be rather persistent throughout childhood. Even more interestingly, they observed three broad categories or patterns of temperaments into which the majority of children can be classified. The first they called "the difficult child," who is characterized by negative reactions to people, intense mood swings, irregular sleep and feeding schedules, frequent periods of crying and violent tantrums when frustrated.

Does that sound familiar?

The second pattern is called "the easy child," who manifests a positive approach to people, quiet adaptability to new situations, regular sleep and feeding schedules, and a willingness to accept the rules of the game. The authors concluded, "Such a youngster is usually a joy to her parents, pediatrician and teachers." Amen.

The third category was given the title "Slow-to-warm-up" or "shy." These youngsters respond negatively to new situations and they adapt slowly. However, they are less intense than difficult children and they tend to have regular sleeping and feeding schedules. When they are upset or frustrated, they typically withdraw from the situation and react mildly, rather than exploding with anger and rebellion.

Not every child fits into these categories, of course, but approximately 65 percent do. Chess and Thomas also emphasize that babies are fully human at birth, being able immediately to relate to their parents and begin learning from their environments. I doubt if that news will come as a surprise to most parents, who never believed in the "blank slate" theory, anyway. Ask the mother who has raised a houseful of children. She will tell you that each of her kids had a different personality . . . a different "feel" . . . the first time she held the little one in her arms. She is right.

It should not be difficult to understand why these findings from longitudinal research have been exciting to me. They confirm my own observations, not only about the wonderful complexity of human beings, but also about the categories of temperament identified by Chess and Thomas. Nevertheless, basic questions remain to be answered.

What do we really know about these strong-willed and compliant children? (We'll leave our consideration of the shy child to a future book.) How persistent are their personality traits as they grow older? What are the teen years like for each? How do their parents feel about raising them? Does the strong-willed child have an advantage over the compliant child socially or academically or in achievement during early adulthood? These questions have never been answered, to my knowledge, since we have only recently admitted that temperamental differences exist. It was this dearth of information that led me to initiate a large-scale inquiry of my own into the subject.

Initially, a questionnaire was developed for use with parents (see Appendix). By completing this research instrument, parents provided extensive information regarding their own temperaments and those of their children. Specifically, they were asked to evaluate each member of the family on a five-point scale as follows: (1) very compliant; (2) rather compliant; (3) average; (4) rather strong-willed; (5) very strong-willed. No effort was made to define these categories because my interest was only in those children at the extremes, (categories [1] and [5]). The other records were ignored, except for the provision of demographic information.

I then asked detailed questions about the children and how their parents felt about raising them. More than 35,000 families participated in the study and the data were analyzed at the University of Southern California Computer Center. I was assisted in the analysis by my good friend, Malcolm Williamson, Ph.D., whose specialties are measurement and statistics. We generated a mountain of computerized information that could fill five books this size, but we will just hit the highlights here. Let me say that this has been a fascinating journey into human nature, and I wish to express appreciation to the families who shared their experiences with me. I believe the information I have learned through this effort is available nowhere else in the world.

We'll discuss those findings in the next two chapters.

---

*I recognize that this is deep water theologically speaking. Jacob was not rejected by God, and yet he, like Esau, was sinful and disobedient. Who among us can explain God's greater judgment on one than the other? In reference to the analogy between Jacob and Esau and the temperaments of children, I want to make it clear that the strong-willed child is no more evil or ungodly than his compliant sibling. His *inclination* toward disobedience may be greater, but I am certainly not casting them in terms of "good" vs. "bad." They are simply different, and one is more difficult to handle than the other.

3

What 35,000 Parents Said about Their Children

All right, class. I'm ready to distribute your midterm examination. We will soon see how well you understand the differences between very strong-willed and very compliant children. Close your books, please, and clear your desks of everything but pencils. Do not copy from your neighbor. We will discuss the correct answers after you have turned in your completed examination. Any questions? Good. Oh, by the way—if you fail this test you will be required to baby-sit with nine strong-willed toddlers for the next six weeks! You may begin.

Multiple Choice

1. It would be interesting to know when a baby is due whether he is likely to be difficult or easy to raise. Based on our data, we can take an educated guess.

293

What do you think the ratio is between very strong-willed and very compliant children?

(1) There are about twice as many very compliant children.

(2) There are almost three times as many very strong-willed children.

(3) There is about the same number of both.

(4) There are about twice as many strong-willed children.

2. Is it tougher to raise boys or girls? The answer may depend in part on the temperaments of each. When we consider only strong-willed children, what is the ratio of males to females?

(1) Males outnumber females by about 5 percentage points.

(2) Females outnumber males by about 9 percentage points.

(3) Males outnumber females by about 31 percentage points.

(4) There is no difference between the sexes.

3. Let's consider only easy-to-raise children now. What is the ratio of males to females among these compliant children?

(1) Males outnumber females by about 10 percentage points.

(2) Females outnumber males by about 6 percentage points.

(3) Males outnumber females by about 19 percentage points.

(4) There is no difference between the sexes.

4. Select the accurate statement below:

(1) Firstborn children are more likely to be very strong-willed.

    (2) Secondborn children are more likely to be very strong-willed.

    (3) Thirdborn children are more likely to be very strong-willed.

    (4) There is no strong tendency for temperament to be related to birth order.

5. Select the accurate statement below:

(Answers relate to when the temperament is identified)

    (1) Less than 10 percent of very strong-willed children are recognizable at birth to 3 months.

    (2) About a third of very strong-willed children are recognizable at birth to 3 months.

    (3) The vast majority of very strong-willed children are recognizable at birth to 3 months.

    (4) Only a few very strong-willed children are recognizable until toddlerhood, when 98 percent "show up."

6. Is the temperament of the child inherited from the parents?

    (1) The data suggest that it is.

    (2) The data suggest that it is not.

7. What happens to the rebellious nature of very strong-willed children as they move through the years?

    (1) Very few rebel until mid-adolescence, when a peak of 30 percent occurs.

    (2) After a peak of 20 percent rebel in toddlerhood, very little rebellion occurs until early adolescence.

    (3) Approximately 40 percent rebel in toddlerhood, and the percentages rise in every age category through adolescence, reaching a peak of 74 percent in the teen years.

      (4) Rebellion remains hidden, more or less, until early adolescence when an "explosion" occurs, reaching a peak of 63 percent at 15 years of age.

8. This next item refers to one of the most important findings from our study. It asks the question, what can be expected from compliant children—those easy, happy, cooperative kids—as they go through adolescence and young adulthood? Do they rebel? If so, how commonly? First, please indicate the percentage of these kids whom you think go into *severe* rebellion in either adolescence or young adulthood.
      (1) 3 percent
      (2) 26 percent
      (3) 52 percent
      (4) 76 percent
      (5) 89 percent

9. What percent of very compliant children eventually go into *mild* rebellion in either adolescence or young adulthood?
      (1) 14 percent
      (2) 33 percent
      (3) 41 percent
      (4) 79 percent
      (5) 91 percent

10. Which individual has an edge in academic achievement during the teen years?
      (1) The very strong-willed child.
      (2) The very compliant child.
      (3) Neither; there is no significant difference between them.

11. Which individual typically makes the best social adjustment in adolescence?
      (1) The very strong-willed child.

(2) The very compliant child.

(3) Neither; there is no significant difference between them.

12. One of the characteristics of the compliant child during the early years is the ease with which his parents
can mold and shape him. He is very responsive to
their leadership. Given that flexibility, how does he
respond to peer pressure? Or, asked another way,
which child (strong-willed or compliant) is more
likely to be "peer dependent" during adolescence?

(1) The very strong-willed child.

(2) The very compliant child.

(3) Neither; there is no significant difference between them.

13. Which individual is more likely to have the higher
self-esteem in adolescence?

(1) The very strong-willed child.

(2) The very compliant child.

(3) Neither; there is no significant difference between them.

14. Parents were asked to indicate how their grown sons
and daughters had achieved in adult pursuits. Which
group do you think succeeded best?

(1) The very strong-willed.

(2) The very compliant.

(3) There was no significant difference between
them.

Well, that's the end of our little quiz. I hope you
won't feel too badly if you flunked it. Honestly, I'm not
sure I could have passed it before seeing the findings
from our study. Apparently, there is broad misunderstanding among parents of these special children with
unusually tough or easy attitudes toward authority.

Indeed, I administered this quiz to many groups of young parents before writing my book. They didn't do so hot, either. In fact, it was typical for them to get from 4 to 6 items correct. One man answered 12 of the 14 items accurately, and he was given the "Superdad of the Year" award. When asked how he knew so much about very strong-willed and very compliant kids, he replied, "I raised one of each!"

Now. I'll repeat a simplified version of each question from the test, give the correct answer and then provide additional information about the issue at hand.

Question 1: What is the ratio of very strong-willed to very compliant children?
Answer: (4) There are about twice as many very strong-willed children. The entire distribution of 37,372 children was as follows:

TABLE 1

	Very Compliant	Rather Compliant	Average	Rather Strong-Willed	Very Strong-Willed	Totals
Number of cases	4,340	10,821	9,331	4,981	7,899	37,372
Percentage in category	11.6%	29.0%	25.0%	13.3%	21.1%	100.0%

Actually, the true ratio of very strong-willed to very compliant children is more like 3 to 1 than 2 to 1. Why? Because many of the 4,340 children in the very compliant category, above, were infants who had not yet been recognized as strong-willed. Their parents reported them to be compliant but a surprise is coming their way. When those children under 30 months are eliminated from our analysis, 74 percent of the children being studied were very strong-willed and 24 percent very compliant.

Question 2: What is the ratio of males to females within the category of very strong-willed children?
Answer: (1) Males outnumber females by about 5 percentage points . . . 52.5 to 47.5.

Question 3: (2) What is the ratio of males to females within the category of very compliant children?
Answer: (2) Females outnumber males by about 6 percentage points . . . 53 to 47.

Question 4: Select the accurate statement below (regarding birth order and temperament).
Answer: (4) There is no strong tendency for temperament to be related to birth order.

There is a slight trend toward compliance for firstborn children and strong-willed for secondborn. However, our assumption is that these characteristics are *inborn,* and should not be highly influenced by an environmental factor such as birth order. That is what we found.

Question 5: Select the accurate statement below (regarding the age when the strong-willed child is recognized).
Answer: (2) About a third (36 percent) of very strong-willed children are recognized at birth.

By one year of age, 66 percent are identified and 92 percent by age 3. Compliant children tend to be recognized earlier: 43 percent between birth and three months, 74 percent by one year and 93 percent by the third birthday.

> *Question 6:* Is the temperament of the child inherited from the parents?
> *Answer:* (1) *Yes.* The data suggest that it is.

Though there are many exceptions, there does seem to be a tendency for the temperaments of the parents to be reproduced in their children. Perhaps the environment has influenced our findings here, but I think genetics played the dominant role. There does seem to be an inherited component, even though it sometimes fails to materialize. It is not uncommon, for example, to produce three or four easy-to-raise children followed by a pistol.

> *Question 7:* What happens to the rebellious nature of very strong-willed children as they move through the years?
> *Answer:* (3) Approximately 40 percent rebel in toddlerhood, and the percentages rise in every age category through adolescence, reaching a peak of 74 percent in the teen years.

The data clearly reveal that the percentage of very strong-willed children who rebel begins high in toddlerhood, (40 percent), and never lets up until adulthood. There is no lull of any significance between toddlerhood and adolescence. This is important information, even though somewhat unpleasant, for parents who want to predict the patterns of behavior from their tough-minded kids. To assist in that understanding, I have plotted the data on the graph below. It depicts the percentage of *strong-willed children only* who rebel at each age category, (upper line), and the percentage who choose to cooperate (lower line). Note that the numbers do not add up to 100 percent because of the uncharted children in the middle who neither rebel nor make a special effort to cooperate.

TABLE 2

Rebellion and Cooperation in Strong-willed Children

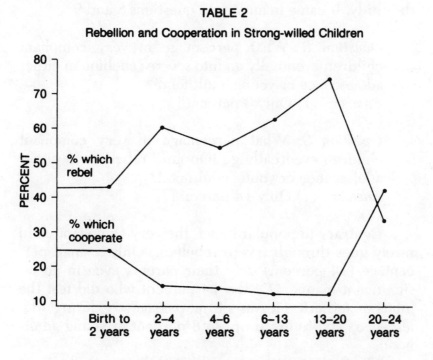

I hope this information will not be discouraging to parents of strong-willed children. It is true that a significant percentage will be in rebellion at any one time, (from 40 to 74 percent) while the percentage who cooperate ranges from 23 percent to a low of 11 percent in adolescence. It is encouraging, however, to see the rapid decline of rebellion in young adulthood, dropping precipitously from 74 to 36 percent. In fact, the lines cross slightly at that point, with more strong-willed children cooperating than rebelling. The battles are still in progress for about a third of the individuals, but most of the fire is spent. They'll soon join the human race again. I'll share other good news in a moment.

Now we come to a most surprising discovery from the study. It came in answer to questions 8 and 9.

> *Question 8:* What percentage of very compliant children eventually go into *severe* rebellion in either adolescence or young adulthood?
> *Answer:* (1) Only 3 percent!!

> *Question 9:* What percentage of very compliant children eventually go into *mild* rebellion in either adolescence or young adulthood?
> *Answer:* (1) Only 14 percent!

Contrary to popular belief, the very compliant child rarely goes through severe rebellion. Only a small percentage (14 percent) defy their parents even in an insignificant manner. Of the 14 percent who did test the limits of authority, it was a brief passageway during adolescence. The figure drops to 8 percent in young adulthood.

The findings about *compliant* children are depicted in Table 3, which parallels the one above for strong-willed children. It tells a remarkable story of cooperation and harmony at home.

Isn't it amazing that the vast majority of these compliant children (91 percent) do not become difficult

TABLE 3

Rebellion and Cooperation in Compliant Children

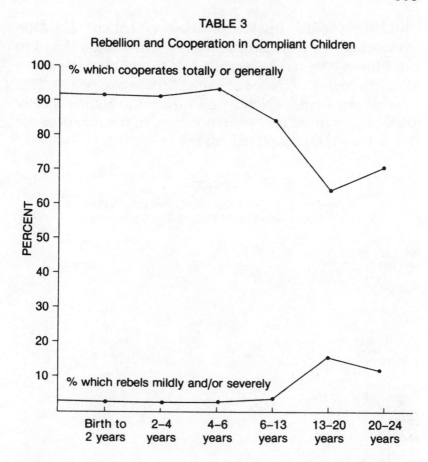

during the terrible twos, and then they remain cooperative up to the time of the adolescent valley? Even during
the teen years, only 17 percent go into rebellion (that
figure includes mild and severe rebellion).

Finally, we need to look at this same issue from
another angle to learn (1) how stable is the tendency
to rebel across time, and (2) at what age does the highest
percentage of rebellion occur? To get at these issues
we asked parents to evaluate their very strong-willed

children (upper line) and very compliant children (lower line) in various time frames from toddlerhood to adulthood. We were interested in the individuals going through severe defiance at each of those age points. This is what we found. (Note, again, that the figures below reflect only those in *severe* rebellion, so the numbers are lower than those depicted earlier.)

TABLE 4

Percent of Strong-willed and Compliant Children in
Severe Rebellion at Various Age Categories

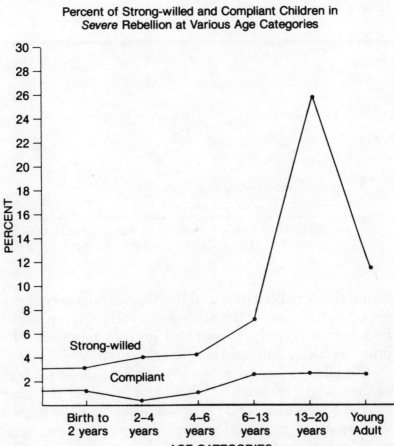

According to these figures, *severe* rebellion is relatively rare before 13 years of age, even for the very strong-willed child. It then spikes to 26 percent during adolescence before expending its energy in early adulthood. By contrast, 97 percent of compliant children do not experience severe rebellion at all.

> *Question 10:* Which individual is more likely to have an edge in academic achievement?
> *Answer:* (2) The very compliant child.

More than three times as many very strong-willed teenagers made D's and F's during the last two years of high school as did compliant teenagers (19% vs. 5%). Conversely, twice as many compliant adolescents made A's (45% vs. 25%). Of all very compliant teenagers, 79 percent were A and B students, compared with 53 percent of very strong-willed kids. The same pattern was also evident in Grades 6, 9, and to a lesser degree, in college.

> *Question 11:* Which individual typically makes the best social adjustment in adolescence?
> *Answer:* (2) The very compliant child.

Again, there is a remarkable difference between these two categories of children, favoring the compliant child by a wide margin. During adolescence, 35 percent of the compliant children were said to have "no social problems," compared with only 15 percent of the strong-willed. Likewise, 5 percent of the compliant had "many social problems" compared with 16 percent of the strong-willed. Only 2 percent of the compliant were "generally disliked," but 9 percent of the strong-willed were given this designation. A similar pattern was seen for younger children, as well.

It would appear that the youngster who is challenging the authority of his parents and starting little insurrections at home is also more likely to behave offensively with his peers. We should point out, however, that the majority of strong-willed children do not have great social problems.

Question 12: Which individual is more likely to be "peer dependent" in adolescence . . . that is, which is more easily influenced by group opinion and peer pressure?
Answer: (1) The very strong-willed child.

The compliant teenagers turned out to be considerably less peer dependent than the strong-willed. I had assumed that these kids who had been so easy for their parents to mold and influence would also be more vulnerable to pressure from their peer group. After all, one of their unique characteristics is the desire to please other people. Why wouldn't that sensitivity extend to friends and associates? I even made a statement to that effect in my first film series, "Focus on the Family," during which I stated:

I am not speaking derogatorily of the strong-willed child. I don't think it's "bad kid vs. good kid." I think the defiant child has greater potential for character development and for accomplishment and leadership. Yes, it is more difficult to raise him.

But maybe the same characteristics that cause a toddler to stamp his foot and say "No" to you will cause him, thirteen years later, to say "No" to the peer group when they offer him drugs. We need to shape his will and give him the ability to shape his own impulses.

I was wrong. But no one is perfect. There was an *enormous* difference in the degree of peer dependency between the two groups of adolescents. Some 58 percent of the strong-willed teenagers were judged by their parents to have been greatly influenced by agemates. This compares with only 24 percent of the compliant adolescents. Since peer dependency is one of the demons behind drug abuse, alcoholism and sexual promiscuity, this characteristic of strong-willed teenagers is of serious concern to us.

Question 13: Which individual is more likely to have the higher self-esteem in adolescence?
Answer: (2) The very compliant child.

It is difficult to overestimate the importance of this finding in favor of the compliant child. He is *much* more likely to feel good about himself than his strong-willed sibling. Only 19 percent of the teenagers in this category either disliked themselves (17 percent) or felt extreme self-hatred (2 percent). Of the very strong-willed teenagers, however, 43 percent either disliked themselves (35 percent) or experienced extreme self-hatred (8 percent). The differences were also evident at the positive end of the scale, although they were not quite so dramatic. A picture is emerging of the compliant child being more at peace with himself, as well as being at peace with his parents.

Why do strong-willed children have a greater tendency to doubt their own worth in this way? It is difficult to say, except to affirm that they are more unsettled in every aspect of their lives. We do know that lower self-esteem is related to the excessive peer dependency, academic difficulties, social problems and even the rebellion we have seen. Acceptance of one's intrinsic worth is the core of the personality. When it collapses, everything else begins to quiver.

Question 14: Finally, parents were asked to indicate how their grown sons and daughters had achieved in their adult pursuits. Which group do you think succeeded best, the strong-willed or the compliant?
Answer: (2) The very compliant.

Again, the pattern held . . . 69 percent of compliant children, then as young adults, were considered to be successful or highly successful by their parents. Only 56 percent of the strong-willed were given this accolade. When one looks at the frequency of failure in the same context, the compliant come out winners once more: 11 percent vs. 22 percent.

Most of the parents with whom I have shared these findings have been surprised by the outcome. They expected strong-willed individuals to emerge on top in this category. Their aggressiveness should have produced a faster start, or so the common wisdom goes. On closer examination, however, the compliant young man or woman succeeds in early business pursuits because he plays by the rules. He finds out what the boss wants and promptly gives it to him. It would also appear that he is going through less personal turmoil in this postadolescent era. He is thereby freer to get on with the business of living.

These findings would not surprise Bill Haughton, a successful real estate broker and former Marine living in

Dallas, Texas. He was in the industrial distribution business for thirty years, starting as the first employee and eventually selling the company in 1980 when there were 450 employees in 40 locations. Bill and I have become good friends, and I once asked him how he had selected new employees. His answer was surprising. He said the first thing he wanted to know about any young man who applied for a job was the nature of his relationship with his father. If it was stormy, he would not hire him.

Bill explained his reasoning: "If a boy learned to accept authority under his dad, the chances were good that he would later accept the leadership of his employers. But if he was a rebel, he was more likely to cause difficulties in my business."

I then asked Bill how he screened women. Again, his perspective was unique, even if controversial. He said, "Women are more difficult to assess in the beginning. You don't really know them until they are on the job. Unfortunately, they can be meaner than men. When I realize I have hired an office malcontent, someone who is always working to get to the head of the pecking order, then I know I have erred. She will create continual morale problems. She must go or my shop will be chaotic!"

Bill Haughton's philosophy of employee-hiring represents a practical application of the findings confirmed in our study. It explains, perhaps, why the strong-willed man or woman typically gets off to a slower start in business than the more compliant individual. Bosses and supervisors want employees who will follow instructions and avoid hassles with co-workers. Incidentally, in another study of people who were fired from their places of employment, fewer than 20 percent lost their jobs for the lack of technical knowledge and skill. More than 80 percent were released because of their inability to get along with *people*. That is their Achilles heel, despite their aptitude for a particular kind of work. Thus, the easy-going young man or woman has a distinct advantage in early positions of employment. That is precisely what we found.

But let me speculate about how this picture might change with the passage of time. Since our study was limited to those individuals 24 years of age and younger, I have wondered what happens to those who are 40 and older. It is my supposition that strong-willed individuals will eventually emerge as the entrepreneurs and leaders. Their desire for independence and their aggressive temperaments might cause them to outproduce their compliant counterparts in the long run.

My good friend, Dr. Malcolm Williamson, whom I referred to earlier, has assessed the personality traits of thousands of adults in the work force. His research shows clearly that corporation presidents are characteristically dominant (strong-willed), aggressive, self-confident, fast-paced and highly independent. Conversely, he finds a high percentage of vice presidents and middle-management executives are "servants." They carry out company policy very well. They tend to be loyal, dedicated perfectionists who do not want to be wrong. And yes, they tend to be compliant.

I believe our study would have confirmed these findings if we had extended the time frame for two more decades. Perhaps we will do so some day.

Conclusion

Now that I have thoroughly depressed the parents of very strong-willed children, let me make two summarizing comments and offer a few encouraging thoughts.

First, there was another finding from our study which should provide hope to every mother and father on the battlefield today. It concerns the return to parental values by these most difficult individuals when they reach adulthood. Depicted on the chart below is what we were told by 853 parents:

TABLE 5

Acceptance or Rejection of Parental Values

	Accepted Parental Values	Rejected Parental Values	Somewhat Accepted Parental Values
Very compliant children, now grown	79%	5%	15%
Very strong-willed children, now grown	53%	15%	32%
Total	60%	12%	32%

As can be observed, 53 percent of even the *most* strong-willed and rebellious children eventually return to the values of their parents, outright. When that figure is combined with those who are "somewhat" accepting of parental perspectives, that means 85 percent of these hard-headed, independent individuals will eventually lean toward their parents' point of view by the time adolescence is over. Only 15 percent are so headstrong that they reject everything their family stood for, and I'll wager that there were other problems and sources of pain in most of those cases.

What this means, in effect, is that these tough-minded kids will fuss and fight and complain throughout their years at home, but the majority will turn around as young adults and do what their parents most desired. Remember, also, that there was a category of individuals whom we described as "rather strong-willed," who have not been considered in any of these analyses. It is virtually certain that the percentage of these less antagonistic kids who accept parental values is higher than those represented above. It is also reassuring to know, in this context, that even the *most* defiant individuals who go through awful rebellion in adolescence are likely to come back to parental values . . . partially if not entirely. Furthermore, if we could evaluate these individuals at 35 instead of 24 years of age, even fewer would still be in rebellion against parental values.

Second, I urge you as parents of strong-willed children not to feel "cheated" or depressed by the assignment of raising such individuals. All human beings arrive with a generous assortment of flaws, including the very compliant child. Yes, it is more difficult to raise an independent little fellow, but you can do it! You can, through prayer and supplication before the Lord, bring him to that period of harmony in early adulthood that makes the effort worthwhile. I also believe that you can increase the odds of transmitting your values to these individuals by following some time-honored principles which we will discuss. So hang in there! Nothing of any real value in life comes easy anyway, except the free gift of salvation from Jesus Christ.

Let's look now, in Chapter 4, at the ways parents react to defiant and compliant children. You might find your own reflection somewhere in the discussion that follows.

What 35,000 Parents Said about Themselves

You will recall from the first chapter that many parents told us they were *intensely* frustrated by their child-rearing responsibilities. More than 30 percent responding to our survey said, in effect, "I am a failure as a parent!" and "I simply can't cope with my kids." But who are these mothers and fathers who have felt such despair at home? I believe we now have revealing answers to that and other important questions.

The 35,000 parents who participated in our study not only gave us valuable information about their strong-willed and compliant children (reported in Chapter 3), but they also described their own feelings and attitudes about raising them. Their responses were surprising in many contexts. Let's look at a few of the more relevant findings, some of which were alarming.

One of the items on the questionnaire (see Appendix)

asked parents to rate the amount of stress that was created by their children's temperaments. Then we divided
the sample to compare the responses of parents of very
compliant children vs. those of the very strong-willed.
This is what we found:

TABLE 6

Parental Response to Strong-willed and Compliant Children

	Total Joy	Generally Pleasant	Average	Generally Difficult	Unpleasant
Parents of very compliant children	44%	51%	4%	1%	0%
Parents of very strong-willed children	1%	10%	17%	55%	17%

What a dramatic story these statistics tell. If we combine the two positive categories (total joy and generally
pleasant), we find that 95 percent of parents raising very
compliant children felt good about the job they were
doing, compared with only 11 percent of the parents of
strong-willed children. On the negative side, 1 percent
of the parents of compliant children rated the assignment
generally difficult or unpleasant, compared with 72 percent of those raising strong-willed kids. Obviously, we
have identified the bulk of frustrated parents from this
one item on our questionnaire.

A second item was intended to explore further the
reactions of parents to children with easy or difficult
personalities. We asked for this information: "Generally
speaking, select the sentence that best describes how you
feel about raising your very strong-willed or very compliant children." The four alternative statements were:

1. "It has been a struggle that has often left me depressed, guilt-ridden and exhausted."
2. "It has been difficult but exciting and rewarding too."
3. "It has been a very positive experience."

Parents of strong-willed children were then given this fourth choice:

4. "He/she was difficult in the early years, but the adolescent years were less stormy and difficult."

Parents of compliant children were then given this fourth choice:

4. "He/she was a joy in the early years, but adolescence was extremely stressful for both generations."

Having obtained responses from 4,801 parents, we divided the sample into eight subgroups in an attempt to identify the parents in greatest distress. We were looking at both strong-willed and compliant mothers and fathers as they interacted with their very strong-willed and very compliant children. The findings are provided in Table 7 (see next page).

Even a cursory examination of these responses makes it clear that strong-willed children are a source of great frustration not only to their mothers, which we expected, but also to their fathers. Lynn Caine, writing in her book *What Did I Do Wrong?*, said this about men: ". . . fathers . . . seemed not to share either the guilt or the blame . . . . They did not feel hated or inadequate or responsible for them. *That* was for women to feel . . . I have seldom met a guilty father . . . . Perhaps our guilt

TABLE 7

Parent-Child Interactions According to Temperaments of Both Generations

Parent/Child Temperaments	1 Struggle	2 Difficult	Negative Factor (1 and 2 Combined)	3 Positive	4 Variable
Very compliant mothers with very compliant children	3%	11%	14%	71%	15%
Very compliant mothers with very strong-willed children	43%	44%	87%	6%	7%
Strong-willed mothers with compliant children	5%	13%	18%	64%	18%
Strong-willed mothers with strong-willed children	34%	56%	90%	6%	4%
Very compliant fathers with very compliant children	3%	14%	17%	71%	12%
Very compliant fathers with very strong-willed children	41%	50%	91%	4%	5%
Very strong-willed fathers with very compliant children	6%	12%	18%	65%	17%
Very strong-willed fathers with very strong-willed children	39%	51%	90%	6%	4%

Number of Parents Polled:
Very compliant mothers 980
Very compliant fathers 710
Very strong-willed mothers 1,684
Very strong-willed fathers 1,427
Totals 4,801

316

is a condition of womankind, a weakness of the sex, the natural softness of the nurturer."*

According to our findings, Mrs. Caine is wrong. Fathers *do* struggle when their children rebel. This fact is verified by adding the first two columns to create what might be called a "negative factor," appearing in the middle column. This combined percentage shows that strong-willed children not only affect mothers and fathers equally, but they create about the same degree of stress for strong-willed and compliant parents. The lowest positive rating (4 percent) occurred for very compliant fathers raising very strong-willed children. In short, every adult who works with these rambunctious youngsters is affected by the tension they create! We will come back to this point in a moment.

Let's turn our attention now from how parents *feel* to how they *discipline*. Some equally dramatic findings turned up at this point. Our primary interest was in the handling of very strong-willed vs. very compliant children. We asked those completing the questionnaire to indicate which parent related best to the children at various age levels. Table 8 (see next page) depicts the response of parents to very strong-willed children only.

From this analysis and several dozen others, it was apparent that mothers of strong-willed children are especially vulnerable to their rebellious kids. As indicated earlier, fathers also struggle and feel guilty in reference to them. Nevertheless, men appear willing to accept an increasing share of the child-rearing responsibility with the passage of time. Mothers begin in complete charge of their young children, handling 78 percent of their strong-willed toddlers. From there, they slide downhill in every age category through adolescence. Fathers actually related to the greater percentage of individuals

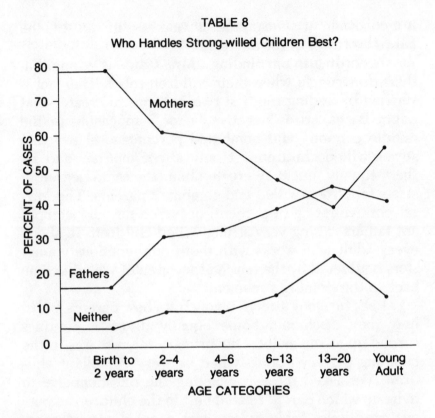

TABLE 8

Who Handles Strong-willed Children Best?

between 13 and 20 years of age by a few percentage points. A rebound then occurs in young adulthood, favoring mothers again. We are assuming that this transfer of parenting responsibilities from women to men occurs because mothers dislike confrontation and are less comfortable than fathers with the power games played by these tougher sons and daughters.

Of greater significance in this context is the bottom line of the graph, showing the percentage of children to whom *neither* parent related very well. The peak of 24 percent of cases in the adolescent years spells trouble! One-fourth of all tough-minded youngsters do not get along well with *either* mother or father, and 14 percent are still charting their own course in young adulthood. Like their parents, these are the teens who desperately need outside influence of the right type.

When responses to the question, "Who handles the child best?" were plotted by sex, it was noted that fathers carry an even greater responsibility for strong-willed sons than they do with their daughters. Surprisingly, however, girls were just as rebellious as boys during adolescence.

Let's compare responses, now, from parents of very compliant children. The pattern is dramatically different.

TABLE 9

Who Handles Compliant Children Best?

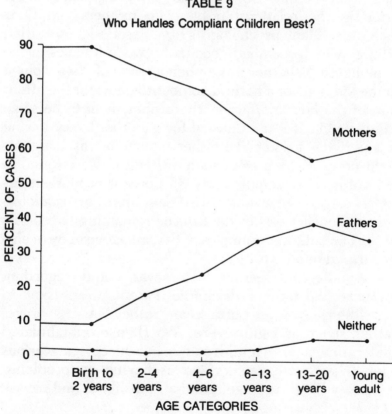

It does not require a statistician to draw meaning from these data. Clearly, mothers love compliant children. Fathers are fond of them, too, but Mom is in the driver's seat throughout childhood. Notice the small percentage of compliant children who feel alienated from both parents (a maximum of 5 percent during adolescence).

Upon seeing these figures for the first time, a struggling mother of a strong-willed tribe said to me wearily, "Where do I get some of those compliant kids?!" I don't know, but the chances are great that *her* parents would also have wanted that information.

From the outset of this study I was especially interested in the relationship between mothers and their daughters. Many psychologists have described a so-called "thing" which seemingly occurs between females in the same house. Whether it is a phenomenon of "two women in the kitchen" or a natural competitiveness for the attention of the husband/father, there does seem to be some validity to it. It is not unusual for a mother to say during this period, "I don't like either my son *or* my daughter right now." Evidences of such difficulties were found in our study. For example, only 36 percent of mothers related best to their strong-willed daughters during adolescence. Conflict was evident in the remaining two thirds of the cases. Other examples of that antagonism were also unearthed in our study.

Another interesting factor was noted regarding mothers' and fathers' discipline. Parents were asked to rate themselves as permissive, rather easy, average, rather strict or rigid/severe. We then cross-tabulated that rating against children's social success at various ages. They were categorized as having no problems, generally liked, average, generally disliked, and having many problems. This is what we found: for the children with many problems, their parents tended to be either permissive with them or they were rigid/severe. The pattern held through many analyses and at virtually each age category from childhood to adulthood. The conclusion is that when children are beset by major social problems, their parents react in extreme ways—either by throwing up their hands and refusing to discipline them at all, or by becoming so rigid and severe as to oppress them. This analysis and several others made it clear that the kind of discipline a parent applies is a function of the child's well-being and of his temperament. When he is unusually difficult or beset by numerous problems, parenting effectiveness sometimes suffers accordingly.

Summary

As indicated earlier, I could fill many books with the massive amount of information generated from this study of 35,000 parents. Admittedly, this was a *retrospective* investigation instead of a more scientific *longitudinal* effort. Nevertheless, the findings speak for themselves. The gap between strong-willed and compliant children is indeed a chasm, and those differences in temperament and behavior have a dramatic effect on those who are raising them.

Perhaps it is now evident why I am especially concerned about the four groups of parents raising very strong-willed children (see Table 7 again). I believe many of these mothers and fathers are near the breaking point today. Their sense of guilt is overwhelming, and yet they have typically carried their pain in silence. I would expect the incidences of child abuse, child abandonment, parental alcoholism and other evidences of family disintegration to be inordinately high in this category. And of course, it is not a category or a group at all. I'm talking about real *people*—living, breathing mothers and fathers who are going down for the count.

If you are one of those struggling parents who has wept in the midnight hours, the balance of this book is for you. While we will also address the special problems encountered by compliant children, the greater urgency must be on the rebellious individual and his family. There is hope for him and for you, his parents.

°Lynn Caine, *What Did I Do Wrong? Mothers, Children, Guilt* (New York: Arbor House, 1985), 136.

With Love to Parents Who Hurt

Several weeks ago, I attended a wedding ceremony held in a beautiful garden setting. After the minister instructed the groom to kiss his bride, approximately 150 colorful, helium-filled balloons were released into the blue California sky. It was a pleasant sight that reminded me of a similar moment during the 1984 Olympics in Los Angeles. Within a few seconds, the balloons were scattered across the heavens—some rising hundreds of feet overhead and others cruising toward the horizon. The distribution was curious. They all began from a common launching pad, were filled with approximately the same amount of helium, and ascended into the same conditions of sun and wind. Nevertheless, within a matter of several minutes they were separated by a mile or more. A few balloons struggled to clear the upper branches of trees, while the show-offs became mere pinpoints of color on

their journey to the sky. How interesting, I thought—
and how symbolic of children.

We have already agreed that babies do not begin
life's journey from a common launching pad. They also
vary in their ability to fly. Let's face it. Some carry more
helium than others. But even if they were identical at
birth, they would not remain equivalent for long. Environmental influences would carry them in infinite directions within the span of a few days. From that point
forward, they only drift farther apart. Some kids seem to
catch all the right breezes. They soar effortlessly to the
heights. Their parents beam with pride for having created superior balloons. Others wobble dangerously close
to the trees. Their frantic folks run along underneath,
huffing and puffing to keep them airborne. It is an exhausting experience.

I want to offer a word of encouragement at this
point to the parents of every low-flying kid in the world
today. There's usually one or more in each family.
They're not all strong-willed and rebellious, of course.
Some are physically handicapped. Others have learning
disabilities, or peculiar personalities, or serious illnesses.
Some have other characteristics that bring ridicule from
their peers. What is it that worries you about your different child? Is he overweight, or underweight, or very
short or tall or clumsy or lazy? Or is he so terribly selfish
and unpleasant that he has alienated everyone he's
met except (or including) you? Is the story of your family
written somewhere within the flight plan of your
"special balloon"?

May I gently put my arm around you through the
pages of this book? I understand your pain and your fears.
Your hopes rise and fall with the altitude of this different

youngster. You awaken in the wee hours of the morning, worrying and praying for his survival. You have nightmares that his balloon will go into a frantic loop-the-loop and then plunge in a power dive to the earth. You would give your life to prevent this catastrophe, but that wouldn't help. You're all he has.

If you've launched only high-flying sons and daughters, then you won't comprehend the sentiment of these words. You may even think them foolish. It is very difficult to understand the depression and apprehension that can accompany the rearing of such a child unless you've been through it. It is also embarrassing. Why? Because of the crazy notion that parents are responsible for everything their child becomes. They are praised or blamed for his successes and failures—all of them. If he is gorgeous, brilliant, artistic, athletic, scholarly and polite, his folks get an A+ for having made him that way. But if he is ordinary, uncoordinated, indolent, homely, unpleasant and dull, they fail the course. Mom and Dad are particularly accountable for their child's misbehavior, even years after he is beyond their control or influence. I hear from parents almost every day who share stories similar to this one:

> Dear Dr. Dobson:
> We have four children including a boy and girl in college. They are doing beautifully and have become everything parents dream of. We also have a twelve-year-old boy whose brain was damaged at birth. He's a beautiful child who works extremely hard to keep his head above water. Finally, we have a thirteen-year-old boy who has been strong-willed from "day one," as you often say.
> We've been Christians for seven years, and we've

done everything possible to help this child—from prayer, to moving this past year, to putting him in a Christian school, to weekly family counseling sessions.

Tonight we had to sit with our son in front of the pastor, the minister of education and members of the Christian school board to request that he not be kicked out of school with only six weeks left. The verdict: He's out! The comment was made by the minister of education to this effect, "What kind of parents are you not to have more control over your son?"

We are desperate! Everything we can think of has been tried with this child. We love him dearly, but I sure see why parents abuse their children. I'm an X-Ray technician, and I see too many brain damaged children from abuse. Maybe at this moment that is what keeps me from beating him. But why do these school administrators put more guilt on us when people like you try so hard to help us handle it? We have enough guilt already, knowing that we are failures at parenting.

Please help. We are desperate!!

God bless you,
Elaine

If we talked to the school board and the minister of education, we might hear a different story about these parents and their rebellious son. Perhaps they did cause his defiant behavior, but I doubt it. When we look at their other children we see they are doing fine. No, I think the parents are victims of the cruel misunderstanding of which we have spoken. They and other contemporary parents have been taught that children are born neutral and good. If the children go wrong, it is because someone wreaks havoc upon them. All behavior is *caused*, say the experts. The child chooses nothing. He merely responds to his experiences.

As indicated earlier, this theory is called *determin-ism*, and if it is valid, then the responsibility for every lie, every school failure, every act of defiance eventually circles around to his family—and especially to his mother. This is why she has been blamed for all the problems and even the silly imperfections that beset her children. Is it any wonder that 1,000 mothers and fathers who responded to our "frustrations of parenthood poll" gave as their most common answer, "I am a failure as a parent"?

I remember boarding a commercial airliner a few years ago on a trip from Los Angeles to Toronto. No sooner had I become comfortable than a mother sat down two seats from me and promptly placed her three-year-old son between us. *O boy!* I thought. *I get to spend five hours strapped next to this little livewire.* I expected him to drive his mother and me crazy by the time we landed. If my son Ryan had been strapped in a chair at that age and given nothing to do, he would have dismantled the entire tail section of the plane by the time it landed. My father once said about Ryan, "If you allow that kid to become bored, you *deserve* what he will do to you."

To my surprise, the toddler next to me sat pleasantly for five long hours. He sang little songs. He played with the ash tray. For an hour or two he slept. But mostly, he engaged himself in thought. I kept expecting him to claw the air, but it never happened. His mother was not surprised. She acted as though all three-year-olds were able to sit for half a day with nothing interesting to do.

Contrast that uneventful episode with another flight I took a few months later. I boarded a plane, found my seat and glanced to my left. Seated across from me this time was a well-dressed woman and a *very* ambitious two-year-old girl. Correction! The mother was seated but her daughter was most definitely not. This little girl had no intention of sitting down—or slowing down. It was also obvious that the mother did not have control of the child, and indeed, Superman himself might have had difficulty harnessing her. The toddler shouted "No!" every few seconds as her mother tried to rein her in. If Mom persisted, she would scream at the top of her lungs while kicking and lunging to escape. I looked at my watch and thought, *What is this poor woman going to do when she is required to buckle that kid in her seat?*

I could see that the mother was accustomed to losing these major confrontations with her daughter. Obviously, the child was used to winning. That arrangement might have achieved a tentative peace at home or in a restaurant, but this was different. They were faced with a situation on the plane where the mother *couldn't* give in. To have allowed the child to roam during takeoff would have been dangerous and impermissible under FAA regulations. Mom *had* to win—perhaps for the first time ever.

In a few minutes, the flight attendant came by and urged the mother to buckle the child down. Easy for her to say! I will never forget what occurred in the next few minutes. The two-year-old threw a tantrum that must have set some kind of international record for violence and expended energy. She was kicking, sobbing, screaming and writhing for freedom! Twice she tore loose from her mom's arms and scurried toward the aisle. The mortified woman was literally begging her child to settle down and cooperate. Everyone in our section of the plane was embarrassed for the humiliated mother. Those of us within ten feet were also virtually deaf by that point.

Finally, the plane taxied down the runway and took off with the mother hanging onto this thrashing toddler with all her strength. Once we were airborne, she was able at last to release the little fireball. When the crisis was over, the mother covered her face with both hands and wept. I felt her pain, too.

Why didn't I help her? Because my advice would have offended the mother. The child desperately needed the security of strong parental leadership at that moment, but the woman had no idea how to provide it. A few sharp slaps on the legs would probably have taken some of the fire out of her. The affair could have ended with a sleeping child curled in her mother's loving arms. Instead, it set the stage for even more violent and costly confrontations in the years ahead.

It is interesting to speculate on how the mothers on these two airplanes probably felt about themselves and their very different toddlers. I would guess that the woman with the passive little boy was significantly overconfident. Raising kids for her was duck soup. "You tell 'em what to do and expect 'em to do it!" she could have said. Some mothers in her comfortable situation hold unconcealed disdain for parents of rebellious children. They just can't understand why others find child-rearing so difficult.

The mother of the second toddler, on the other hand, was almost certainly experiencing a great crisis of confidence. I could see it in her eyes. She wondered how she had managed to make such a mess of parenting in two short years! Somehow, she had taken a precious newborn baby and twisted her into a monster. But how did it happen? What did she do to cause such outrageous behavior? She may ask those questions for the rest of her life.

I wish she had known that at least part of the problem resided in the temperament of the child. It was her nature to grab for power, and the mother was making a serious mistake by granting it to her.

This is my point: parents today are much too willing

to blame themselves for everything their children (or adolescents) do. Only in this century have they been so inclined. If a kid went bad 100 years ago, he was a bad kid. Now it's the fault of his parents. Admittedly, many mothers and fathers *do* warp and twist their children during the vulnerable years. I am not pleading their cases. Believe me, I know that our society today is peppered with terrible parents who don't care about their kids. Some are addicted to alcohol, gambling, pedophilia, pornography, or just plain selfishness. This book is not written to soothe their guilt. But there are others who care passionately about their sons and daughters and they do the best they can to raise them properly. Nevertheless, when their kids entangle themselves in sin and heartache, guess who feels responsible for it? Behavior is caused, isn't it? The blame inevitably makes a sweeping U-turn and lodges itself in the hearts of the parents.

I am particularly concerned about the mother and father who give the highest priority to the task of parenthood. Their firstborn child is conceived in love and born in great joy. They will neither talk nor think of much else for the next three years. The first smile; the first word; the first birthday; the first step. Every milestone is a cause for celebration. They buy him a tricycle and they teach him to fly a kite. And they patch up the bird with the broken wing. Only the best will do for this inheritor of the family name. They buy him Child-Craft® books and teach him to sing. They show him how to pray. It is a labor of love that knows no limits.

Before they know it, their precious little lad is ready for kindergarten. How time flies! They buy him new clothes and cut his hair and get him a Snoopy lunch pail. "Hurry, now," says his mom on the first day of school.

"Let's don't be late." She walks with him across the street and waits for the big yellow bus that stops on the corner. It arrives presently and the door opens. She places the child on the first step and then moves backward to take his picture. The door closes and the bus rumbles slowly down the street. Mom watches as long as it is in sight and then she turns toward her house. She cries quietly as she crosses the street. Her baby is growing up.

The years pass so quickly but it is a happy time. The boy learns to ride a bicycle and soon he's heavily into bugs and snakes and spiders. He gives Little League a try and Dad attends every game. You'd think it was the World Series! There is nothing this father would not do for his son. The boy loves his mom and dad, too, although he has a mind of his own. He has always been somewhat assertive and independent. His cousins think he is a brat. Some of the church folks think he is spoiled. His parents think he's just immature. All three are right.

The tenth, eleventh and twelfth years are marked by increasing tension in the house, but major blow-ups have not yet occurred. Then, suddenly, the roof falls in. The boy turns thirteen and a dramatic change settles over him. Overnight, almost, he has become distant and edgy. He explodes whenever he is frustrated, which seems to happen every few days. He also resents his parents for the first time. He shrinks back when they touch him and he objects to the pet names they have always used. He hates his mom's cooking and complains about the way she irons his shirts. It is a very tough year.

At fourteen, he spends long hours in his room with his door closed. Because life has become intolerable at home he talks vaguely about running away. His parents are utterly bewildered. What did they do? How have they changed? They feel no different, yet this son whom they love so much has targeted them as his enemies. Why? They are hurt and confused.

When he is fifteen, Mom is cleaning his room one day and finds some weird-looking cigarettes behind a bookend. "Could it be? Would he really? Oh no! Not our son!" Then they discover a bottle of little red pills in the bottom drawer of his dresser. "Where is he getting the money?"

Every day is a struggle now for his mother and father. He will not yield to their leadership. This young man, whom they have cherished, seems bent on destroying himself before he is grown. He comes home at all hours of the night reeking of alcohol and smoke. If they demand to know where he's been, he blows up. "Get off my back!" he screams. They are worried sick.

Dad talks to the juvenile authorities on the phone. "I just can't control him," he says. "Sorry," the officer replies, "there's nothing we can do until he commits a serious crime. Even then we can be of little help. There are so many . . . ."

At sixteen, the boy buys himself a car. Now he is really emancipated. His folks rarely see him. He fails four classes as a sophomore and quits school as a junior. From there to his nineteenth year, he is involved in three automobile accidents, gets seven tickets for speeding, and finally, is arrested for driving under the influence. He spends a night in the tank for that one, which nearly kills his mother. Dad's car insurance policy is summarily cancelled.

Now, at twenty, he's living with a girl who is not his wife. She had an abortion last year and is pregnant again. They fight continually over money. He's never held a job for more than three months and they're living on food stamps and State assistance. A friend tells his parents that their son is snorting cocaine now.

Most painful of all to his mother and father is his rejection of their faith. He says he hates their religion and never accepted a word of it. "You can believe what you want," he sneers, "but don't try to sell it to me." Long-term, unrelenting depression settles over their home like a thick black cloud.

Does this frightening scenario actually occur in solid, secure, loving Christian homes? Yes, occasionally it does. And when it happens to *you* and your family, it might as well be a world-wide plague. I feel great tenderness toward parents who have been there. One of them, a mother of three grown daughters, wrote to me recently. This is what she said:

> Dear Dr. Dobson:
> Your radio interview with Dr. John White was so helpful. I had already read his book, *Parents in Pain*, but it ministered to me again. [Incidentally, I recommend this book highly to my readers.]
> We have three daughters, ages 20, 23, and 24, raised as well as we could do it. I read Kesler and I read Trobisch. I did the best I could to be a good example and to follow Christian standards. I spent hours trying to show them that each one was valued and loved immensely. I tried to give them room to be individuals and we both enjoyed watching them develop into adults. In our zeal we never even bought a TV set!!!
> Results: we have two daughters who couldn't have turned out better and one who couldn't have turned out worse. Our oldest daughter is a college graduate, has a productive job, is loving her Christian walk and is a joy to have around.

Daughter #3 caused us untold grief and worry and finally at age 18 ran off with a 29-year-old thrice-married ex-convict (who was still married to wife #3). For 3 weeks I sat at the kitchen table all day in shock.

I didn't know that anyone could endure that much pain and still live. At first I thought I would commit suicide. Then I thought I would go around forever with FAILURE branded on my forehead. My husband and I had long discussions about whether we should drop out of the church and not attempt to minister to others because of our failure. It shook our marriage to the roots. We felt like 26 years went down the drain. It was so embarrassing to see people who knew what had happened. It was worse to run into people who didn't know, because they might ask how our girls were. I would cut people absolutely dead so they wouldn't have a chance to ask.

I complained to God for "letting it happen." For many weeks I considered giving up the Christian walk, but on the other hand I could hardly wait for church and the Bible study because of the help I knew was there. Finally I did come to the point where I had to admit to God that I had to stick with Him because only He had the words of eternal life, but I could hardly pray for months because my heart was like a rock.

Now, almost exactly two years have passed. We finally know where she is, and only this week she has decided that she would even write us a letter.

There is a special group of parents at church who have formed an unspoken brotherhood because their children have broken their hearts, and other parents with all good kids lightly compare notes while the rest of us sit silently with aching hearts.

I tell you, Dr. Dobson, that it would be easier to bury the children than it would be to see them using their bodies for such shameful purposes—those bodies that we've lovingly washed, bandaged, dressed, stuffed good food and vitamins into, kept out of the lake and off of the roads—using their lives to advance the cause of Satan. I sincerely hope that *you* never hear your kid say, "I hate you. You've ruined my life and I never want to see you again," and walk out coolly.

I want to tell you something else about the effect this has had on our family that we didn't expect. Our oldest daughter says: "I will never have any children. Parents spend years doing their best for the children, and suddenly at age 14 the parents become despised enemies. I refuse to put up with that for myself."

I could go on for several more paragraphs, but I think you get the idea, as much as you could, not having gone through it yourself.

God bless you. Keep up the good work.

Sincerely,
Mary Alice

This mother was right. I have never experienced the kind of pain she has described, for which I'm grateful. But I believe I understand it. I have witnessed the same trauma in hundreds of families. It is one of the most devastating experiences in living. Most of the parents I have known who are dealing with adolescent or postadolescent rebellion respond precisely as Mary Alice did. They blame themselves. Note that she felt as though the word "failure" had been branded across her forehead. She was so humiliated she contemplated suicide. She and her husband thought of dropping out of church because they considered themselves no longer worthy as Christians. These are the words of guilt-ridden parents who have believed the great lie. In their minds, they had destroyed their own precious daughter. They were convinced that even God could not forgive so great a sin.

Guilt is one of the most painful emotions in human experience. Sometimes it is valid and represents the displeasure of God Himself. When that is the case, it can be forgiven and forgotten. On other occasions, it is entirely of our own creation. Mary Alice and her husband appear to be victims of this self-imposed condemnation, as are thousands of other parents. As with the writer of the earlier letter, this mother and her husband had raised three girls by the same philosophy and technique. If they were such horrid parents, why did two daughters turn out so well? I believe the vast differences between these three young women is traceable more to their own temperaments and choices than to the successes and failures of their parents. Nevertheless, Mary Alice felt totally responsible for the mess her youngest daughter was in. It wasn't fair. But that's the way mothers are made.

This tendency to assume the responsibility for everything our teenagers and grown children do is not only a product of psychological mumbo-jumbo (determinism) but it reflects our own vulnerabilities as parents. We know we are flawed. We know how often we fail. Even under the best of circumstances, we are forced time after time to guess at what is right for our children. Errors in judgment occur. Then our own selfishness surfaces and we do and say things that can never be undone. All these shortcomings are then magnified tenfold when a son or daughter goes bad.

Finally, the inclination toward self-condemnation also reflects the way Christians have been taught to believe. Though I am not a theologian, it is apparent to me that a serious misunderstanding of several key passages has occurred. The error has produced false condemnation for circumstances that exceed parental control or influence.

Consider, for example, the pastor who wrote me in anguish after his twenty-one-year-old son impregnated his girlfriend on a Christian college campus. The minister was devastated. He felt as guilty as though he had personally been caught in an adulterous affair. This anguished man, who was a successful and popular pastor, wrote a letter of confession to his church and resigned as their leader. He cited Titus 1:6 as evidence of his unworthiness to continue in the ministry.

The verse he quoted is a portion of the apostle Paul's statement of qualifications for church leadership. Paul said a bishop must be "the husband of but one wife, a man whose children believe and are not open to the charge of being wild and disobedient." You may draw your own conclusions from this scripture, but I believe it refers to much younger children than the pastor's son. This young man was twenty-one years of age and had gone away to college. He was no longer a child!

Remember, also, that males and females were considered grown much earlier in Paul's day. They often married at fourteen or sixteen years of age. Thus, when Paul referred to a man having his children in proper subjection, I believe he was talking about *children*. He intended to disqualify men who had chaotic families and those who were unable to discipline or manage their young sons and daughters. That is a far cry from holding a man responsible for the rebellious behavior of his grown offspring, or in this instance, for a single sinful event. They are beyond his control.

The pastor who wrote to me might take solace from reading again the book of Genesis. It would appear that

God, Himself would not qualify for Church leadership according to the pastor's interpretation of Titus 1:6, because His wayward "children," Adam and Eve, fell into sin. Obviously, in my view, something is wrong with this interpretation of the Scriptures.

Ezekiel 18 is also helpful to us in assessing blame for the sinful behavior of grown children. God's way of looking at that situation is abundantly clear:

> The word of the Lord came to me: "What do you people mean by quoting this proverb about the land of Israel: The fathers eat sour grapes, and the children's teeth are set on edge"?
>
> As surely as I live, declares the Sovereign Lord, you will no longer quote this proverb in Israel. For every living soul belongs to me, the father as well as the son— both alike belong to me. The soul who sins is the one who will die (Ezekiel 18:1–4).

Then in verse 20 he concludes: "The son will not share the guilt of the father, nor will the father share the guilt of the son. The righteousness of the righteous man will be credited to him, and the wickedness of the wicked will be charged against him."

These words from the Lord should end the controversy once and for all. Each adult is responsible for his own behavior, and that of no one else.

So where does this leave us as Christian parents? Are we without spiritual resources with which to support our sons and daughters? Absolutely not! We are given the powerful weapon of intercessory prayer which must never be underestimated. The Scriptures teach that we can pray effectively for one another and that such a petition "availeth much" (James 5:16 KJV). God's answer to our requests will not remove the freedom of choice from

our children, but He will grant them clarity and understanding in charting their own course. They will be given
every opportunity to make the right decisions regarding
matters of eternal significance. I also believe the Lord
will place key individuals in the paths of the ones for
whom we pray—people of influence who can nudge
them in the right direction.

Shirley and I prayed this prayer for our son and
daughter throughout their developmental years: "Be
there, Father, in the moment of decision when two paths
present themselves to our children. Especially during
that time when they are beyond our direct influence,
send others who will help them do what is righteous and
just."

I believe God honors and answers that kind of intercessory prayer. I learned that from my grandmother, who
seemed to live in the presence of God. She had prayed for
her six children throughout their formative years, but her
youngest son (my father) was a particularly headstrong
young man. For seven years following his high school
graduation, he had left the church and rejected its teachings. Then, as it happened, an evangelist came to town
and a great spiritual awakening swept their local church.
But my father would have no part of it and refused even
to attend.

One evening as the rest of the family was preparing
to go to church, my father (who was visiting his parents'
home) slipped away and hid on the side porch. He could
hear his brothers chatting as they boarded the car. Then
one of them, Willis, said suddenly, "Hey, where's Jim?
Isn't he going tonight?"

Someone else said, "No, Willis. He said he isn't ever
going to church again."

My father heard his brother get out of the car and

begin searching for him all over the house. Willis had experienced a personal relationship with Jesus Christ when he was nine years old and he loved the Lord passionately. He had held tightly to his faith throughout adolescence when his brothers (including my father) mocked him unmercifully. They had called him "Preacher Boy," "Sissy" and "Goody-Goody." It only made him more determined to do what was right.

My dad remained silent as Willis hurried through the house calling his name. Finally, he found his brother sitting silently in the swing on the side porch.

"Jim," he said, "aren't you going with us to the service tonight?"

My dad said, "No, Willis. I'm through with all of that. I don't plan to ever go back again."

Willis said nothing. But as my father sat looking at the floor, he saw big tears splashing on his brother's shoes. My father was deeply moved that Willis would love him that much, after the abuse he had taken for his Christian stand.

I'll go just because it means that much to him, my dad said to himself.

Because of the delay my father had caused, the family was late arriving at the church that night. The only seats left were on the second row from the front. They streamed down the aisle and were seated. A song evangelist was singing and the words began to speak to my dad's heart. Just that quickly, he yielded. After seven years of rebellion and sin, it was over. He was forgiven. He was clean.

The evangelist at that time was a man named Bona Fleming, who was unusually anointed of God. When the singer concluded, Reverend Fleming walked across the platform and put his foot on the altar rail. He leaned forward and pointed his finger directly at my dad.

"You! Young man! Right there! Stand up!"

My father rose to his feet.

"Now, I want you to tell all these people what God did for you while the singer was singing!"

My dad gave his first testimony, through his tears, of the forgiveness and salvation he had just received. Willis was crying too. So was my grandmother. She had prayed for him unceasingly for more than seven years.

To the day of his death at sixty-six years of age, my father never wavered from that decision. His only passion was to serve the God with whom he fell in love during a simple hymn. But where would he have been if Willis had not gone to look for him? How different life would have been for him . . . and for me. God answered the prayers of my grandmother by putting a key person at the critical crossroads.

He will do as much for your children, too, if you keep them in your prayers. But until that moment comes, pray for them in *confidence*—not in regret. The past is the past. You can't undo your mistakes. You could no more be a perfect parent than you could be a perfect human being. Let your guilt do the work God intended and then file it away forever. I'll bet Solomon would agree with that advice.

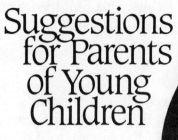

Suggestions for Parents of Young Children

6

The best way to deal with parental guilt, of course, is to prevent it from occurring in the first place. We've taken a step in that direction by exposing false guilt resulting from circumstances beyond our control. But we must not go too far in that direction. Parents are accountable before God to meet their responsibilities to their children, and He is vitally concerned about their welfare. Jesus said that anyone who would hurt the faith of a little child would be better off sinking in the sea with a millstone attached to his neck. That warning is relevant to us as mothers and fathers. Our failure to love and discipline our children often inflicts upon them a weak and damaged faith. There is no greater tragedy in life!

We also want to do our best for our kids because we love them dearly. In that spirit, then, let me offer a few suggestions to parents of babies and children who have not yet reached their thirteenth birthdays.

1. Go with the Flow

I took my son Ryan and one of his friends on a ski trip when they were about twelve years of age. As we rode the gondola to the top of the mountain, I decided to snap the boys' picture with the beautiful scenery visible behind them. While I focused the shot, Ryan began clowning and waving at the camera. Ricky, on the other hand, sat glumly and quietly beside him.

"Come on, Rick!" said Ryan. "Loosen up! Smile for the camera!"

Ricky never changed his expression but simply said dryly, "I'm *not* that kind of person."

He was right. Ricky is reserved and dignified while Ryan is spontaneous and flamboyant. It's the way they are constructed. In a thousand years of practice Ricky could not be like Ryan, and Ryan would come unstitched if he had to be as controlled as Ricky. It was interesting to see how the boys recognized and accepted their differences in basic temperaments.

A surprising degree of diversity can occur even between children born to the same parents. For example, there were five boys in my father's family. The oldest two were twins who developed into great athletes. One went on to coach football at Byrd High School in Shreveport, Louisiana. The next eldest was Willis, who wore thick glasses and could neither catch nor throw a ball. He earned a Ph.D. in Shakespearean literature at the University of Texas and then taught college English for forty-five years.

The next in line was a gifted businessman who saved

part of every dollar he ever earned. He was president of two Coca-Cola® bottling plants when he died.

Finally, there was my dad—a sensitive artist by desire and a minister by the calling of God. With the exception of the twins, these brothers could not have been more unique if they had come from four different families. My father didn't even look like his brothers, being 6′ 4″ tall while the others were 5′ 9″ or less. Obviously, God had taken a common genetic pool and fashioned five unique and distinct individuals from it.

Some of my readers might be wondering if we are absolutely sure that my grandfather was really the sire of this crew, but there's no doubt about that. I am reminded, however, of a man who lay dying and called his wife to his bedside. He then turned to her and said, "Mildred, I've always wanted to ask you about the youngest of our twelve children. He just doesn't look like me and I've waited all these years to confront you. Is he really mine?"

"Yes, George, he's yours," said Mildred, "but the other eleven aren't."

That's a terrible joke but it illustrates the diversity of offspring that can come from two fertile parents. It also raises an important question: what happens when you as a mother or father don't like the particular temperament with which your child is equipped? That is a common source of agitation among parents. Though they may never even admit their negative feelings to each other, they struggle with the fact one child is a profound disappointment to them. He is an embarrassment in public and an irritant at home. It may be his extreme shyness that galls them, or his extrovertish personality—or maybe his giddiness. Perhaps it is an athletic father with an uncoordinated son, or an overweight mother who desperately wanted, but didn't get, a thin daughter. For whatever reason, they had hoped to see the signs of greatness emerging in this child; instead, he turns out to be an intolerable misfit in the family. What then, my friends? What happens if *you* are the mother or father who dislikes one or more of your offspring?

Let's acknowledge that some children are easier to love than others. Haven't you heard it said about a particular boy or girl, "That is the sweetest kid I've ever known. I could just hug him to pieces"? We've all seen children like that who naturally attract us to them. But there are other children, millions of them, who lack that natural charm. They push people away from them, including their own families, without even understanding why.

When bonding fails to occur between parents and a particular child, both generations stand to suffer. The mother, especially, is likely to experience great feelings of guilt for her lack of affection for this individual. She recognizes his emotional needs and knows it is her responsibility to meet them, but something inside makes it difficult to respond. Instead, she reacts negatively toward this son or daughter. Ordinary childish behavior that would have been ignored in one of her other kids may bring flashes of anger toward this "problem" individual. Then she experiences more guilt for hurting someone so innocent and vulnerable. It is an emotional pit into which many parents have tumbled.

Such rejection is even more destructive from the child's point of view. Even if he can't explain it, he can feel the wall that separates him from his parents. He is especially sensitive to any preference or bias in favor of his siblings. By comparing himself with them, he gets a clearer picture of his standing in the family. If he concludes he is unloved and hated in that inner circle, his pain may manifest itself in unrestrained rebellion during the adolescent years. I've seen it happen a thousand times.

A recent guest on our Focus on the Family radio broadcast, who I'll call Susan, described her own experiences as a rejected child. Her father had returned from World War II in 1945 to discover that his wife had given birth to a baby girl who wasn't his. Susan was that infant. As the living symbol of his wife's infidelity, she was hated by her father. When she was nine years old, she found a loaded 38-caliber pistol hidden in a drawer. She was showing it to a friend when her mother burst into the room. The woman grabbed the gun from Susan and said "I hid this pistol so your dad wouldn't shoot you with it. He hates your guts and one of these days he *will* kill you."

For the next five years, Susan was subjected to the most terrible rejection at home. Then when she was fourteen, her mother said with intensity, "I just have to be really honest with you, Susan. You've been a problem in our marriage since the day you were born, and your dad hates you. He will never change. The best thing for you to do is to leave." Susan packed a bag and headed for California.

A person of lesser character would have been shattered by such mistreatment at home. Susan, however, managed to land on her feet. She was introduced to Jesus Christ while still a teenager, and she has devoted her life to helping others cope with their own pressures and fears.

Susan's story illustrates the intense hatred that parents can harbor for one or more of their children. When it occurs during the formative years, the despised son or daughter usually becomes twisted and crippled for the rest of his or her life. But we have been describing a more subtle and less deliberate form of rejection. It occurs in response to what might be called a parent's "private disappointment." It is not as overt as the hatred inflicted on Susan, but its pain can be almost as devastating.

Let me offer a few suggestions that may help. First, I believe it is possible in many cases to override one's emotions by an iron-clad determination of the will. Feelings often follow behavior. If you make up your mind to love and care for each of your children equally, you might be surprised to find that the barriers isolating that "special" boy or girl are crumbling. What I'm saying is that human emotions are flighty and fickle. You *must* rule them with the rational mind. Do not permit yourself to be repelled from that youngster who needs and depends on you for his very sustenance. The stakes are too high!

Second, be especially wary of the game called "comparison." It is a killer! I'm convinced that most parents indulge regularly in this practice of comparing their kids with everyone else's. They want to know who is brightest, tallest, prettiest, healthiest, most mature, most athletic, and most obedient. It is fun to play as long as they win. Sooner or later, however, they're bound to lose. Their son's or daughter's greatest weakness will glow in the light of another child's strengths. It is an unsettling experience.

Our concern, of course, is for the parents whose child compares unfavorably with every other child around him. Perhaps he is mentally slow or physically handicapped or emotionally unbalanced. His parents hammer themselves with his shortcomings every day of his life. They strain to make him become what he is not . . . what he can never be. Little things gnaw at their insides. The children's program at church, for example, features the bright cutie who wows the congregation. *Just once,* they think, *would it hurt to choose our daughter? Would it violate some unwritten law of the universe to feature the least remarkable child in the starring role?* They think these thoughts, but they say nothing. No one would understand.

Have you played the comparison game? Have you thought to yourself, "If only Laurie was more like April, who is so soft and feminine. Laurie is so . . . so brash, you know? There are times when I just wish she could be—different"?

Don't do it, parents. I've lived long enough to know that circumstances may not be as they seem. April may turn out to be the problem child in the long run. Laurie may be the jewel. Either way, the worth of these kids is not dependent on the characteristics that separate them. None of us is perfect, and there is room in this world for every individual into whom an eternal soul has been breathed. My advice is to take the child God sends to you and "go with the flow." You and he will be much more contented for it!

I know this is difficult advice to follow. Parents of the shy child, for example, often ask me how they can pull him out of his shell and make him outgoing with strangers. At home he says the most profound things and shares his observations on the universe. But in public, his tongue becomes wedged to the side of his cheek. His neck curves downward and he appears deaf.

"Billy," says his exasperated father, "can't you say hello to Pastor Wilson? Billy? Billy! Has the cat got your tongue?"

The cat does *not* have Billy's tongue. It is merely stuck to his jaw, to the embarrassment of his father.

Why is Billy so introverted? Is it because he has been hurt or rejected in the past? Perhaps. But it is more likely that he was born that way, and no amount of goading by his parents will make him outgoing, flamboyant or confident. It is a function of his temperament. Thus, I am again recommending that his parents go with the flow— accepting Billy the way God made him.

On behalf of the parent who has the greatest difficulty accepting a child the way he is, it might be helpful to ventilate those feelings with a husband, wife or close friend. Then determine to love this unlovable boy or girl come what may. You *can* do it! There are qualities in your special youngster that may not have been seen before. Find them. Cultivate them. And then give God time to make something beautiful in his little life!

2. Grab the Reins of Authority Early

I cannot overemphasize the importance of "taking charge" of a strong-willed child during the early years of his life. This is not accomplished by being harsh, gruff or stern. Instead, the relationship is produced by confident and steady leadership. You are the boss. You are in charge. If you believe it, the child will accept it also.

Unfortunately, many mothers are tentative and insecure in approaching their young children today. A pediatrician friend told me about a telephone call he received from the anxious mother of a six-month-old baby.

" I think he has a fever," she said nervously.

"Well," the doctor replied, "did you take his temperature?"

"No," she said, "he won't let me insert the thermometer."

I genuinely hope this woman's baby does not turn

out to be a gutsy toddler bent on world dominion. He'll blow his shaky mother right out of the saddle. Like the little girl on the airplane, he will sense her insecurity and step into the power vacuum she has created.

Susannah Wesley, mother of eighteenth-century evangelists John and Charles Wesley, reportedly raised seventeen vigorous and healthy children. Toward the end of her life, John asked her to express her philosophy of mothering to him in writing. Copies of her reply are still in existence today. As you will see from the excerpts that follow, her beliefs reflect the traditional understanding of child-rearing:

> In order to form the minds of children, the first thing to be done is to conquer the will, and bring them into an obedient temper. To inform the understanding is a work of time, and must with children proceed by slow degrees as they are able to bear it; *but the subjecting of the will is a thing which must be done at once, and the sooner the better!*
>
> For by neglecting timely correction, *they will contract a stubbornness and obstinancy which is hardly ever after conquered*, and never without using such severity as would be painful to me as to the children. In the esteem of the world, those who withhold timely correction would pass for kind and indulgent parents, whom I call cruel parents, who permit their children to get habits which they know must afterward be broken. Nay, some are so stupidly fond as in sport to teach their children to do things which in the after while, they must severely beat them for doing.
>
> Whenever a child is corrected, it must be conquered; and this will be no hard matter to do, if it be not grown headstrong by too much indulgence. And, if the will of a child is totally subdued, and if it be brought to revere and stand in awe of the parents, then a great many

childish follies and inadvertencies may be passed by. Some should be overlooked and taken no notice of, and others mildly reproved. *But no willful transgressions ought ever to be forgiven children, without chastisement, more or less as the nature and circumstances of the offense shall require.*

I cannot dismiss this subject. *As self-will is the root of all sin and misery, so whatever cherishes this in children insures their after wretchedness and faithlessness. whatever checks and mortifies, promotes their future happiness and piety.* This is still more evident if we further consider that Christianity is nothing less than doing the will of God, and not our own; that the one grand impediment to our temporal and eternal happiness being this self-will. No indulgence of it can be trivial, no denial unprofitable.

Does that sound harsh by twentieth-century standards? Perhaps. I might use different words to guard against parental oppression and overbearance. Nevertheless, in my view, Mrs. Wesley's basic understanding is correct. If the strong-willed child is allowed by indulgence to develop "habits" of defiance and disrespect during his early childhood, those characteristics will haunt him for the next twenty years. Note also that Mrs. Wesley recommended overlooking "childish follies and inadvertencies," but never to ignore "willful transgressions." What did she mean?

I attempted to distinguish between these categories of behavior in my earlier book, *Dare to Discipline*. It is interesting to see the congruity between my perspective and that of Mrs. Wesley, in spite of the 200 years separating our times. Perhaps we drew our understandings from the same source . . . ? This is what I wrote about seventeen years ago:

The issue of respect can be a useful tool in knowing when to punish and how excited one should get about a given behavior. First, the parent should decide whether an undesirable behavior represents a direct challenge of his authority—to his position as the father or mother. Punishment should depend on that evaluation. For example, suppose little Walter is acting silly in the living room and he falls into a table, breaking many expensive china cups and other trinkets. Or suppose he loses his bicycle or leaves Dad's best saw out in the rain. These are acts of childish irresponsibility and should be handled as such. Perhaps the parent should have the child work to pay for the losses—depending on the age and maturity of the child, of course. However, these examples do not constitute direct challenges to authority.

Thus far, I was dealing with what Mrs. Wesley called "follies and inadvertencies." Then we turned a corner.

They do not emanate from willful, haughty disobedience. In my opinion, spankings should be reserved for the moment a child (age ten or less) expresses a defiant "I will not!" or "You shut up!" When a youngster tries this kind of stiff-necked rebellion, you had better take it out of him, and pain is a marvelous purifier. When nose to nose confrontation occurs between you and your child, it is not the time to have a discussion about the virtues of obedience. It is not the occasion to send him in his room to pout. It is not appropriate to wait until poor, tired old dad comes plodding in from work, just in time to handle the conflicts of the day. You have drawn a line in the dirt, and the child has deliberately flopped his big hairy toe across it. Who is going to win? Who has the most courage? Who is in charge here? If you do not answer these questions conclusively for the child, he will precipitate other battles designed to ask them again and again. It is the ultimate paradox of childhood that a youngster wants to be controlled, but he insists that his parents earn the right to control him.[1]

The tougher the temperament of the child, the more critical it is to "shape his will" early in life. However, I must hasten to repeat the familiar disclaimers that have accompanied all my other writings on this subject. I am not recommending harshness and rigidity in child-rearing techniques! I don't believe in parental oppression, and indeed, our own children were not raised in such an atmosphere. Furthermore, I want to make it clear that corporal punishment is not to be imposed on babies.

Parents should not even shake their infants in anger. As a child's head is being jerked back and forth his brain can strike the inside of the skull, causing concussions and even death. Frustrated and exhausted parents will sometimes do this to a colicky baby or one who has other irritating characteristics. It is tragic and it is against the law. If you fear you will inflict this or some other kind of violence on your child or if you have already hurt him, please call a local hotline (or 1-800-422-4453); you should seek immediate professional assistance. You owe it to your little one to get help before it is too late.

No. The philosophy I am recommending is not born of harshness. It is conceived in love. Corporal punishment is reserved specifically for moments of willful, deliberate, on-purpose defiance by a child who is old enough to understand what he is doing. These challenges to authority will begin at approximately fifteen months of age and should be met with loving firmness. A thump on the fingers or a single stinging slap on the upper legs will be sufficient to say, "You must listen when I tell you no." By your persistence you will establish yourself as the leader to whom the child owes obedience. At the same time, however, you must seek numerous and continual ways of telling this youngster how much you adore him. That formula of love and discipline has been tested and validated over many centuries of time, and it will work for you.

But why have we stressed the necessity of bringing a strong-willed child into subjection during the younger years? Can't it be accomplished later if necessary? Yes, it can, but as Susannah Wesley said, the cost becomes much higher even at four or five years of age. Why is that true?

Perhaps we can explain the process this way: Have you ever wondered why young children can learn to speak perfect Russian, Chinese, Spanish, Hebrew or any other language to which they are exposed? No trace of an accent will be manifested. But twenty or more years later, most individuals will only be able to approximate the sounds made by natives of the particular region. Researchers now know why this is true. It is explained by a process known as "phoneme contraction" (or "sound dropout"). The larynx of a young child assumes a shape necessary to make the sounds he is learning to use at the time. It then solidifies or hardens in those positions, making it impossible or very difficult to make other sounds later in life. Thus, there is a brief window of opportunity when anything is possible, linguistically. It will soon be history.

A child's attitude toward parental authority is also like that. He passes through a brief window of opportunity during late infancy and toddlerhood when respect and "awe" can be instilled. But that pliability will not last long. If his early reach for power is successful, he will not willingly give it up—ever.

Before we leave this topic of early discipline, let me issue a warning about a common mistake made by parents of more than one child. Psychologist Bruce Baldwin calls it "sibling drift." By that he refers to the tendency of parents to require more of first- or secondborn children. They must earn or fight for everything they get. But as subsequent children come along, the parents begin to wear down. They are preoccupied elsewhere. We obtained definite evidence of this sibling drift from our survey of parents. With the arrival of each new child, the discipline of parents tended to loosen. Tables 10 and 11 display this weakening of authority by compliant mothers and fathers. The pattern was not quite so

TABLE 10

Changing Patterns of Discipline among Compliant Fathers

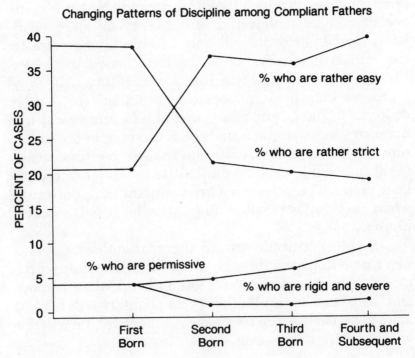

TABLE 11

Changing Patterns of Discipline among Compliant Mothers

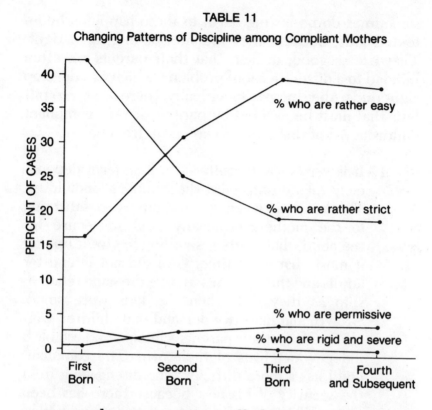

pronounced among strong-willed parents, but it occurred nevertheless.

Without seeing these findings, Dr. Baldwin wrote, "The net effect is less stringent parental discipline and consequently diminished self discipline in younger children. As a parent, you must exert constant energy to counter this trend so younger children grow up as responsible adults, too."[2] We obviously agree.

3. Raising the Compliant Child

Early discipline is not nearly so critical for the easygoing youngster. Even extremely permissive parents sometimes do no lasting harm to these happy and contented kids, because they are not looking for a fight. They are so good, in fact, that their parents are often blinded to a different set of problems which can develop right under their noses. Specifically, there are three pitfalls that must be avoided by parents of very compliant children. All of them tend to creep up from behind.

1. It is very easy to cultivate a long-term dependency relationship with the compliant individual. The bond between generations is so satisfying to the mother, especially, and so secure for the child, that neither is willing to give it up. Yet it must change in time. God did not intend for adults and their parents to have the same relationship as they did when the kids were small. Growth and maturity demand that children wiggle free from their parents' clutches and establish independent lives of their own. The compliant child has a more difficult time disengaging from the security of his nest because there has been no conflict there. By contrast, the strong-willed child is often desperate to get free. This process by which late adolescents and grown "children" are granted their independence is so important that I've devoted an entire chapter (11) to that topic.
2. The compliant child often has difficulties holding his own with his siblings.
3. The compliant child is more likely to internalize his anger and look for ways to reroute it.

These last two items deserve additional explanation because they represent a serious (but very quiet) threat to the well-being of the compliant child. My greatest concern for him is the ease with which he can be underestimated, ignored, exploited or shortchanged at home. Haven't you seen two-child families where one youngster was a stick of dynamite who blew up regularly, and the other was an All-Star sweetheart? Under those circumstances it is not unusual for parents to take their cooperative sibling for granted. If there is an unpleasant job to be done, he will be expected to do it. Mom and Dad just don't have the energy to fight with the tiger.

If one child is to be chosen for a pleasant experience, it will probably go to the brattier of the two. He would scream bloody murder if excluded. When circumstances require one child to sacrifice or do without, you know who will be elected. Parents who favor the strong-willed child in this way are aware that they are being unfair, but their sense of justice has yielded to the pressures of practicality. They are simply too depleted and frustrated to risk irritating the tougher kid.

The consequences of such inequity should be obvious. Even though the compliant child goes along with the program and does not complain, he may accumulate a volume of resentment through the years. Isn't that what seems to have occurred to the brother of the Prodigal Son? He was the hard-working, responsible, *compliant* member of the family. Apparently, his kid brother was irresponsible, flighty and very strong-willed. If we may be permitted to extrapolate a bit from the biblical account in Luke 15:11–32, it seems likely that there was little love lost between these sons, even before the prodigal's impulsive departure.

Disciplined elder brothers usually resent the spoiled brat who gets everything he asks for. Nevertheless, the older brother kept his thoughts to himself. He would not want to upset his father, whom he respected enormously. Then came that incredible day when little brother demanded his entire inheritance in one lump sum. The compliant son overheard the conversation and gasped in shock. *What audacity!* he thought. Then, to his amazement he heard his father grant the playboy's request. He could hear the clink of numerous gold coins being counted. Elder brother was furious. We could only assume that the departure of this sibling meant he would have to handle double chores and work longer hours in the fields. It wasn't fair that the load should fall on him. Nevertheless, he said nothing. Compliant people are inclined to hold their feelings inside.

The years passed slowly as the elder brother labored to maintain the farm. The father had grown older by then, placing a heavier strain on this firstborn son. Every day he labored from dawn to dusk in the hot sun. Occasionally, he thought about his brother living it up in the far country, and he was briefly tempted. But no. He would do what was right. Pleasing his father was the most important thing in his life.

Then, as we remember, the strong-willed goof-off ran out of money and became exceedingly hungry. He thought of his mom's cooking and the warmth of his father's fire. He clutched his rags around him and began the long journey home. When he was yet afar off, his father ran to meet him—embracing him and placing the royal robes around his shoulders. The fatted calf was killed and a great feast planned. That did it. The compliant brother could take no more. The prodigal son had secured through his folly what the elder brother could not gain through his discipline: the approval and affection of his father. His spirit was wounded!

Whether my interpretation of this parable is or is not true to the Scriptures will be left to the theologians to decide. Of this I am certain, however: strong-willed and compliant siblings have played out this drama since the days of Cain and Abel, and the responsible kid often feels like the loser. He holds his feelings inside and then pays a price for storing them. He is more susceptible as an adult to ulcers, hypertension, colitis, migraine headaches and a wide range of other illnesses. Furthermore, his sense of utter powerlessness can drive his anger underground. It may emerge in less obvious quests for control.

That introduces the significance of food as an instrument of power, which we will discuss presently. It also calls to mind the twin eating disorders of anorexia and bulimia. The anorectic individual can literally starve herself to death if not treated. She either reduces her intake of food radically or else she eats a normal meal and then promptly vomits. Sometimes she exercises compulsively while ingesting only 200–400 calories per day. Before long a 130-pound woman may weigh less than 80 pounds, and yet she may still believe herself to be overweight. The bulimic person follows the opposite pattern. She gorges uncontrollably and then "purges" herself by vomiting or the use of laxatives. Bulimia is called a "closet" disease because it often occurs in secret. It has been estimated that 20 to 30 percent of all American women of college age engage in bulimic activity! Jane Fonda has admitted to having been one of them.

Both anorexia and bulimia are thought to be minimally related to food itself. Instead, they represent a desire for *control*. The typical anorectic patient is a female in late adolescence or early adulthood. She is usually a compliant individual who was always "a good little girl."

She did not play power games to any great extent. She conformed to her parents' expectations, although resenting them quietly at times. She withheld her anger and frustration at being powerless throughout the developmental years. Her father, and perhaps her mother, were strong individuals who took her submission for granted. Then one day, her need for control was manifested in a serious eating disorder. There, at least, was one area where she could be the boss.

Treatment for anorectic and bulimic individuals is a lengthy therapeutic process, and must remain the subject for another day. However, prevention of this and other common difficulties among formerly compliant children is definitely of concern to us here. I would offer these rather obvious recommendations to the parents of compliant children—especially the female of the species.

1. Treat them with respect, even when it is not demanded at gunpoint.
2. Keep them talking. Urge them to express their feelings and frustrations. Show them how to ventilate.
3. Give them their fair share in comparison to other children in the family and help them hold their own with more aggressive siblings. Remember that fences make good neighbors!
4. Grant them power commensurate with their ages. Within reason, they should make their own choices regarding clothing, hair styles, food preferences, selections of courses in school, etc. It would be quicker and more efficient to impose these decisions on the compliant individual. Resist the temptation!
5. Hold them close and then let them go. Do not

    continue to "parent" them after the task should
be completed.
6. Keep an eye on your daughter's weight after thirteen years of age. Seek prompt help from specialists if signs of trouble develop.

There's nothing simple about raising kids, is there?
Even in the case of the "easiest" children, being a parent
requires all the intelligence, tact, wisdom and cunning
we can muster. Obviously, it is no job for cowards.

4. Keep Your Sense of Humor

Laughter is the key to survival during the special
stresses of the child-rearing years. If you can see the
delightful side of your assignment, you can also deal with
the difficult. Almost every day I hear from mothers who
would agree. They use the ballast of humor to keep their
boats in an upright position. They also share wonderful
stories with me.

One of my favorites came from the mother of two
small children. This is what she wrote.

Dear Dr. Dobson:
    A few months ago, I was making several phone calls
in the family room where my three-year-old daughter,
Adrianne, and my five-month-old son, Nathan, were
playing quietly. Nathan loves Adrianne, who has been
learning how to mother him gently since the time of his
birth.
    I suddenly realized that the children were no longer
in view. Panic-stricken, I quickly hung up the phone and
went looking for the pieces. Down the hall and around
the corner, I found the children playing cheerfully in
Adrianne's bedroom.

Relieved and upset, I shouted, "Adrianne, you know you are not allowed to carry Nathan! He is too little and you could hurt him if he fell!"

Startled, she answered, "I didn't, Mommy."

Knowing he couldn't crawl, I suspiciously demanded, "Well, then, how did he get all the way into your room?"

Confident of my approval for her obedience, she said with a smile, "I rolled him!"

He is still alive and they are still best friends.

Sincerely

Can't you imagine how this kid felt during his journey down the hall? I'll bet the walls and ceiling are still spinning past his eyes! He didn't complain, however, so I assume he enjoyed the experience.

Another parent told me that her three-year-old daughter had recently learned that Jesus will come to live in the hearts of those who invite Him. That is a very difficult concept for a young child to assimilate, and this little girl didn't quite grasp it. Shortly thereafter she and her mother were riding in the car and the three-year-old suddenly came over and put her ear to her mother's chest.

"What are you doing?" asked the mother.

"I'm listening to Jesus in your heart," replied the child. The woman permitted the little girl to listen for a few seconds, and then she asked, "Well. What did you hear?"

The child replied, "Sounds like He's making coffee to me."

Who else but a toddler would come up with such a unique and delightful observation? If you live or work around kids, you need only listen. They will punctuate your world with mirth. They will also keep you off balance much of the time. I learned that fact several years before I became a father. As part of my professional training at the University of Southern California, I was required to teach elementary school for two years. Those were among the most informative years of my life, as I quickly learned what kids are like. It was also an initiation by fire.

Some days were more difficult than others, like the morning a kid named Thomas suddenly became ill. He lost his breakfast (37 scrambled eggs) with no warning to his fellow students or to me. I can still recall a room full of panic-stricken sixth-graders climbing over chairs and desks to escape Thomas' volcanic eruptions. They stood around the walls of the room, holding their throats and going "eeeeuuuuuyuckk!" One of them was more vocal in his disgust than the others, prompting a fellow student to say, "I wouldn't talk, Norbert. You did it last year!"

It was quite a morning for a new teacher. The lunch bell saved me, and having lost my appetite, I went outside to supervise students on the playground. Since I had not grown up in California, I was interested in an apparatus called tetherball. As I stood there watching two boys competing violently with each other, a cute little sixth-grade girl named Doris came and stood beside me. Presently she asked, "Would you like to play?"

"Sure," I said. It was a mistake.

Doris was twelve years old and she was a tetherball freak! I was twenty-five years old and I couldn't get the hang of the game. The tether would change the trajectory of the ball and I kept swinging wildly at the air. My students gathered around and I became very self-conscious about my performance. There I was, 6' 2" tall and a self-proclaimed jock, yet I was getting clobbered by this little girl. Then it happened.

Doris decided to go for broke. She spiked the ball with all her might and drove it straight up my nose. I never even saw it coming. The whole world began spinning and my nose was vibrating like a tuning fork. I really thought I was going to die. My eyes were streaming tears and my ears were humming like a beehive. Yet, what could I do? Twenty kids had seen Doris ring my bell and I couldn't let them know how badly I was hurt. So I went on playing even though I couldn't see the ball. It's a wonder Doris didn't whack me again.

Thank goodness for the afternoon bell. I took my pulsating nose back to the classroom and resolved to accept no more challenges from seventy-five-pound girls. They're dangerous.

5. The Establishment of Faith

Finally, may I urge you as parents of young children, whether compliant or strong-willed, to provide for them an unshakable faith in Jesus Christ. This is your *most* important function as mothers and fathers. How can anything else compare in significance to the goal of keeping the family circle unbroken in the life to come? What an incredible objective to work toward!

If the salvation of our children is really that vital to us, then our spiritual training should begin before children can even comprehend what it is all about. They should grow up seeing their parents on their knees before God, talking to Him. They will learn quickly at that age and will never forget what they've seen and heard. Even if they reject their faith later, the remnant of it will be with them for the rest of their lives. This is why we are instructed to ". . . bring them up in the nurture and admonition of the Lord" (Ephesians 6:4 KJV).

Again, I was fortunate to have had parents who understood this principle. After I was grown they told me that I attempted to pray before I learned to talk. I watched them talk to God and then attempted to imitate the sounds I had heard. Two years later, at three years of age, I made a conscious decision to become a Christian. You may think it impossible at such an age, but it happened. I remember the occasion clearly today. I was attending a Sunday evening church service and was sitting near the back with my mother. My father was the pastor, and he invited those who wished to do so to come pray at the altar. Fifteen or twenty people went forward, and I joined them spontaneously. I recall crying and asking Jesus to forgive my sins. I know that sounds strange, but that's the way it occurred. It is overwhelming for me to think about that event today. Imagine the King of the universe, Creator of all heaven and earth, caring about an insignificant kid barely out of toddlerhood! It makes no sense, but I know it happened.

Not every child will respond that early or dramatically, of course, nor should they. Some are more sensitive to spiritual matters than others, and they must be allowed to progress at their own pace. But in no sense should we as their parents be casual or neutral about their training. Their world should sparkle with references to Jesus and to our faith. That is the meaning of Deuteronomy 6:6–9, "These commandments that I give you today are to be upon your hearts. Impress them on your children. Talk about them when you sit at home and when you walk along the road, when you lie down and when you get up.

Tie them as symbols on your hands and bind them on your foreheads. Write them on the doorframes of your houses and on your gates."

I believe this commandment from the Lord is one of the most crucial verses for parents in the entire Bible. It instructs us to surround our children with godly teaching. References to spiritual things are not to be reserved just for Sunday morning or even for a bedtime prayer. They should permeate our conversation and the fabric of our lives. Why? Because our children are watching our every move during those early years. They want to know what is most important to us. If we hope to instill within them a faith that will last for a lifetime, then they must see and feel our passion for God.

As a corollary to that principle, I must remind you that children miss nothing in sizing up their parents. If you are only half convinced of your beliefs, they will quickly discern that fact. Any ethical weak spot—any indecision on your part—will be incorporated and then magnified in your sons and daughters. Like it or not, we are on the hook. Their faith or their faithlessness will be a reflection of our own. As I've said, our children will eventually make their own choices and set the course of their lives, but those decisions will be influenced by the foundations we have laid. Someone said, "The footsteps a boy follows are the ones his father thought he covered up." It is true.

That brings me to another extremely important point, even though it is controversial. I firmly believe in acquainting children with God's judgment and wrath while they are young. Nowhere in the Bible are we instructed to skip over the unpleasant scriptures in our teaching. The wages of sin is death, and children have a right to understand that fact.

I remember my mother reading the story of Samson to me when I was about nine years old. After this mighty warrior fell into sin, you will recall, the Philistines put out his eyes and held him as a common slave. Some time later, Samson repented before God and he was forgiven. He was even given back his awesome strength. But my mother pointed out that he never regained his eyesight nor did he ever live in freedom again. He and his enemies died together as the temple collapsed upon them.

"There are terrible consequences to sin," she told me solemnly. "Even if you repent and are forgiven, you will still suffer for breaking the laws of God. They are there to protect you. If you defy them, you will pay the price for your disobedience."

Then she talked to me about gravity, one of God's physical laws. "If you jump from a ten-story building, you can be certain that you will crash when you hit the ground. It is inevitable. You must also know that God's *moral* laws are just as real as his physical laws. You can't break them without crashing sooner or later."

Finally, she taught me about heaven and hell and the great Judgment Day when those who have been covered by the blood of Jesus will be separated eternally from those who have not. It made a profound impression on me.

Many parents would not agree with my mother's decision to acquaint me with the nature of sin and its consequences. They have said to me, "Oh, I wouldn't want to paint such a negative picture for my kids. I want them to think of God as a loving Father, not as a wrathful judge who punishes us." In so doing, they withhold a portion of the truth from their children. He is both a God of love and a God of judgment. There are 116 places in the Bible where we are told to "fear the Lord." By what authority do we eliminate these references in describing who God is to our children?

I am thankful that my parents and my church had the courage to acquaint me with the "warning note" in Scripture. It was this awareness of sin and its consequences that kept me moral at times when I could have fallen into sexual sin. Biblical faith was a governor—a checkpoint beyond which I was unwilling to go. By that time I was not afraid of my parents. I could have fooled them. But I could not get away from the all-seeing eye of the Lord. I knew I would stand accountable before Him someday, and that fact gave me the extra motivation to make responsible decisions.

I can't overstate the importance of teaching divine accountability to your strong-willed children, especially. Since their tendency is to test the limits and break the rules, they will need this internal standard to guide their behavior. Not all will listen to it, but some will. But while doing that, be careful to *balance* the themes of love and justice as you teach your children about God. To tip the scales in either direction is to distort the truth and create confusion in a realm where understanding is of utmost significance.

---

[1] *Dare to Discipline* (Wheaton, IL: Tyndale House Publishers, 1970), 27–28.
[2] Bruce A. Baldwin, "Growing Up Responsible (Part 2), Parental Problem with Discipline Procedures," *Piedmont Airline* (December 1985): 11.

Power
Games

In our efforts to understand the strong-willed child, we must ask ourselves why he or she is so fond of conflict. If given the opportunity to choose between war and peace, most of us would prefer tranquility. Yet the tough-minded kid goes through life like a runaway lawn mower. He'll chew up anything that gets in his way. The taller the grass, the better he survives and thrives. What makes him like that? What drives him to challenge his mother and defy his father? They are not his enemies. Why would he resist their loving leadership from the earliest days of childhood? Why does he seem to enjoy irritating his siblings and goading his neighbors? Why does he throw erasers when his teachers turn their backs and why won't he do his homework? Indeed, why can't he be like his compliant brothers and sisters?

These are interesting questions that I have pondered

for years. Now I believe I'm beginning to understand some of the motivating forces that drive the strong-willed kid to attack his world. Deep within his or her spirit is a raw desire for *power*. We can define power in this context as control—control of others, control of our circumstances and, especially, control of ourselves. The strong-willed child is not the only one who seeks power, of course. He differs from the rest of the human family only in degree, not in kind. We all want to be the boss and that desire is evident in very young children. Remember the toddler who rode his tricycle into the street and shouted angrily at his mother? The real issue between them was a matter of power and who would hold it. We see the same struggle when an adolescent slams doors and flees in his car, or when a husband and wife fight over finances, or when an elderly woman refuses to move to a nursing home. The common thread is the desire to run our own lives—and that of everyone else if given the chance. We vary in intensity of this impulse, as we will see, but it seems to motivate all of us to one degree or another.

The desire for control appears to have its roots in the very early hours after birth. Studies of newborns indicate that they typically "reach" for the adults around them on the first or second day of life. By that I mean they behave in ways designed to entice their guardians to meet their needs. Some will perfect the technique in the years that follow.

Even mature adults who ought to know better are usually involved in power games with other people. It happens whenever human interests collide, but it is especially prevalent in families. Husbands, wives, children, siblings, in-laws and parents all have reason to manipulate each other. It is fascinating to sit back and watch them push, pull and twist. In fact, I've identified sixteen techniques that are used to obtain power in another person's life. Perhaps you will think of additional approaches as you read the list that follows:

1. *Emotional Blackmail:* "Do what I want or I'll get very angry and go all to pieces."
2. *The Guilt Trip:* "How could you do this to me after I've done so much for you?"
3. *Divine Revelation:* "God told me you should do what I want."
4. *The Foreclosure:* "Do what I want or I won't pay the bills."
5. *The Bribe:* "Do what I want and I'll make it worth your time."
6. *By Might and by Power:* "Shut up and do what I tell you!"
7. *The Humiliation:* "Do what I want or I'll embarrass you at home and abroad."
8. *The Eternal Illness:* "Don't upset me. Can't you see I'm sick?"
9. *Help from Beyond the Grave:* "Your dear father (or mother) would have agreed with me."
10. *The Adulterous Threat:* "Do what I want or I'll find someone who will."
11. *The In-law Ploy:* "Do what I want and I'll be nice to your sweet mother."
12. *The Seduction:* "I'll make you an offer you can't afford to refuse," or as Mae West said to Cary Grant, "Why doncha come up and see me some time?" She also said she used to be Snow White but she drifted.

Special approaches used by adolescents:

13. *Teenage Terror:* "Leave me alone or I'll pull a stupid adolescent stunt" (suicide, drugs, booze, wrecking the car or hitch-hiking to San Francisco).
14. *The Flunkout:* "Let me do what I want or I'll get myself booted out of Woodrow Wilson Junior High School."
15. *Fertile Follies:* "Do what I want or I'll present you with a baby!" (This threat short-circuits every nerve in a parent's body.)
16. *The Tranquilizer:* "Do what I want and I won't further complicate your stressful life."

Manipulation! It's a game any number can play, right in the privacy of your own home. The objective is to obtain power over the other players, as we have seen. It will come as no surprise to parents, I'm sure, that children can be quite gifted at power games. That is why it is important for mothers and fathers to consider this characteristic as they attempt to interpret childish behavior. Another level of motivation lies below the surface issues that seemingly cause conflicts between generations. For example, when a three-year-old runs away in a supermarket, or when a nine-year-old refuses to straighten his room, or when a twelve-year-old continues to bully his little brother, or when a sixteen-year-old smokes cigarettes or drinks liquor, they are making individual statements about power. Their rebellious behavior usually represents more than a desire to do what is forbidden. Rather, it is an expression of independence and self-assertion. It is also a rejection of adult authority, and therein lies the significance for us.

Power games begin in earnest when children are between twelve and fifteen months of age. Some get started even earlier. If you've ever watched a very young child continue to reach for an electric plug or television knob while his mother shouts, "No!", you've seen an early power game in progress. It is probably not a conscious process at this stage, but later it will be. I'm convinced that a strong-willed child of three or older is inclined to challenge his mom and dad whenever he believes he can win. He will carefully choose the weapons and select the turf on which the contest will be staged. I've called these arenas "the battlefields of childhood." Let's look at some of the Gettysburgs, Stalingrads or Waterloos that have gone down in family history.

Bedtime

One of the earliest contests begins at eighteen months and one day of age, give or take a few hours. At precisely that time, a toddler who has gone to bed without complaining since he was born will suddenly say, "I'm not getting back in that crib again for as long as I live." That is the opening salvo in what may be a five-year battle. It happens so quickly and unexpectedly that parents may be fooled by it. They will check for teething problems, a low-grade fever or some other discomfort. "Why *now*?" they ask. I don't know. It just suddenly occurs to toddlers that they don't want to go to bed anymore, and they will fight it tooth and nail.

Although the tactics change a bit, bedtime will continue to be a battlefield for years to come. Any creative six-year-old can delay going to bed for at least 45 minutes by an energetic and well-conceived system of stalling devices. By the time his mother gets his pajamas on, brings him six glasses of water, takes him to the bathroom twice, helps him say his prayers, and then scolds him for wandering out of his bedroom a time or two, she is thoroughly exhausted. It happens night after night.

A college friend of mine named Jim found himself going through this bedtime exercise every evening with his five-year-old son, Paulie. Jim recognized the tactics as a game and decided he didn't want to play anymore. He sat down with his son that evening and said, "Now, Paulie, things are going to be different tonight. I'm going to get you dressed for bed; you can have a drink of water and then we'll pray together. When that is done I'm walking out the door and I don't intend to come back. Don't call me again. I don't want to hear a peep from you until morning. Do you understand?"

Paulie said, "Yes, Daddy."

When the chores were completed, final hugs were exchanged and the lights were turned out. Jim told his son good night and left the room. Sweet silence prevailed in the house. But not for long. In about five minutes, Paulie called his father and asked for another drink of water.

"No way, Paulie," said his dad. "Don't you remember what I said? Now go to sleep."

After several minutes, Paulie appealed again for a glass of water. Jim was more irritated this time. He spoke sharply and advised his son to forget it. But the boy would not be put off. He waited for a few minutes and then re-opened the case. Every time Paulie called his dad, Jim became more irritated. Finally, he said, "If you ask for water one more time I'm going to come in there and spank you!"

That quieted the boy for about five minutes and then

he said, "Daddy, when you come in here to spank me would you bring me a glass of water please?"

The kid got the water. He did not get the spanking.

One of the ways of enticing children (perhaps age four to eight) to go to bed is by the use of fantasy. For example, I told my son and daughter about "Mrs. White's Party" when they were little. Mrs. White was an imaginary lady who threw the most fantastic celebrations in the middle of the night. She ran an amusement park that made Disneyland boring by comparison. Whatever was of interest to the children was worked into her repertoire— dogs, cats, sweets of all varieties, water slides, cartoons, thrilling rides and anything else that excited Danae and Ryan's imagination. Of course, the *only* way they could go to Mrs. White's Party was to be asleep. No one who was awake would ever get an invitation. It was fun to watch our son and daughter jump into bed and concentrate to go to sleep. Though it never happened, I wish I could have generated such interest that they would have actually dreamed about Mrs. White. Usually, the matter was forgotten the next morning.

By hook or crook, fantasy or reality, you must win the great bedtime battle. The health of your child (and maybe your own) is at stake.

Food

The dinner table is another major battlefield of childhood, but it should be avoided. I have strongly advised parents not to get suckered into this arena. It is an ambush. A general always wants to engage the other army in a place where he can win, and mealtime is a lost cause. A mother who puts four green beans on a fork and

resolves to sit there until the child eats them is in a powerless position. The child can outlast her. And because
meals come around three times a day, he will eventually
prevail.

Instead of begging, pleading, bribing and threatening a child, I recommend that good foods be placed before him cheerfully. If he chooses not to eat, then smile
and send him on his way. He'll be back. When he returns, take the same food out of the refrigerator, heat it
and set it before him again. Sooner or later, he will get
hungry enough to eat. Do not permit snacking or substituting sweets for nutritious foods. But also do not fear
the physical effects of hunger. A child will not starve
in the presence of good things to eat. There is a gnawing
feeling inside that changes one's attitude from "Yuck!" to
"Yum!", usually within a few hours.

We have already talked about anorexia and bulimia,
eating disorders related to parental power. Obviously,
food can be the focal point of great struggles between
generations.

Schoolwork

Perhaps there is *no* greater source of conflict between generations today than schoolwork, and especially
that portion assigned to be done at home. This is another
battlefield where all the advantages fall to the youngster.
Only he knows for sure what was assigned and how the
work is supposed to be done. The difficult child will
capitalize on this information gap between home and
school, claiming that "I got it all done in school," or "I
have nothing to do tonight." He reminds me of the kid
who brought home 4 F's and a C on his report card.
When his dad asked what he thought the problem was,

he said, "I guess I've been concentrating too hard on one subject."

Parents should know that *most* students go through an academic valley sometime between the sixth and ninth grades in school. Some will quit working altogether during this time. Others will merely decrease their output. Very few will remain completely unaffected. The reason is the massive assault made on adolescent senses by the growing-up process. Self-confidence is shaken to its foundation. Happy hormones crank into action and sex takes over center stage. Who can think about school with all that going on? Or better yet, who wants to? As parents, you should watch for this diversion and not be dismayed when it comes. We'll discuss the underachiever later in this book.

Vacations and Special Days

Tell me why it is that children are the most obnoxious and irritating on vacations and during other times when we are specifically trying to please them? By all that is fair and just, you would expect them to think, "Boy! Mom and Dad are really doing something nice for us. They are taking us on this expensive vacation when they could have spent the money on themselves. And Dad would probably have preferred to go fishing (that's true) or something else he wanted to do. But they care about us and have included us in their plans. Wow! I'm going to be as nice and cooperative as possible. I'll try to get along with my sister and I won't make any unusual demands. What a fun trip this will be!"

Do kids think that way? Fat chance! There is no such thing as intergenerational gratitude.

Before the family has even left town, the troops are

fighting over who gets to sit by the window and which one will hold the dog. Little Sister yells, "I'm telling!" every few minutes. Tensions are also building in the front seat. By the time they get to Phoenix, dad is ready to blow his cork. It was tough enough for him to complete his office work and pack the car. But this bickering is about to drive him crazy. For four hundred miles, he has endured arguments, taunts, jabs, pinches, tears, tattling and unscheduled bathroom breaks. Now he's starting to lose control. Twice he swings wildly at writhing bodies in the back seat. He misses and hurts his shoulder. He's driving faster by this time but he's quit talking. The only clues to what he's feeling are his bloodshot eyes and the occasional twitch in his left cheek. Happy vacation, Pop. You have thirteen days to go.

Recently I received a letter from a mother who had just returned from a stressful vacation similar to the one I described. For days, their two sons had whined and complained, insulting and fighting with each other. They kicked the back of their father's seat for hours at a time. Finally, his fuse burned down to the dry powder. He pulled the car over to the side of the road and jerked the boys outside. Judgment Day had arrived. After spanking them both, he shoved them back into the car and warned them to keep their mouths shut. "If I hear a peep from either of you for thirty minutes," he warned, "I'll give you some more of what you just had!" The boys got the message. They remained mute for thirty minutes, after which the older lad said, "Is it all right to talk now?"

The father said sternly, "Yes. What do you want to say?"

"Well," continued the boy. "When you spanked us back there my shoe fell off. We left it in the road."

It was the only good pair of shoes the kid owned. This time Mom went berserk and flailed at the back seat like a crazy lady. So ended another great day of family togetherness.

Is this the way parents should deal with a period of irritation from their children? Of course not, but let's face it. Parents are people. They have their vulnerabilities and flash points too. The children should have been separated or perhaps offered spankings much earlier in the journey. It is when parents are desperately trying to avoid punishment that their level of irritation reaches a dangerous level. By then, anything can happen. That is why I have contended that those who oppose corporal punishment on the grounds that it leads to child abuse are wrong. By stripping parents of the ability to handle frustrating behavior at an early stage, they actually increase the possibility that harm will be done to children as tempers rise.

Before we leave the matter of family vacations, let's deal with why it is that children seem to become more obnoxious on those special days. There are two good reasons for it. First, adults and children alike tend to get on each other's nerves when they are cooped up together for extended periods of time. But also, a difficult child apparently feels compelled to reexamine the boundaries whenever he thinks they may have moved. This was certainly true of our children. On days when we planned trips to Disneyland, ski trips or other holidays, we could count on them to become testy. It was as though they were obligated to ask, "Since this is a special day, what are the rules now?" We would sometimes have to punish or scold them during times when we were specifically trying to build relationships. Your strong-willed kids may do the same. Perhaps that's why Erma

Bombeck said, "The family that plays together gets on one another's nerves."

Other battlefields of early childhood include clothing and hair styles, doing the dishes and household chores, demands for candy and treats in supermarkets, getting up in time to catch the school bus, taking regular baths, talking sassy to mom and keeping the child's room clean. (One mother told me her ten-year-old's bedroom was such a mess that she would have to get a tetanus shot to walk through it.) The number of these routine skirmishes between parents and children is virtually endless. A child can use almost any pretext to launch a new crusade—or had you already noticed?

To repeat our thesis, these trouble spots between generations are not simply matters of differing opinion. If the conflicts amounted to no more than that, then negotiation and compromise would resolve them very quickly. Instead, they represent staging areas where the authority of the parent can be challenged and undermined. The question being asked is not so much, "Can I have my way?" as it is, "Who's in charge here?" (Remember, now, that I'm describing the motivation of very strong-willed children. The compliant child is more subtle in his maneuvers for power.)

With the passage of time, the battles do tend to become more intense. What began as relatively minor struggles over bedtime or homework can develop into the most terrible conflicts. Some teenagers put their parents through hell on earth. Deep, searing wounds are inflicted that may never fully heal. For now, however, I want to conclude this discussion by explaining the great significance of power and its ramifications for parents. Everything said to this point is merely prologue to the message in paragraphs that follow. Please give special emphasis to this remaining section as you read.

The sense of power that is so attractive to children and to the rest of humanity is actually a very dangerous thing. Men have deceived, exploited and killed to get it. Those who have achieved it have often been destroyed in its grasp. Lord Acton said, "Power corrupts, and absolute power corrupts absolutely." History has proved him right.

The most bloodthirsty men who ever lived were driven by an insatiable lust for power. In the effort to dominate the world, Adolph Hitler set off a conflagration that claimed fifty million lives. Joseph Stalin is said to have murdered twenty to thirty million people during his reign of terror. On one occasion, Stalin reportedly sent his secret police to the little town where he was raised with orders to kill the teachers who had instructed him as a child. Imagine the brutality! Apparently, he wanted to leave no witnesses to his mediocre beginnings. This is where the lust for power leads when it is unbridled.

Our concern, however, is not limited to the behavior of dictators and despots. Power has a negative effect wherever it comes to rest. I've known many famous physicians and surgeons, for example, who exercised vast authority in the medical community. Patients worshiped them; nurses feared them; colleagues respected them; and friends envied them. They seemed to have it all. But how did this adulation affect their personalities? Did they grow more humble and self-effacing as their ego needs were met? Hardly! They tended to become more infantile in their demands, or they became tyrannical and sought to crush anyone who got in their way.

Notorious physicians are not the only ones who have

trouble handling power. The same is true of successful actors, musicians, ministers, lawyers and military generals in times of war. Study the historical profiles of great military generals like George Patton or Douglas MacArthur. Most were proud and arrogant men. A story is told about the haughty British general, Bernard Montgomery, who was giving a speech near the end of his life. He said, "You will remember when God said to Moses there in the wilderness—and I think rightly so—" Who but a commander of armies would dare critique the words of the Lord Himself?

United States presidents have also been known to take themselves too seriously, and Lyndon Johnson was among the worst. During his years in the White House, he was a power monger, terrorizing his aides for their minor mistakes and oversights. I'm told, for example, that he became furious when they forgot to restock the presidential airplane with root beer, his favorite soft drink. "No rut beer!?" he would scream in his Texas drawl. "Whaddaya mean no rut beer?!" He couldn't believe anyone would have the audacity to ignore his whims in this way.

It is interesting that five United States presidents in the twentieth century have won landslide electoral victories and achieved the power to which they were entitled. Predictably, perhaps, all five experienced their greatest crises shortly thereafter: Harding and the Teapot Dome Scandal; Roosevelt and the Supreme Court debacle; Johnson and the Vietnam war; Nixon and the Watergate affair; and Reagan and the Iran-Contra connection. Time after time, history illuminates the destructive nature of raw power. Proverbs 27:21 states, ". . . man is tested by the praise he receives."

Chuck Colson lived through the Watergate debacle

that brought down President Richard Nixon. As a senior member of the White House staff during an era when presidential influence was maximal, Colson knew how to use power. He was also quite willing to abuse it. He worked just a few feet from the Oval Office and his orders carried the authority of the president himself. By simply making a phone call, he could send a detachment of troops anywhere in the world. He could have the presidential helicopter land on the White House lawn within minutes to take him where he wished to go. He conferred with the Soviets and with our allies on matters of monumental importance. Yes, Chuck Colson experienced the meaning of political power in all its glory, and his fall from that lofty perch was one of the most dramatic descents in American history.

After his conviction in the Watergate scandal, Colson was sentenced to serve two years in the federal penitentiary at Maxwell Prison Camp in Florida. Upon arrival, this proud governmental leader was systematically shorn of his dignity. He was stripped, searched and dusted for lice. He was placed in an eight-foot cell with a stinking open toilet. A guard came by every two hours and shined a flashlight in his eyes. Colson, who had conferred with prime ministers, emperors and princes, now lived and worked with rapists, murderers, thieves and child molesters. He was utterly powerless for some seven months.

How impressive it is that Chuck Colson chose not to reconstruct his power base when he was released from prison. He could have gone back to his law practice in New York, with its six-figure income, a yacht and the other trappings of opulence. Instead, he founded Prison Fellowship Ministries to assist the down-and-outers of the world. Why would a man deny himself in that way?

Because he found a "higher power" in a personal relationship with Jesus Christ. It totally revolutionized his life. I admire this man greatly and am honored to call him my friend.

If you talk to Chuck Colson today, he will warn you of the dangers of power. He should know. He was nearly destroyed by it. He will also tell you how he manipulated naïve Christians when he was in the White House. He dazzled them with presidential power and molded them to his political purposes. Finally, he will remind you that Jesus came without power and consistently resisted His disciples' desire for it. Jesus taught them, ". . . he who is least among you all—he is the greatest" (Luke 9:48).

Perhaps you have foreseen how this discussion of presidential politics and professional pride is related to the discipline of children, but let me lay it out. If power can be destructive to mature adults who think they know how to handle it, imagine what it will do to a mere child. Think again of the three-year-old boy on the tricycle, described in the second chapter. He had already achieved virtual independence from his mother. There he was, fresh out of *babyhood*, yet he had become his own boss. That's pretty heady stuff for a kid who's only three feet high. How would he choose to use all that power? Well, for starters he insisted on riding his tricycle down a busy boulevard. He is fortunate that his first taste of freedom didn't put him under the wheels of a 4,000-pound automobile. There will be other risks in future years, of course.

One of the characteristics of those who acquire power very early is a prevailing attitude of disrespect for authority. It extends to teachers, ministers, policemen, judges and even to God Himself. Such an individual has never yielded to parental leadership at home.

Why should he submit himself to anyone else? For a rebellious teenager it is only a short step from there to drug abuse, sexual experimentation, running away, and so on. The early acquisition of power has claimed countless young victims by this very process.

What do we recommend, then? Should parents retain every vestige of power for as long as possible? No! Even with its risks, self-determination is a basic human right and we must grant it systematically to our children. To withhold that liberty too long is to incite wars of revolution. My good friend, Jay Kesler, observed that Mother England made that specific mistake with her children in the American colonies. They grew to become rebellious "teenagers" who demanded their freedom. Still she refused to release them and unnecessary bloodshed ensued. Fortunately, England learned a valuable lesson from that painful experience. Some 171 years later, she granted a peaceful and orderly transfer of power to another tempestuous offspring named India. Revolution was averted.

This, then, is our goal as parents: we must not transfer power too early, even if our children take us daily to the battlefield. Mothers who make that mistake are some of the most frustrated people on the face of the earth. On the other hand, we must not retain parental power too long, either. Control will be torn from our grasp if we refuse to surrender it voluntarily. The granting of self-determination should be matched stride for stride with the arrival of maturity, culminating with complete release during early adulthood.

Sounds easy, doesn't it? We all know better. I consider this orderly transfer of power to be one of the most delicate and difficult responsibilities in the entire realm of parenthood. We'll talk more about the "how to" in subsequent chapters.

Too Pooped to Parent

We want to deal now with the problem of parental exhaustion and its effect on mothers and fathers of young children. Chronic fatigue has become an everyday occurrence for the majority of parents in North America, and its implications are difficult to overestimate. Without question, the best book I have read on this subject is entitled *Parent Burnout*, by Dr. Joseph Procaccini and Mark Kiefaber.[1] The authors describe how parents manage to squander their resources and ultimately fail in the task they care about most: raising healthy and responsible children. If you have staggered under the pressures of parenthood, I hope you will buy and read that book. In the meantime, let me provide a broad outline of its central message and add a few thoughts of my own.

Not surprisingly, perhaps, the most likely candidates for early exhaustion are the parents who are radically committed to their children. After all, if there is no "fire" there can be no burnout. These zealous and dedicated mothers and fathers are determined to provide every advantage and opportunity for the next generation from the earliest days of infancy. That is where their hearts lie. That is what they care about most. Their devotion leads them to make what they consider to be small sacrifices on behalf of the children. They often discontinue all recreational, romantic and restful activities that would take them away from home. Even long-term friends with whom they used to associate are now given lame excuses or are ignored altogether.

Compulsive Parenting

Everything focuses on the children. They are often unwilling to leave the kids with a baby-sitter for more than a few moments. Not even Mother Teresa would qualify as guardian for an evening. They would simply never forgive themselves if something went wrong while they were frivolously indulging in fun or entertainment. Imagine how they would feel if the announcer said over the public address system, "May I have your attention? Would Mr. or Mrs. James Johnson come to a house telephone, please? Your baby-sitter needs to know where the fire extinguisher is." No way! It's not worth it. They choose to stay home.

Sometimes this exclusivity with the baby even extends to grandparents, who are enormously insulted by the situation. They have accumulated twenty-five years of parenting experience and yet they are not trusted with the grandkids for a single evening. White-hot anger flows between generations and may be remembered for the rest of their lives. Nevertheless, the parents dig in and isolate themselves further.

In other cases, grandparents are simply not available to help shoulder the load. They may live 1,000 miles away and come to visit only once or twice a year. But let's be honest. Other grandmas don't want to be bothered. They're busily chasing careers of their own. The following poem, shared with me by Florence Turnridge, delightfully makes that case.

WHERE HAVE ALL THE GRANDMAS GONE?

> In the dim and distant past,
>   When life's tempo wasn't fast,
> Grandma used to rock and knit,
>   Crochet, tat and baby-sit.
> When the kids were in a jam,
>   They could always call on "Gram."
> In that day of gracious living,
>   Grandma was the gal for giving.
>
> BUT today she's in the gym,
>   Exercising to keep slim,
> She's off touring with the bunch,
>   Or taking clients out to lunch.
> Going north to ski or curl,
>   All her days are in a whirl.
> Nothing seems to stop or block her,
>   Now that Grandma's off her rocker!!!
>
> Author Unknown[2]

If she's not careful, Grandma will also burn herself out and be back in her rocker again. Either way, she may not be able to offer the support to her children that grandparents provided in centuries past. The extended family is gone, leaving a young mother isolated and alone. She may pass two or four or even ten years without a significant break from the tasks of child-rearing. She feels it is a minor sacrifice to make for so great a purpose. And yet, her perspective on life is distorted. The routine events of her world are interpreted in terms of this one-dimensional value system. Anything that might have the remotest negative influence on her kids becomes deeply disturbing to her, leading to overreaction and conflict. Insignificant childhood squabbles in the neighborhood, for example, or idle comments from church members can bring surprisingly heated responses. And Lord help the teacher or Sunday school worker who fails to deliver!

Compulsive parenting can also be destructive to a marriage, especially when only one parent is so inclined. If it is the mother, she may give herself totally to the children and have nothing left for her husband. He believes she has gone a little wacky with this mothering thing, and may even resent the kids for taking her away from him. She, in turn, despises his selfishness and becomes sole defender and care-giver for their children. A wedge is thereby driven between them that may someday destroy the family.

Superparenting

Please understand that I am not critical of the motives behind what might be called "superparenting." Children *are* worth our very best efforts to raise them properly, and I have spent twenty years urging parents to give them their due. Nevertheless, even a noble and necessary task can be taken to such extremes that it becomes harmful to both the giver and the receiver. In the child's case, there is a direct link between superparenting and overprotection, an egocentric perspective on life, and in some cases, a prolonged dependency relationship with parents. In the adult context, obsessive child-rearing can lead inexorably to the condition known as parental burnout.

Procaccini and Kiefaber have provided an insightful explanation of how burnout occurs in the compulsive parent, or for that matter, in anyone who fails to take care of himself. Their concept is based on five key premises, as follows: (1) human energy is a precious resource that makes possible everything we wish to do; (2) energy is a *finite* quantity—there is a limited supply available to each of us; (3) *whenever the expenditure of energy exceeds the supply, burnout begins*; (4) parents who hope to accomplish the goals they have set for themselves and their children must not squander their vital resources foolishly; and (5) wasteful drains on that supply should be identified and eliminated, and priority given to rebuilding the reserve.

From this explanation it is understandable why burnout is an occupational hazard for parents who reserve nothing for themselves. It should also be clear why superparenting is a natural trap for those of us who share the Christian faith. Deeply ingrained within us is a philosophy that lends itself to compulsive child-rearing. The family ranks near the top of our value system, and our way of life focuses on self-sacrifice and commitment to others. Does it not seen reasonable, therefore, that we would pour every resource into this awesome task? That is our God-given assignment, isn't it?

Well, of course, it is, but I would point out that the apostle Paul advocates moderation in *all* things (Philippians 4:5). Remember too that Jesus took time to rest and care for His body. On one occasion, He got in a boat and rowed away from the multitudes of sick and needy people on the shore. He could have remained there and healed thousands more, but He had apparently reached the limits of His strength. Parents *must* learn to monitor their own bodies, too, and conserve their energy for the long haul. That is, after all, in the very best interest of their children.

Lest we be misunderstood, extremely dedicated mothers and fathers are not the only parents who are inclined to overextend their resources. The routine experiences of living in today's stressful environment are sufficient in themselves to wear us out. Urgent demands are made simultaneously by our jobs, our churches, our children's schools, our friends and our civic responsibilities. The great movement of women into the labor force has left millions of mothers on the brink of nervous collapse as they attempt to combine full-time employment with full-time responsibilities at home. In her book, *Having It All*, Helen Gurley Brown advised women that it is possible to achieve multiple competing goals. She is wrong, except in rare cases. Something has to give. Again, when the demand for energy exceeds the supply, *for whatever reason,* burnout is inevitable. And children are almost always the losers in the competition for that limited resource.

But what is it like to experience parental burnout? According to Procaccini and Kiefaber, it occurs in five progressive stages, each more stressful than the ones before. The first can be called the "Gung-Ho" stage, which has been described in preceding paragraphs. It may actually begin with the discovery of pregnancy and continue for several years. Very subtly, then, parents can move from the first to the second stage of burnout, which is characterized by persistent doubts. They know something is definitely wrong at this point, but may fail to realize how rapidly they are losing altitude. They are frequently irritated by the children and find themselves screaming on occasions. Quite often they feel drained and fatigued. A full range of psychosomatic symptoms may come and go, including back and neck aches, upset stomach, ulcers and colitis, hypertension, headaches, diarrhea and constipation. Still, the individual may wonder, *Why do I feel this way?* Not long ago I received a classic letter from a father in the second stage of parental burnout. This is what he wrote (emphasis mine):

> The reason I'm writing is that the Lord has blessed us so much, and I should be full of joy. But I have been depressed for about 10 months now.
> I don't know whether to turn to a pastor, a physician, a psychologist, a nutritionist or a chiropractor.
> Last September the Lord blessed us with a beautiful baby boy. He is just wonderful. He is cute and smart and strong. We just can't help but love him. *But he has been very demanding.* The thing that made it hardest for me was last semester Margie was taking classes three nights a week to finish her BA degree and I took care of little Danny. He cried and sobbed the whole time we were together. He would eventually go to sleep if I would hold him, but then I was afraid to put him down for fear he would wake up. I was used to being able to pay my bills, work out the budget, read, file mail, answer letters, type lists, etc., in the evening, but all this had to be postponed until Margie was here.
> It was a real depressing time for me. I just couldn't handle all that crying. It was worse because Margie was breast-feeding him. I got very tired and started having a great deal of trouble getting up in the morning to go to work. I started getting sick very easily.

I have not been able to cope with these things. I really should be at work at 8:00, but I haven't been there before 9:00 or 9:30 in months. *It seems like I'm always fighting the flu.* I love our baby a lot and I wouldn't trade him for anything in the world. But I don't understand why I'm so depressed. Sure, Margie gets tired because we can't seem to get Danny to bed before 11 or 12 midnight and he wakes up twice per night to be fed. But she's not depressed. *All this getting awakened at night really gets to me* and I don't even have to get up to feed him.

Another thing that has been a constant struggle is leaving Danny in the nursery at church. He isn't content to be away from us very long so they end up having to track Margie down almost every Sunday. *We hardly ever get to be together.* This has been going on for 11 months now.

There are a couple of other things that probably contribute to my depression. They are (1) responsibilities at work; we're short-handed and I'm trying to do too much; (2) spending too many weekends with yard work or trying to fix up our fixer-upper house; and (3) our finances, which are very limited. Sixty-four percent of our income goes to pay for our house and there's not much left over. We don't want Margie to go to work, so we are on a meticulous budget. It's down to the bare essentials, now. I get so tired of that.

We have all the things we would ever dream of at our age (27). Our own neat little house in a good neighborhood, a job I consider a ministry. We have a fine healthy boy, each other, and not least of all, our life in Christ.

I have no reason to be depressed and tired all the time. I come home from work so exhausted that I don't even want Danny near me. He hangs on to Margie and she can't even fix dinner if I don't get him out of her hair. I just don't know how she stands it.

She must have a higher tolerance as far as not getting anything done is concerned.

If you have any insights as to what I should do, please let me know. Thanks and God bless you.

Jack

This young father of 27 years is well on the way toward burning out. The surprising thing is that Jack is bewildered by it. When one looks at his impossible schedule, it is no wonder that his mind and body are rebelling. After handling an extremely demanding job, he comes home to a fussy baby, a wife in night school and mountains of bills and paperwork to do. On weekends he is rebuilding his run-down house! Finally, Jack made it clear that he and his wife have no time alone together, no fun in their lives, no social life, no regular exercise and no escape from the baby. No wonder!!

In addition to his other pressures, Jack can't even get an uninterrupted night's sleep. He climbs into bed about midnight, but is awakened at least twice before morning. That is probably the key to his depression. Some individuals are extremely vulnerable to loss of sleep and this man appears to be one of them. I am another. Our son, Ryan, did not sleep through the night once in his first four months, and I thought I was going to die. Do you remember what that was like with your newborns? There is no sound on earth quite like the piercing screech of an infant in the wee small hours of the morning. (Incidentally, people who say they "sleep like a baby" probably never had one.)

It may be impossible for this family to make immediate and sweeping changes in their lifestyle, but that's what is necessary to avoid greater problems. Margie is coping for the moment, but she will eventually crack too. I would recommend for starters that they postpone reconstructing their house, spending that money instead on child care and weekend trips to the mountains or beach. They both desperately need at least one day a week away from the baby. Breast-feeding is a problem, but there are solutions to it. Will the child scream when they leave? Yes. Will that hurt him? Not nearly as much as having parents who are too worn out to care for him.

Transition

What will happen if this couple does not find some source of relief? Well, fortunately, their baby will not always be so demanding. But toddlerhood lies ahead and new babies are always a possibility. If they continue to give out without taking in, they will slide from the second stage of burnout into the third. According to Procaccini and Kiefaber, this is the most critical phase. They called it the *transition stage* because decisions are usually made during this period that will determine the well-being of the family for years to come. They will either recognize the downward path they are on and make changes to reverse it, or else they will continue their plunge toward chaos.

What is felt during this third stage is indescribable fatigue, self-condemnation, great anger and resentment. For the first time, a couple in this situation openly blames the kids for their discontent. One of the reasons they were so excited about parenthood was their idealistic expectation of what children are like. They honestly did not know that little boys and girls can be, and usually are, demanding, self-centered, sloppy, lazy and rebellious. It wasn't supposed to be this way! In fact, they expected the kids to meet *their* needs for love and appreciation.

Instead it is give! give! give! take! take! take! Depression and tears are daily visitors.

Pulling Away

The human mind will not tolerate that level of agitation for very long. It will seek to protect itself from further pain. As indicated earlier, this transition phase usually leads either to beneficial changes or to a destructive self-defense. The latter occurs in Stage Four, which the authors call pulling away. The individual withdraws from the family and becomes "unavailable" to the children. The mother may not even hear them, even though they tug at her skirt and beg for her attention. She may slip into alcoholism or drug or tranquilizer abuse to dull her senses further. If forced to deal with the minor accidents and irritants of childhood, such as spilled milk or glue on the carpet, she may overreact violently and punish wildly. Fantasies of "slinging the brat against the wall" or "bashing him good" may recur in this angry and guilt-ridden parent. Obviously, child abuse is only an inch away. It occurs thousands of times daily in most Western countries.

If asked to explain what she is feeling, a mother in the fourth stage of burnout will say something like this, "I just can't deal with the kids right now." I counseled a woman in this situation who told me, referring to her children, "They hang around my ankles and beg for this or that, but I'll tell you, I kick 'em off. I'm not going to let 'em destroy my life!" She was a living, breathing stick of dynamite waiting to be ignited. People who reach this stage not only pull away from their children, but they tend to become isolated from their spouses and other family members too. Thus, being physically and psychologically exhausted, guilt-ridden to the core, drenched in self-hatred and disappointed with life, these parents descend into the fifth stage of burnout.

The Final Phase

The final phase is called *chronic disenchantment* by Procaccini and Kiefaber. It is characterized by confusion and apathy. The individual at this stage has lost all meaning and purpose in living. Identity is blurred. Weeks may pass with nothing of significance being remembered. Sexual desire is gone and the marriage is seriously troubled. Recurring thoughts may focus on suicide, "cracking up" or running away. Clearly, this individual is desperately in need of counseling and a radical shift in lifestyle. If nothing changes, neither generation will ever be quite the same again.

And it is all so unnecessary!

Now let's take a closer look at the typical home today. Most of my readers will never reach the latter stages of burnout described above. Life is hard, but it isn't *that* hard. Some of you, however, will spend your parenting years in a state of general fatigue and stress, perhaps characterized by stage two. You'll crowd your days with junk . . . with unnecessary responsibilities and commitments that provide no lasting benefits. Precious energy resources will be squandered on that which only *seems* important at the moment. Consequently, your parenting years will pass in a blur of irritation and frustration. How can you know if this is happening even now? Well, continual screaming, nagging, threatening, punishing, criticizing and scolding of children is a pretty sure tip-off. There must be a better way to raise our sons and daughters.

One of the most common mistakes of young families is to duplicate the error of the young father who wrote to me. Jack and Margie attempted to accomplish too much too soon. I flinch when a newly married couple tells me they intend during their first two years together to go to school, have a baby, work full time, fix up a house, moonlight for extra money and teach Sunday school class.

It is a hairbrained plan. The human body will not tolerate that kind or pressure. And when one's body is finally exhausted, an interesting thing happens to the emotions. They also malfunction.

You see, the mind, body and spirit are very close neighbors and one usually catches the ills of the other. You'll recall that Jack did not understand his depression. He had every reason to be happy. He was miserable. Why? Because his depleted physical condition greatly affected his mental apparatus. And if the truth were known, his spiritual life probably wasn't all that inspiring either. The three departments of our intellectual apparatus are tightly linked and they tend to move up and down as a unit. (Remember how Elijah became depressed and wanted to die immediately after his exhausting confrontation with the prophets of Baal?) This is why it is so important for us to maintain and support the triad: mind, body and spirit. If one breaks down, the entire engine begins to sputter.

In summary, I join the authors of *Parent Burnout* in urging you to use your physical resources carefully and wisely in the years ahead. Raising children is not unlike a long-distance race in which the contestants must learn to pace themselves. If you blast out of the blocks as though you were running a sprint, you will inevitably tire out. You'll gasp and stumble as the road winds endlessly before you. Then when you come to heartbreak

hill, better known as adolescence, there will be no reserve with which to finish the course. Parenting, you
see, is a marathon, and we have to adopt a pace that we
can maintain for two or even three decades. That is the
secret of winning.

A balanced life makes that possible!

---

[1] Copyright © 1987, Dr. Joseph Procaccini and Mark W. Kiefaber,
Parent Burnout, Doubleday & Company, Inc., New York, NY 10167.
[2] Copyright © 1987, F. Turnridge, reprinted with permission.

Suggestions for Parents of Adolescents

Adolescence is a fascinating and crazy time of life. It reminds me in some ways of the very early space probes that blasted off from Cape Canaveral in Florida. I remember my excitement when Colonel John Glenn and the other astronauts embarked on their perilous journeys into space. It was a thrilling time to be an American.

People who lived through those years will recall that a period of maximum danger occurred as each spacecraft was reentering the earth's atmosphere. The flier inside was entirely dependent on the heat-shield on the bottom of the capsule to protect him from temperatures in excess of 1,000 degrees Fahrenheit. If the craft descended at the wrong angle, the astronaut would be burned to cinders. At that precise moment of anxiety, negative ions would accumulate around the capsule and prevent all communication with the earth for approximately seven minutes. The world waited breathlessly for news of the astronaut's safety. Presently, the reassuring voice of Chris Craft would break in to say, "This is Mission Control. We have made contact with Friendship Seven. Everything is A-Okay. Splashdown is imminent." Cheers and prayers went up in restaurants, banks, airports, and millions of homes across the country. Even Walter Cronkite seemed relieved.

The analogy to adolescence is not so difficult to recognize. After the training and preparation of childhood are over, a pubescent youngster marches out to the launching pad. His parents watch apprehensively as he climbs aboard a capsule called adolescence and waits for his rockets to fire. His father and mother wish they could go with him, but there is room for just one person in the spacecraft. Besides, nobody invited them. Without warning, the mighty rocket engines begin to roar and the "umbilical cord" falls away. "Liftoff! We have liftoff!" screams the boy's father.

Junior, who was a baby only yesterday, is on his way to the edge of the universe. A few weeks later, his parents go through the scariest experience of their lives: They suddenly lose all contact with the capsule. "Negative ions" have interfered with communication at a time when they most want to be assured of their son's safety. Why won't he talk to them?

This period of silence does not last a few minutes, as it did with Colonel Glenn and friends. It may continue for years. The same kid who used to talk a mile a minute and ask a million questions has now reduced his vocabulary to nine monosyllabic phrases. They are, "I dunno," "Maybe," "I forget," "Huh?," "No!," "Nope," "Yeah," "Who—me?'" and "He did it." Otherwise, only "static" comes through the receivers—groans, grunts, growls and gripes. What an apprehensive time it is for those who wait on the ground!

Years later when Mission Control believes the spacecraft to have been lost, a few scratchy signals are picked up unexpectedly from a distant transmitter. The parents are jubilant as they hover near their radio. Was that *really* his voice? It is deeper and more mature than they remembered. There it is again. This time the intent is unmistakable. Their spacey son has made a deliberate effort to correspond with them! He was fourteen years old when he blasted into space and now he is nearly twenty. Could it be that the negative environment has been swept away and communication is again possible? Yes. For most families, that is precisely what happens. After years of quiet anxiety, parents learn to their great relief that everything is A-Okay on board the spacecraft. The "splashdown" occurring during the early twenties can then be a wonderful time of life for both generations.

Isn't there some way to avoid this blackout period and the other stresses associated with the adolescent voyage? Not with some teenagers, perhaps the majority. It happens in the most loving and intelligent of families. Why? Because of two powerful forces that overtake and possess boys and girls in the early pubescent years. Let's talk about them.

The *first* and most important is hormonal in nature. I believe parents and even behavioral scientists have underestimated the impact of the biochemical changes occurring in puberty. We can see the effect of these hormones on the physical body, but something equally dynamic is occurring in the brain. How else can we explain why a happy, contented, cooperative twelve-year-old *suddenly* becomes a sullen, angry, depressed thirteen-year-old? Some authorities would contend that social pressure alone accounts for this transformation. I simply don't believe that.

The emotional characteristics of a suddenly rebellious teenager are rather like the symptoms of premenstrual syndrome or severe menopause in women, or perhaps a tumultuous mid-life crisis in men. Obviously, dramatic changes are going on inside! Furthermore, if the upheaval were caused entirely by environmental factors, its onset would not be so predictable in puberty. The emotional changes I have described arrive right on schedule, timed to coincide precisely with the arrival of physical maturation. Both characteristics, I contend, are driven by a common hormonal assault. Human chemistry apparently goes haywire for a few years, affecting mind as much as body.

If that explanation is accurate, then what implications does it have for parents of early adolescents? First, understanding this glandular upheaval makes it easier to tolerate and cope with the emotional reverberations that are occurring. For several years, some kids are not entirely rational! Just as a severely menopausal woman may accuse her innocent and bewildered husband of infidelity, a hormonally depressed teenager may not interpret his world accurately, either. His social judgment is impaired. Therefore, don't despair when it looks like everything you have tried to teach your kid seems to have been forgotten. He is going through a metamorphosis that has turned everything upside down. But stick around. He'll get his legs under him again!

I strongly recommend that parents of strong-willed and rebellious females quietly plot the particulars of her menstrual cycle. Not only should you record when her period begins and ends each month, but also make a comment or two each day about her mood. I think you will see that the emotional blow-ups that tear the family apart are cyclical in nature. Premenstrual tension at that age can produce a flurry of tornadoes every twenty-eight days. If you know they are coming, you can retreat to the storm cellar when the wind begins to blow. You can also use this record to teach your girls about premenstrual syndrome and how to cope with it. Unfortunately, many parents never seem to notice the regularity and pre-dictability of severe conflict with their daughters. Again, I recommend that you watch the calendar. It will tell you so much about your girls.

Emotional balance in teenage boys is not so cyclical, but their behavior is equally influenced by hormones. Everything from sexual passion to aggressiveness is moti-vated by the new chemicals that surge through their veins.

I indicated that there were two great forces which combine to create havoc during adolescence, the first having an hormonal origin. The other is social in nature. It is common knowledge that a twelve- or thirteen-year-old child suddenly awakens to a brand-new world around him, as though his eyes were opening for the first time. That world is populated by agemates who scare him out of his wits. His greatest anxiety, far exceeding the fear of death, is the possibility of rejection or humiliation in the eyes of his peers. This ultimate danger will lurk in the background for years, motivating him to do things that make absolutely no sense to the adults who watch. It is impossible to comprehend the adolescent mind without understanding this terror of the peer group.

I'll never forget a vulnerable girl named Lisa who was a student when I was in high school. She attended modern dance classes and was asked to perform during an all-school assembly program. Lisa was in the ninth grade and had not begun to develop sexually. As she spun around the stage that day, the unthinkable happened! The top to her strapless blouse suddenly let go (it had nothing to grip) and dropped to her waist. The student body gasped and then roared with laughter. It was terrible! Lisa stood clutching frantically at her bare body for a moment and then fled from the stage in tears. She never fully recovered from the tragedy. And you can bet that her "friends" made sure she remembered it for the rest of her life.

Such a situation would also humiliate an adult, of course, but it was worse for a teenager like Lisa. An embarrassment of that magnitude could even take away the desire to live, and indeed, thousands of adolescents are killing themselves every year. We must ask ourselves, why? How do we explain this paralyzing social fear at an age when other kinds of dangers are accepted in stride? Teenagers are known to be risk-takers. They drive their cars like maniacs and their record for bravery in combat ranks among the best. Why, then, can an eighteen-year-old be taught to attack an enemy gun emplacement or run through a minefield, and yet he panics in the quiet company of his peers? Whence cometh this great vulnerability?

I believe the answer is to be found, again, in the nature of *power* and how it influences behavior. Adolescent society is based on the exercise of raw force. That is the heart and soul of its value system. It comes in various forms, of course. For girls, there is no greater social dominance than physical beauty. A truly gorgeous young woman is so powerful that even the boys are often terrified of her. She rules in a high-school setting like a queen on her throne, and in fact, she is usually elected to some honor with references to royalty in its name

(Homecoming Queen, All-school Queen, Sweetheart's Queen, Football Queen, etc.). The way she uses this status to intimidate her subjects is in itself a fascinating study in adolescent behavior.

Boys derive power from physical attractiveness too, but also from athletic accomplishment in certain pre-scribed sports, from owning beautiful cars and from learning to be cool under pressure. It is also a function of sheer physical strength.

Do you remember what the world of adolescence was like for you? Do you recall the power games that were played—the highly competitive and hostile envi-ronment into which you walked every day? Can you still feel the apprehension you experienced when a popular (powerful) student called you a creep, or a jerk, or he put his big hand in your face and pushed you out of the way? He wore a football jersey which reminded you that the entire team would eat you alive if you should be so foolish as to fight back. Does the memory of the junior-senior prom still come to mind occasionally, when you were either turned down by the girl you loved or were not asked by the boy of your dreams? Have you ever had the campus heroes make fun of the one flaw you most wanted to hide, and then threaten to mangle you on the way home from school?

Perhaps you never went through these stressful en-counters. Maybe you were one of the powerful elite who oppressed the rest of us. But your son or daughter could be on the other end of the continuum. A few years ago I talked to a mother whose seventh-grade daughter was getting butchered at school each day. She said the girl awakened an hour before she had to get up each morning and lay there thinking about how she could get through her day without being humiliated.

Typically, power games are more physical for adolescent males than females. The bullies literally force their will on those who are weaker. That is what I remember most clearly from my own high school years. I had a number of fights during that era just to preserve my turf. There was one dude, however, whom I had no intention of tackling. His name was Killer McKeechern and he was the terror of the town. It was generally believed that Killer would destroy anyone who crossed him. That theory was never tested, to my knowledge. No one dared. At least, not until I blundered along.

When I was fifteen years old and an impulsive sophomore, I nearly ended a long and happy manhood before it had a chance to get started. As I recall, a blizzard had blown through our state the night before and a group of us gathered in front of the school to throw snowballs at passing cars. (Does that tell you something about our collective maturity at the time?) Just before the afternoon bell rang, I looked up the street and saw McKeechern chugging along in his "chopped" 1934 Chevy. It was a junk heap with a cardboard "window" on the driver's side. McKeechern had cut a 3 × 3 inch flap in the cardboard, which he lifted when turning left. You could see his evil eyes peering out just before he went around corners. When the flap was down, however, he was oblivious to things on the left side of the car. As luck would have it, that's where I was standing with a huge snowball in my hand—thinking very funny and terribly unwise thoughts.

If I could just go back to that day and counsel myself, I would say, "Don't do it, Jim! You could lose your sweet life right here. McKeechern will tear your tongue out if you hit him with that snowball. Just put it down and go quietly to your afternoon class. Please, son! If *you* lose, *I* lose!" Unfortunately, no such advice wafted to my ears that day and I didn't have the sense to realize my danger. I heaved the snowball into the upper atmosphere with all my might. It came down just as McKeechern drove by and, unbelievably, went through the flap in his cardboard window. The missile obviously hit him squarely in the face, because his Chevy wobbled all over the road. It bounced over the curb and came to a stop just short of the Administration Building. Killer exploded from the front seat, ready to rip someone to shreds (me!). I'll never forget the sight. There was snow all over his face and little jets of steam were curling from his head. My whole life passed in front of my eyes as I faded into the crowd. *So young!* I thought.

The only thing that saved me on this snowy day was McKeechern's inability to identify me. No one told him I had thrown the snowball, and believe me, I didn't volunteer. I escaped unscathed, although that brush with destiny must have damaged me emotionally. I still have recurring nightmares about the event thirty-five years later. In my dreams, the chimes ring and I go to open the front door. There stands McKeechern with a shotgun. And he still has snow on his face. (If you read this story, Killer, I do hope we can be friends. We were only kids, you know? Right, Killer? Huh? Right! Howsa car?)

Why have I reminded you of the world of adolescent power? Because your teenagers are knee deep in it right now. That is why they are nervous wrecks on the first day of school, or before the team plays its initial game, or any other time when their power base is on the line. The raw nerve, you see, is not really dominance, but self-esteem. One's sense of worth is dependent on peer acceptance at that age, and that is why the group holds such enormous influence over the individual. If he is mocked, disrespected, ridiculed and excluded—in other words, if he is stripped of power—his delicate ego is torn to shreds. As we have said, that is a fate worse than death itself. Social panic is the by-product of that system.

Now, what about your sons and daughters? Have you wondered why they come home from school in such a terrible mood? Have you asked them why they are so jumpy and irritable through the evening? They cannot describe their feelings to you, but they may have engaged in a form of combat all day. Even if they haven't had to fight with their fists, it is likely that they are embroiled in a highly competitive, openly hostile environment where emotional danger lurks on every side. Am I overstating the case? Yes, for the kid who is coping well. But for the powerless young man and woman, I haven't begun to tell their stories.

To help parents cope with these special stresses of the adolescent years, let me offer five suggestions that have been beneficial to others, as follows:

1. Boredom Is Dangerous to Energetic Teenagers. Keep Them Moving.

The strong-willed adolescent simply must not be given large quantities of unstructured time. He will find destructive ways to use such moments. My advice is to get him involved in the very best church youth program you can find. If your local congregation has only four bored members in its junior high department and seven sleepy high schoolers, I would consider changing churches. I know that advice could be disruptive to the entire family and I'm sure most pastors would disagree, but you must save that volatile kid. Obviously, such radical action is not as necessary for the more compliant individual or for one who has other wholesome outlets for his energy. But if you're sitting on a keg of dynamite, you have to find ways to keep the powder dry! Not only can this be done through church activities, but also by involvement with athletics, music, horses or other animals, and part-time jobs. You *must* keep that strong-willed kid's scrawny legs churning!

2. Don't Rock the Boat.

In my second film series entitled, "Turn Your Heart Toward Home," I offered this advice to parents of teenagers: "Get 'em through it." That may not sound like such a stunning idea, but I believe it has merit for most families—especially those with one or more tough-minded kids. The concept is a bit obscure, so I will re-sort to a couple of pictures to illustrate my point.

When parents of strong-willed children look ahead to the adolescent river, they often perceive it to be like this.

9 10 11 12 13 14 15 16 17

Ages

In other words, they expect the early encounter with rapids to give way to swirling currents and life-threatening turbulence. If that doesn't turn over their teenagers' boat, they seem destined to drown farther downstream when they plunge over the falls.

Fortunately, the typical journey is much safer than anticipated. Most often it flows like this.

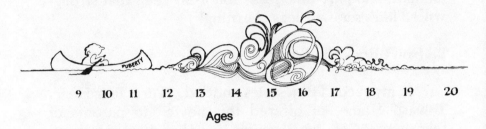

Ages

What I'm saying is that the river usually descends not into the falls but into smooth water once more. Even though your teenager may be splashing and thrashing and gasping for air, it is not likely that his boat will capsize. It is more buoyant than you might think. Yes, a few individuals do go over the falls, usually because of drug abuse. Even some of them climb back in the canoe and paddle on down the river. In fact, the greatest danger of sinking the boat could come from . . . *you*!

This warning is addressed particularly to idealistic and perfectionistic parents who are determined to make their adolescents—*all* of them—perform and achieve and measure up to the highest standard. A perfectionist, by the way, is a person who takes great pains with what he does and then gives them to everyone else. In so doing, he rocks a boat that is already threatened by the rapids. Perhaps another child could handle the additional turbulence, but our concern is for the unsteady kid—the one who lacks common sense for a while and may even lean toward irrational behavior. Don't unsettle his boat any more than you must!

I'm reminded of a waitress who recognized me when I came into the restaurant where she worked.

She was not busy that day and wanted to talk about her twelve-year-old daughter. As a single mother, she had gone through severe struggles with the girl, whom she identified as being *very* strong-willed.

"We have fought tooth and nail for this entire year," she said. "It has been awful! We argue nearly every night, and most of our fights are over the same issue."

I asked her what had caused the conflict, and she replied, "My daughter is still a little girl but she wants to shave her legs. I feel she's too young to be doing that and she becomes so angry that she won't even talk to me. This has been the worst year of our lives together."

I looked at the waitress and exclaimed, "Lady, buy your daughter a razor!"

That twelve-year-old girl was paddling into a time of life that would rock her canoe good and hard. As a single parent, Mom would soon be trying to keep this rebellious kid from getting into drugs, alcohol, sex and pregnancy, early marriage, school failure and the possibility of running away. Truly, there would be many ravenous alligators in her river within a year or two. In that setting, it seemed unwise to make a big deal over what was essentially a nonissue. While I agreed with the mother that adolescence should not be rushed into prematurely, there were higher goals than maintaining a proper developmental timetable.

I have seen other parents fight similar battles over nonessentials such as the purchase of a first bra for a flat-chested preadolescent girl. For goodness sake! If she wants it that badly, she probably needs it for social reasons. Run, don't walk, to the nearest department store and buy her a bra. The objective, as Charles and Andy Stanley wrote, is to *keep your kids on your team.* Don't throw away your friendship over behavior that has no great moral significance. There will be plenty of real issues that require you to stand like a rock. Save your big guns for those crucial confrontations.

Let me make it very clear, again, that this advice is not relevant to every teenager. The compliant kid who is doing wonderfully in school, has great friends, is disciplined in his conduct and loves his parents is not nearly so delicate. Perhaps his parents can urge him to reach even higher standards in his achievements and lifestyle. My concern, however, is for that youngster who *could* go over the falls. He is intensely angry at home and is being influenced by a carload of crummy friends. Be very careful with him. Pick and choose what is worth fighting for, and settle for something less than perfection on issues that don't really matter. *Just get him through it!*

What does this mean in practical terms? It may indicate a willingness to let his room look like a junkyard for awhile. Does that surprise you? I don't like lazy, sloppy, undisciplined kids any more than you do, but given the possibilities for chaos that this angry boy or girl might precipitate, spit-shined rooms may not be all that important.

You might also compromise somewhat regarding the music you let him hear. I'm *not* condoning hard rock and heavy metal, which is saturated with explicit and illicit sex and violence today. But neither can you ask this go-go teenager to listen to your "elevator music." Perhaps a compromise can be reached. Unfortunately, the popular music of the day is the rallying cry for rebellious teenagers. If you try to deny it altogether to a strong-willed kid, you just might flip his canoe upside down. You have to ask yourself this question, "Is it worth risking everything of value to enforce a particular standard upon this son or daughter?" If the issue *is* important enough to defend at all costs, then brace yourself and make your stand. But think through those intractable matters in advance and plan your defense of them thoroughly.

The philosophy we applied with our teenagers (and you might try with yours) can be called "loosen and tighten." By this I mean we tried to loosen our grip on everything that had no lasting significance, and tighten down on everything that did. We said "yes" whenever we possibly could, to give support to the occasional "no." And most importantly, we tried never to get too far away from our kids emotionally.

It is simply not prudent to write off a son or daughter, no matter how foolish, irritating, selfish or insane a child may seem to be. You need to be there, not only while their canoe is bouncing precariously, but after the river runs smooth again. You have the remainder of your life to reconstruct the relationship that is now in jeopardy. Don't let anger fester for too long. Make the first move toward reconciliation. And try hard not to hassle your kids. They *hate* to be nagged. If you follow them around with one complaint after another, they are almost forced to protect themselves by appearing deaf. And finally, continue to treat them with respect, even when punishment or restrictions are necessary. Occasionally, you may even need to say, "I'm sorry!"

My father found it very difficult to say those words. I remember working with him in the back yard when I was fifteen years of age, on a day when he was particularly irritable for some reason. I probably deserved his indignation, but I thought he was being unfair. He crabbed at me for everything I did, even when I hustled. Finally, he yelled at me for something petty and that did it. He capsized my canoe. I threw down the rake and quit.

Defiantly I walked across our property and down the street while my dad demanded that I come back. It was one of the few times I ever took him on like that! I meandered around town for a while, wondering what would happen to me when I finally went home. Then I strolled over to my cousin's house on the other side of town. After several hours there, I admitted to his father that I had had a bad fight with my dad and he didn't know where I was. My uncle persuaded me to call home and assure my parents that I was safe. With knees quaking, I phoned my dad.

"Stay there," he said. "I'm coming over."

To say that I was apprehensive for the next few minutes would be an understatement. In a short time Dad arrived and asked to see me alone.

"Bo," he began. "I didn't treat you right this afternoon. I was riding your back for no good reason and I want you to know I'm sorry. Your mom and I want you to come on home now."

He made a friend for life.

3. Maintain a Reserve Army.

A good military general will never commit all his troops to combat at the same time. He maintains a reserve force that can relieve the exhausted soldiers when they falter on the front lines. I wish parents of adolescents would implement the same strategy. Instead, they commit every ounce of their energy and every second of their time to the business of living, holding nothing in reserve for the challenge of the century. It is a classic mistake which can be disastrous for parents of strong-willed adolescents. Let me explain.

The problem begins with a basic misunderstanding

during the pre-school years. I hear mothers say, "I don't plan to work until the kids are in kindergarten. Then I'll get a job." They appear to believe that the heavy demands on them will end magically when they get their youngest in school. In reality, the teen years will generate as much pressure on them as did the preschool era. An adolescent turns a house upside down . . . literally and figuratively. Not only is the typical rebellion of those years an extremely stressful experience, but the chauffeuring, supervising, cooking and cleaning required to support an adolescent can be exhausting. *Someone* within the family must reserve the energy to cope with those new challenges. Mom is the candidate of choice. Remember, too, that menopause and a man's mid-life crisis are scheduled to coincide with adolescence, which makes a wicked soup! It is a wise mother who doesn't exhaust herself at a time when so much is going on at home.

I know it is easier to talk about maintaining a lighter schedule than it is to secure one. It is also impractical to recommend that mothers not seek formal employment during this era. Millions of women have to work for economic reasons, including the rising number of single parents in our world. Others choose to pursue busy careers. That is a decision to be made by a woman and her husband, and I would not presume to tell them what to do.

But decisions have inevitable consequences. In this case, there are biophysical forces at work which simply must be reckoned with. If, for example, 80 percent of a woman's available energy in a given day is expended in getting dressed, driving to work, doing her job for eight or ten hours, and stopping by the grocery store on the way home—then there is only 20 percent left for everything else. Maintenance of the family, cooking meals, cleaning the kitchen, relating to her husband and all other personal activities must be powered by that diminishing resource. It is no wonder that her batteries are spent by the end of the day. Weekends should be restful, but they are usually not. Thus, she plods through the years on her way to burnout.

This is my point: a woman in this situation has thrown all her troops into front-line combat. As we saw in the previous chapter on burnout, she is already exhausted but there is no reserve on which to call. In that weakened condition, the routine stresses of raising an adolescent can be overwhelming. Let me say it again. Raising boisterous teenagers is an exciting and rewarding but also a frustrating experience. Their radical highs and lows affect our moods. The noise, the messes, the complaints, the arguments, the sibling rivalry, the missed curfews, the paced floors, the wrecked car, the failed test, the jilted lover, the wrong friends, the busy telephone, the pizza on the carpet, the ripped new blouse, the rebellion, the slammed doors, the mean words, the tears—it's enough to drive a *rested* mother crazy. But what about our career woman who already "gave at the office," then came home to this chaos? Any unexpected crisis or even a minor irritant can set off a torrent of emotion. There is no reserve on which to draw. In short, the parents of adolescents should save some energy with which to cope with aggravation!

Whether or not you are able to accept and implement my advice is your business. It is mine to offer it, and this is my best shot: to help you get through the turbulence of adolescence, you should:

1. Keep the schedule simple.
2. Get plenty of rest.

3. Eat nutritious meals.
4. Stay on your knees.

When fatigue leads adults to act like hot-tempered teenagers, anything can happen at home.

4. The Desperate Need for Fathers.

It is stating the obvious, I suppose, to say that fathers of rebellious teenagers are desperately needed at home during those years. In their absence, mothers are left to handle disciplinary problems alone. This is occurring in millions of families headed by single mothers today, and I know how tough their task has become. Not only are they doing a job that should have been shouldered by two; they must also deal with behavioral problems that fathers are more ideally suited to handle. It is generally understood that a man's larger size, deeper voice and masculine demeanor make it easier for him to deal with defiance in the younger generation. Likewise, I believe the exercise of authority is a mantle ascribed to him by the Creator.

Not only are fathers needed to provide leadership and discipline during the adolescent years, but they can be highly influential on their sons during this period of instability. (We will discuss fathers and daughters presently.) Someone has said, "Link a boy to the right man and he seldom goes wrong." I believe that is true. If a dad and his son can develop hobbies together or other common interests, the rebellious years can pass in relative tranquility. What they experience may be remembered for a lifetime.

I recall a song, written by Dan Fogelberg, that told about a man who shared his love of music with his elderly father. It is called "Leader of the Band," and its message touches something deep within me. *This* is the way it should be:

> An only child
> Alone and wild
> A cabinet maker's son
> His hands were meant
> For different work
> And his heart was known to none—
> He left his home
> And went his lone
> And solitary way
> And he gave to me
> A gift I know I never can repay.
>
> A quiet man of music
> Denied a simpler fate
> He tried to be a soldier once
> But his music wouldn't wait
> He earned his love through discipline
> A thundering, velvet hand
> His gentle means of sculpting souls
> Took me years to understand.
>
> The leader of the band is tired
> And his eyes are growing old
> But his blood runs through my instrument
> And his song is in my soul—
> My life has been a poor attempt
> To imitate the man
> I'm just a living legacy
> To the leader of the band.
>
> My brothers' lives were different
> For they heard another call
> One went to Chicago
> And the other to St. Paul

And I'm in Colorado
When I'm not in some hotel
Living out this life I've chose
And come to know so well.

I thank you for the music
And your stories of the road
I thank you for the freedom
When it came my time to go—
I thank you for the kindness
And the times when you got tough
And, papa, I don't think I
Said 'I love you' near enough—

The leader of the band is tired
And his eyes are growing old
But his blood runs through my instrument
And his song is in my soul—
My life has been a poor attempt
To imitate the man
I'm just a living legacy
To the leader of the band.
I am the living legacy to
The leader of the band.[1]

Can't you see this man going to visit his aged father today, with a lifetime of love passing between them? That must have been what God had in mind when he gave dads to boys. Let me address the reader directly: what common ground are you cultivating with *your* impressionable son? Some fathers build or repair cars with them; some construct small models or make things in a woodshop. My dad and I hunted and fished together. There is no way to describe what those days meant to me as we entered the woods in the early hours of the morning. How could I get angry at this man who took time to be with me? We had wonderful talks while coming home from a day of laughter and fun in the country.

I've tried to maintain that kind of contact with my son, Ryan. We're rebuilding a Model A Ford together, now. We've also hunted rabbits, quail, pheasant and larger game since he turned twelve. As it was with my father, Ryan and I have had some meaningful conversations while out in the fields together. Last year, for example, we got up one morning and situated ourselves in a deer blind before the break of day. About twenty yards away from us was a feeder which operated on a timer. At seven A.M. it automatically dropped kernels of corn into a pan below.

Ryan and I huddled together in this blind, talking softly about whatever came to mind. Then through the fog, we saw a beautiful doe emerge silently into the clearing. She took nearly thirty minutes to get to the feeder near where we were hiding. We had no intention of shooting her, but it was fun to watch this beautiful animal from close range. She was extremely wary, sniffing the air and listening for the sounds of danger. Finally, she inched her way to the feeder, still looking around skittishly as though sensing our presence. Then she ate a quick breakfast and fled.

I whispered to Ryan, "There is something valuable to be learned from what we have just seen. Whenever you come upon a free supply of high quality corn, unexpectedly provided right there in the middle of the forest, be careful! The people who put it there are probably sitting nearby in a blind, just waiting to take a shot at you. Keep your eyes and ears open!"

Ryan may not always remember that advice, but *I* will. It isn't often a father says something that he considers profound to his teenage son. One thing is certain: This interchange and the other ideas we shared on that day would not have occurred at home. Opportunities for that kind of communication have to be created. And it's worth working to achieve.

Before we leave the subject of fathers interacting with their sons, I want to reflect briefly on a *mother's* contribution to that relationship. Women can help the generations bond together or they can drive a wedge between them. This concept was expressed beautifully in a book entitled *Fathers and Sons* by Lewis Yablonsky. The author observed that mothers are the *primary* interpreters of fathers' personality, character and integrity to their sons. In other words, the way boys see their fathers is largely a product of the things their mothers have said and the way she feels. In Yablonsky's case, his mother destroyed the respect he might have had for his father. This is what he wrote:

> I vividly recall sitting at the dinner table with my two brothers and father and mother and cringing at my mother's attacks on my father. "Look at him," she would say in Yiddish. "His shoulders are bent down, he's a failure. He doesn't have the courage to get a better job or make more money. He's a beaten man." He would keep his eyes pointed toward his plate and never answer her. She never extolled his virtues or persistence or the fact that he worked so hard. Instead she constantly focused on the negative and created an image to his three sons of a man without fight, crushed by a world over which he had no control.
>
> His not fighting back against her constant criticism had the effect of confirming its validity to her sons. And my mother's treatment and the picture of my father did not convey to me that marriage was a happy state of being, or that women were basically people. I was not

especially motivated to assume the role of husband and father myself from my observations of my whipped father.

My overall research clearly supports that the mother is the basic filter and has enormous significance in the father-son relationship.[2]

Though Yablonsky did not say so, it is also true that fathers can do great damage to the conception their children may have of their mother. Very early on I found that when I was irritated with Shirley for some reason, my attitude was instantly picked up by our son and daughter. They seemed to feel, "If Dad can argue with Mom, then we can too." It became clear to me just how important it was for me to express my love and admiration for Shirley. However, I could *never* do that job of building respect for my wife as well as she did for me! She made me a king in my own home. If our son and daughter believed half of what she told them about me, I would have been a fortunate man. The close relationship I enjoy with Danae and Ryan today is largely a product of Shirley's great love for me and the way she "interpreted" me to our kids. I will always be grateful to her for doing that!

Fathers and Daughters

Let's talk now about fathers and daughters. Most psychologists believe, and I am one of them, that all future romantic relationships to occur in a girl's life will be influenced positively or negatively by the way she perceives and interacts with her dad. If he is an alcoholic and a bum, she will spend her life trying to replace him in her heart. If he is warm and nurturing, she will look for a lover to equal him. If he thinks she is beautiful, worthy and feminine, she will be inclined to see herself that way. But if he rejects her as unattractive and uninteresting, she is likely to carry self-esteem problems into her adult years.

I have also observed that a woman's willingness to accept the loving leadership of her husband is significantly influenced by the way she perceived the authority of her father. If he was overbearing, uncaring or capricious during her developmental years, she may attempt to grab the reins of leadership from her future husband. But if dad blended love and discipline in a way that conveyed strength, she will be more willing to yield to the confident leadership of her husband.

None of these tendencies or trends is absolute, of course. Individual differences can always produce exceptions and contradictions. But this statement will be hard to refute: a good father will leave his imprint on his daughter for the rest of her life.

Many fathers are also called upon to perform another vitally important role during the adolescent years. It occurs when tension begins to develop between mothers and teenage girls. That conflict is very common among the ladies of the house, and as you recall, it showed up in the findings from our study of temperaments. Several years may pass when they don't even *like* each other very much.

In that setting, fathers are desperately needed as peacemakers and mediators. I have found that teenagers who are greatly irritated with one parent will sometimes seek to preserve their relationship with the other. It's like a country at war in search of supportive allies. If fathers are chosen in that triangle, they can use the opportunity to settle their daughters and "interpret" their mothers in a more favorable light. They may also be able to help their wives ventilate their anger and understand their role in perpetuating the conflict. Without this masculine influence, routine skirmishes can turn into World War III.

In conclusion, I have this recurring message for today's fathers—especially to those who have teenagers at home: don't let these years get away from you. Your contributions to your kids could rank as your greatest accomplishments in life—or your most oppressive failures. If you're not yet convinced of your importance at home, read the article that follows. If it doesn't touch your heart you may not have one.

Dad Coming Home Was the Real Treat

by Howard Mann

When I was a little boy I never left the house without kissing my parents goodbye.

I liked kissing my mother because her cheek felt mushy and warm, and because she smelled of peppermints. I liked kissing my father because he felt rough and whiskery and smelled of cigars and witch hazel.

About the time I was 10 years old, I came to the conclusion that I was now too big to kiss my father. A mother, OK. But with a father, a big boy should shake hands—man to man, you see.

He didn't seem to notice the difference or to mind it. Anyway, he never said anything about it. But then he never said much about anything, except his business.

In retrospect, I guess it was also my way of getting even with him. Up until then, I had always felt I was something special to him. Every day, he would come home from that mysterious world of his with a wondrous treat, just for me. It might be a miniature baseball bat, engraved with Babe Ruth's signature. It might be a real honeycomb with waffle-like squares soaked in honey. Or it might be exotic rahat, the delectable, jellied Turkish candies, buried in powdered sugar and crowded into a little wooden crate.

How I looked forward to his coming home each night! The door flung open and there he stood. I would run to him, hug him while he lifted me high in his arms.

I reached my peak the day of my seventh birthday. I woke up before anyone else in the family and tiptoed into the dining room. There, on the heavy mahogany table, was a small, square wristwatch with a brown leather strap, stretched out full length in a black velvet box. Could it really be for me? I picked it up and held it to my ear. It ticked! Not a toy watch from the 5-and-10, but a real watch like grown-ups wore. I ran into his bedroom, woke up father and covered him with kisses. Could any boy possibly be as happy as me?

Later, it began to change. At first, I wasn't aware it was happening. I supposed I was too busy with school and play and having to make new friends all the time. (We moved every two years, always seeking a lower rent.)

The flow of treats dried up. No more bats or honeycombs. My father gradually disappeared from my life. He would come home late, long after I had gone to sleep. And he would come home with his hands empty. I missed him very much, but I was afraid to say anything. I hoped that he would come back to me as strangely as he had left. Anyhow, big boys weren't supposed to long for their fathers.

Years after he died, my mother talked about how the Depression had "taken the life out of him." It had crushed his dream of being a "big man." He no longer had money for treats. He no longer had time for me.

I am sorry now. I look at his picture and his crinkly hazel eyes and wish that he were here today. I would tell him what is happening with me now and talk about things that he might like to hear—politics, foreign events and how business is doing. And I would put my arms around his neck and say, "Pop, you don't have to bring me anything—just come home early."

And I would kiss him.[3]

5. Handling the Very Toughest Cases.

Go back with me now to the story I told about my dad's apology during our brief disagreement in the back yard. He took all the blame for that confrontation and in essence, "ate humble pie." I must make it clear that it is not always wise to assume this posture. In fact, I believe most parents of very difficult teenagers go too far in that direction. There is a time for parents to get off their knees and *quit* apologizing. They have sought to avoid conflict by groveling and appeasing their strong-willed adolescents, and in so doing, they have made what turns out to be a tragic mistake. Please remember this fact: To a power-hungry tyrant of any age, appeasement only inflames his lust for more power. Behavioral research has now demonstrated this relationship between insecure, permissive parents and violent, delinquent teenagers.

Dr. Henry Harbin and Dr. Denis Madden observed a significant increase in the number of vicious attacks on parents by their unruly children. Working at the University of Maryland's Medical School, these psychiatrists also studied the circumstances surrounding this form of family violence. Surprisingly, they found that "parent battering" usually occurs when "one or both parents have abdicated the executive position" and when no one is in charge. No one, that is, except possibly the violent child.

Harbin and Madden also observed that "an almost universal element" in the parent-battering cases was the parents' unwillingness to admit the seriousness of the situation. They did not call the police, even when their lives were in danger; they lied to protect the children and they continued to give in to their demands. Parental authority had collapsed.

One father was almost killed when his angry son pushed him down a flight of stairs. He insisted that the boy did not have a bad temper. Another woman was stabbed by her son, missing her heart by an inch. Nevertheless, she continued letting him live at home.

Drs. Harbin and Madden concluded that appeasement and permissiveness are related to youthful violence, and that both parents should lead with firmness. "Someone needs to be in charge," they said.[4]

Obviously, I agree wholeheartedly with these psychiatrists. Having been appointed by President Ronald Reagan to serve on the National Advisory Commission to the Office of Juvenile Justice and Delinquency Prevention, I am very familiar with the pattern of youthful violence. I've seen cold-blooded killers who were no more than thirteen years of age. Many of them came from homes where authority was weak or nonexistent. It is a formula for cranking out very tough criminals at an early age.

That brings us to the most difficult question with which parents are ever confronted: what can be done in those cases when parental leadership collapses altogether? What resources are available to mothers and fathers when an adolescent continually breaks the law, intimidates or attacks his family and does precisely what he wishes? If appeasement makes matters worse, as we have seen, what other approaches can we suggest?

Though it would be glib to imply that there are simple answers to such awesome questions, I believe one organization is on the right track. It is called TOUGHLOVE,
founded by Phyllis and David York. TOUGHLOVE is dedicated to helping out-of-control parents regain the upper
hand in their own homes. Their basic philosophy is one of
confrontation that is designed to bring a belligerent
teenager to his senses.

The TOUGHLOVE concept began during the early
1980s, after counselors Phyllis and David York had
run into serious problems with their eighteen-year-
old daughter. She broke every rule and eventually held
up a cocaine dealer in Landsdale, Pa. She was soon
arrested at gunpoint in the Yorks' home. That got their
attention.

From this painful experience, the Yorks began to
formulate the TOUGHLOVE principles. They are simple
enough: forgiveness and understanding are laudable responses to defiance, but they do not work with the most
difficult cases. As York said, "I started out being this nice
therapist. 'Let me listen, let me be this daddy to you
guys.' And what really needs to happen is to grab these
kids and say, 'You really can't do that. You've got to follow the rules here, and if you don't we're going to call the
police and have you locked up!'"

Instead of groveling and whining, parents of rebellious teens are encouraged to stand firm and take appropriate action. This may include taking away the family
car, restricting use of the telephone and refusing to intervene when the teen is in jail. It may also involve lock-
ing a drug user out of his home. A note on the front door
informs him that he will be welcome there only if he
enrolls in a drug rehab program. A teen who comes

home hours after his curfew may find a note instructing him to spend the night with another family that is willing to take him in.

Time magazine, 8 June 1981, quoted TOUGHLOVE mothers as follows, "It's just old-fashioned discipline, where the parents run the home and there is cooperation among the family members." Another said she turned in her son, Jeff, 17, to the police after he confessed to robbing a nearby home to support his drug habit. "Police enrolled him in a rehabilitation program," said *Time*, "and now he is back home, working and attending Narcotics and Alcoholics Anonymous."

Many similar examples are cited in the Yorks' book *Toughlove*. But as might be expected, most parents lack the confidence and understanding needed to implement the principles on their own. They need the support of other parents who are going through the same trauma. That's why the TOUGHLOVE organization was founded. It puts harassed parents in touch with one another. Then if a teenager is sent to prison, for example, his distressed mother and father may ask other members of their local TOUGHLOVE group to visit him first, or to accompany them to the prison. It is an idea whose time has come.

The article in *Time* magazine concluded with this statement:

> TOUGHLOVE brings parents together to buck up one another at meetings and to follow the progress of problem youngsters. If a runaway is picked up in another state or a youngster is arrested, members in the group are ready to go to the scene. Says Ted Wachtel, president of the Community Service Foundation in Sellersville, Pa., which sponsors the TOUGHLOVE movement: "If a child winds up in prison, it is sometimes too much of an

emotional experience for the parents to go at first, so other members of the group make the visits."

TOUGHLOVE does not work all the time, but so far it has been an effective way of uniting parents to square off against the youngsters' own powerful peer group that endorses drug taking and rebelliousness. One tactic of TOUGHLOVE is to make a list of a youngster's closest friends, then go out and meet the parents of the friends and try to make an alliance. The message: Don't feel guilty; don't get into shouting matches with youngsters; don't be a victim; get over disillusionment. Says the TOUGHLOVE self-help manual for parents: "We really were not prepared for such a rapidly changing culture full of distractions like dope, violence, and a peer group that means more to our children than a home and family." In TOUGHLOVE's view, the time has come for parents to stand up against a hostile culture.[5]

What has been the public response to the TOUGHLOVE concept? There were twenty-five groups scattered around the United States in 1981. Today there are more than 1,500 in all fifty states and in Canada. It has become a national movement.

If you are among those fed-up parents who have reached the end of your rope, you might want to contact TOUGHLOVE's national headquarters. Their address is:

TOUGHLOVE
Community Service Foundation
P.O. Box 1069
Doylestown, PA 18901

Do I recommend them personally? Yes, with two reservations: (1) TOUGHLOVE is not a Christian organization, although I have not known them to contradict our basic beliefs. I wish a similar national program existed that emphasized prayer and Scripture, but I know of none. In the meantime, TOUGHLOVE is getting the job done. (2) Any franchised program like this will be no better than the people who operate it on a local level. You could get a lemon, so to speak. I will say this, however: I have heard very little criticism of the TOUGHLOVE program in all these years. Hundreds of grateful parents wrote to me after the Yorks were guests on our Focus on the Family radio broadcast. One woman told our program director, "TOUGHLOVE literally saved my life. I would not have survived without it."

Whether or not you are in need of the radical support provided by TOUGHLOVE, I invite you to read an interesting article written about it by Columnist Ann Landers. This article was also published in 1981, the year TOUGHLOVE burst on the scene, and was originally incorporated in *Family Circle* magazine, November 3 of that year. Note the similarity in philosophy to what we have been discussing throughout this book. Obviously, I do not agree with Landers's criticism of the Bible, and I will deal with her misinterpretation of Proverbs 22:6 in the upcoming question-and-answer chapter.

Here's the way Ann Landers sees it:

I never thought I'd live to see the day when I'd actually argue with the Bible . . . especially since I've frequently quoted the very passage I no longer feel applies: "Train up a child in the way he should go . . . and . . . he will not depart from it," meaning that if you carefully train your child, he or she will turn out well. Yet, unfortunately, the last 15 years have produced a great deal of evidence disproving this Biblical directive. My desk is groaning from the weight of letters that sound a lot like this one.

Dear Ann Landers:

We took our children to church, we didn't send them. We never had sitters. If we couldn't get his mother or mine to stay, the children came with us or we didn't go. We invested so much love and time and energy in our sons and daughters, yet they became involved with truancy, drugs, shoplifting, a pregnancy—every kind of trouble you might expect from street kids. What went wrong?

Being a firm believer that the twigs grew in the direction they were bent, I didn't know how to respond to these anguished, guilt-ridden parents. Their letters describing years of tender loving care didn't square with what was happening to their children. Many carefully nurtured twigs seemed to be growing in bizarre and unpredictable directions. I had to rethink my answers and come up with something better.

A few years ago I printed a letter that said volumes. It was from a high school student who came across her mother's diary; the letter contained an entry the mother had written:

All adolescent kids have diaries these days. Well, I think it's time for mothers to have diaries, too. We ought to keep a daily chronicle reporting the heartaches of parents who did the best they could with their mixed-up sons and daughters. Only the kids suffer, do they? Only their feelings are hurt? Well, move over, children, your parents are having a very hard time trying to bring you up to be self-reliant, decent citizens. It seems like the cards are stacked against us. The more we give, the less we get back.

What's gone wrong? Obviously something has. I don't pretend to know all the answers, but after reading thousands of letters from teenagers in trouble, teachers who see them almost every day, guidance counselors who listen to them and parents who are wringing their hands in despair. I have concluded that peer pressure is a far more dominant factor in shaping teenage behavior than parental influence.

The experts with whom I checked (juvenile authorities, drug-abuse and mental health counselors, some psychologists, a few psychiatrists) supported my notion. I'm not suggesting that parental training and role models mean nothing. What I am saying is that in our present-day culture what a teenager's peers think of him carries more weight than what his parents say.

The need to be accepted, the fear of being outside the charmed circle, the desire to be "in" is vitally important to adolescents today. And, all too often that means keg parties, getting drunk, smoking dope, popping uppers and downers, snorting cocaine, using angel dust and acid and having sex.

Moreover, a generation that has grown up with its eyeballs hooked onto a TV screen is constantly searching for ways to combat boredom and anesthetize themselves against the pain of growing up. Teenagers (and adults, as well) have discovered that alcohol and drugs can put troubles on the back burner and make you feel "different."

According to a report put out in 1980 by the Department of Health, Education and Welfare (now called Department of Health and Human Services), one out of 10 high school students regularly uses pot. This means these kids smoke at least one or two joints every day. I happen to believe that this figure is too low. High school teachers have written to tell me that on Monday mornings, at least one-third of the juniors and seniors walk into classrooms stoned. An even more frightening fact is that some of these students drive themselves to school, which helps explain why auto accidents are today's leading cause of death among teenagers. And emergency room attendants tell us that approximately 65 percent of all fatal teenage accidents are alcohol or drug-related.

How can parents combat outside influences that run counter to everything they have tried to teach their children? What advice do I have for them? Plenty. And I've already had responses telling me it works. The following letter opened my eyes and sent me in a completely new direction. It came from Bucks County, Pennsylvania.

Dear Ann:
Please print this for parents with unreachable, mixed-up, always-in-trouble teenagers. I know where they are coming from. My husband and I have been there and there's no hell like it.

We, too, were desperate and without hope. Our son was a bum, in debt, stealing from us, on drugs, breaking up the furniture, cursing and hitting us. We were beside ourselves with anxiety and fear. We tried everything to please him, and nothing worked. The nicer we were, the worse he got.

Finally we called the police. They gave us the phone number of an organization called TOUGHLOVE. From that day on we became members of a community network of parents who are successfully coping with their kids' hostile, antisocial behavior.

Before we came to TOUGHLOVE, we were ashamed and felt weak and guilty because we couldn't stand up to our son. We thought that no other parents in the community had failed as miserably as we had. Then we met other members of TOUGHLOVE and discovered that we were no longer helpless. We had the support of other parents, the police, the schools, the courts, and rehabilitation facilities.

We didn't have to throw our son out of the house, nor did we have to continue to take his abuse. We laid down a whole new set of rules and gave him a choice. He could live by our rules or get out. He chose to stay.

I'm enclosing a pamphlet that tells you more about TOUGHLOVE. Please, Ann, share it with your readers. It's the greatest thing that happened to us and we want to spread the word. Thanks for your help.

Forever Grateful

I read the pamphlet and it made a lot of sense. It explained a program designed to help parents who feel heartsick and helpless about their teenagers. The program asks parents to choose which road they want to take. Will it be confrontation, firm guidelines and mutual respect—or excuses (as usual), denial, gutlessness, continued indulgence and bribery? It encourages parents to meet the crisis head on, take a stand and demand cooperation.

Actually, the permissive method of child-rearing surfaced in the '40s, blossomed in the '50s and gained total respectability in the '60s. Psychiatrists and psychologists told us that if we spoke softly to our children; held, rocked and cuddled them; let them stop soiling their diapers and panties when they decided it was time to stop; allowed them to get the anger out of their systems, being careful never to say, "No, you can't do that" unless they started to burn down the house, they would develop healthy egos and grow up to be well-adjusted young men and women, self-assured, highly motivated and a joy to us.

We beat down our natural instincts, slavishly adhered to the teachings of these "experts" and developed dark circles and high blood pressure while our kids talked back to us, spit on us, hit us, broke their toys and threw themselves in the aisles of supermarkets (or department stores) until they got their way. These same kids turned out to be selfish, spoiled, hostile, disrespectful, lazy and unmotivated. They had no respect for us, their teachers or the law.

To add insult to injury, some psychiatrists charged up to $100 an hour to tell us, "There are no bad children . . . only bad parents."

The sad truth of the matter is that for too many years parents have been bamboozled by "experts," and have sopped up half-baked theories in "how-to" books instead of using the brains God gave them and reacting to their natural instincts when their kids pushed them too far in an attempt to test limits.

I'll never forget a letter I received from a 19-year-old

just three years ago. She had no friends and couldn't hold a job because she was always shooting her mouth off, telling acquaintances, colleagues and bosses exactly what she thought of them. "I was brought up that way . . . " she declared. "I was allowed to say anything to anybody. My parents raised me that way and now I am all messed up and it's their fault. Any suggestions, Ann?"

I replied, "Yes . . . accept responsibility and quit blaming your parents for your mean mouth and foul moods. If you don't like the way you are—go to work on yourself and become something different. Enough of this 'You damaged me. Now take care of me' nonsense. It's a cop-out. Guilt laid on parents by you kids is so thick you can cut it with a knife—and all it does is perpetuate financial and emotional dependence and create a climate of hostility and ultimate failure."

So what can parents do with kids who have them backed against the wall? They can make a 180-degree turn and go the TOUGHLOVE route. Heaven knows reasoning, pleading, crying, threatening and bribing hasn't worked. It's time to try something else, and I believe self-help groups like TOUGHLOVE are the most effective approach to problem-solving.

People who have shared the same problems and triumphed over them give one another tremendous strength. They say, "I did it; you can do it too. I'll help show you how."

Parents today encounter the following problems all too often:

- You are confused when your teenager comes home in varying states of intoxication or completely stoned—yet denies he's had alcohol or dope even though you've found drug paraphernalia in his room.
- You're heartsick and don't know what to do because your child is failing in school.
- Your 15-year-old takes things that belong to others.
- Your sophomore student lives in a filthy room and refuses to do any chores in the house.

- Your star-athlete son gets into trouble with the law.
- Your daughter stays out past curfew.

So mothers and fathers ask themselves why they're such rotten parents and say, "I'd like to kill that kid for putting us through this" . . . or, "A lot of our friends have the same trouble, they just don't talk about it." Or, "It's all our fault, so now we have to take care of them."

Bullfeathers!!!!!!!!!!

You need TOUGHLOVE if you feel helpless and unable to cope with your teenagers' behavior or if you feel victimized by them, disappointed in yourself as a parent, guilty because you think you have done a rotten job and are frightened by the potential for violence in yourself and your children. These feelings are experienced by the affluent, the disadvantaged, middle income families, the uneducated, intellectual, single, divorced, married, permissive, repressive, black and white. Anybody.

Remember, you have the right to a night's sleep without worrying where your kid is—or being awakened by a phone call from the police or a hospital or a drunk teenager who's stranded somewhere. It's time you started taking care of yourself and letting your teenager be responsible for his or her actions. That's where the concepts of TOUGHLOVE come in.

You must find the courage to withdraw your money, influence, affection, anger, guilt and pleas that he or she learn to shape up. You must begin to make real demands entailing severe consequences. You must make it clear that you will not live in a house with people who mistreat you and do not respect the rules you have laid down. You do not need your teenager's approval. You're the boss. The sooner your youngster understands this, the better.

Of course, after years of accepting blame and guilt laid on by some psychiatrists, it's not easy to make this turn-about alone. You'll need help. Telephone the parents of your kids' friends. Tell them, "I'm worried about my children's behavior. Will you come to a meeting at my house tonight?" They'll probably say, "Thank heaven you called. I have been worried sick about mine, too."

Call your neighbors even if they don't have children. You'll need allies in this battle and they can help. Call an understanding clergyman and sympathetic schoolteachers. Call those you know who work with delinquent children. They know the ropes.

Once you start a support group, other parents will want to join. Your local school may become interested. They're just as eager as you are to learn how to deal with difficult kids. Never in the history of our country has there been so much trouble disciplining children. Last year there were over 70,000 assaults on teachers in our public schools. When principals and teachers learn that parents are banding together to demand that their kids be respectful, law-abiding citizens, they'll want to be part of this effort.

Of course, it's unrealistic to expect unruly, antisocial children to change overnight. Some will become extremely hostile and resentful when they discover they are no longer in control. This is where the support of friends and neighbors comes in.

When Johnny does not come home at midnight, which was the curfew you laid down, lock the door and bolt it. Tack a note on the outside saying, "It's past midnight. You are not welcome here. Go to the Pattersons or the Smiths" or some other neighbors.

Arrange with these people to take your kid when he breaks the house rules. Agree to take their kids when they do the same. Often teenagers will talk more easily with their friends' parents than with their own. This can be an excellent beginning. Then negotiate with the Pattersons or Smiths about the terms under which Johnny will be allowed to return home.

Not all kids are in trouble. We see many children who are law-abiding, generous, kind and a pleasure to have around. They're not spaced out on drugs; they're not running away from home and they're not driving their parents crazy. Chances are that these children were not raised by books.

They were raised according to clearly defined guidelines. If they went beyond these guidelines, the consequences were sure and swift.

If you have a kid in trouble whom you've always catered to, don't feel guilty. Most of the child-rearing teachings of the past 25 years encouraged parents to treat children as equals and let them learn by doing their own thing.

Remember, too, as I said earlier—peer pressure means more to most children than what their parents say. There are countless factors over which parents have no control.

The economics of the country, for example, the post-World War II money boom, with TV showing us all those wonderful things we simply couldn't live without . . . all have created a wildly acquisitive society.

And let's not forget Vietnam—the biggest mistake this country ever made. The richly deserved disgrace of losing to a small country 10,000 miles away not only infuriated a whole generation of young people, but made them anti-American and provided them with an excuse to look like bums. It also helped them get heavily involved with drugs.

But that belongs to history and now we must look to the future. We must get back to the basics and love our children enough to stop protecting them against their destructive, self-defeating behavior. Because in the end, if we allow them to destroy themselves, they will destroy us, too.[6]

[1] "Leader of the Band" by Dan Fogelberg. © 1981 APRIL MUSIC INC. and HICKORY GROVE MUSIC. All rights controlled and administered by APRIL MUSIC INC. All rights reserved. International copyright secured. Used by permission.

[2] Lewis Yablonsky, *Fathers and Sons* (New York: Simon and Schuster, Fireside Books, 1984), 134.

[3] *Los Angeles Times*, 16 June 1985. Used with permission of the author, Howard Mann, Van Nuys, California.

[4] "'Giving In' Often Seen When Kids Hit Parents,"*Omaha World-Herald*, 6 July 1979.

[5] *Time* Magazine, 8 June 1981.

[6] Reprinted from the November 3, 1981 issue of *Family Circle* Magazine. Copyright © 1981 THE FAMILY CIRCLE, INC.

Questions and Answers

Our discussion to this point has dealt with some heavy and troublesome issues. Other topics have been complex and difficult to explain. To help gather up the loose ends and clarify the areas we've touched superficially, we will devote this chapter to a question-and-answer format. We will hopscotch through the preceding discussions to anticipate the questions that would have been asked if I were talking directly to parents instead of writing to them.

Let's proceed, now, with the first question, which relates to the scripture misunderstood by Ann Landers.

Q. *You have said that the children of godly parents sometime go into severe rebellion and never return to the faith they were taught. I have seen that happen to some wonderful families that loved the Lord and were* *committed to the church. Still, it appears contradictory to Scripture. How do you interpret Proverbs 22:6, which says, "Train up a child in the way he should go, and when he is old, he will not depart from it"? Doesn't that verse mean, as it implies, that the children of wise and dedicated Christian parents will never be lost? Doesn't it promise that all wayward offspring will return, sooner or later to the fold?*

A. I wish Solomon's message to us could be interpreted that confidently. I know the common understanding of the passage is to accept it as a divine guarantee, but it was not expressed in that context. Psychiatrist John White, writing in his excellent book, *Parents in Pain*, has helped me understand that the Proverbs were never intended to be absolute *promises* from God. Instead, they are *probabilities* of things which are likely to occur. Solomon, who wrote the Proverbs, was the wisest man on the earth at that time. His purpose was to convey his divinely inspired observations on the way human nature and God's universe work. A given set of circumstances can be expected to produce certain consequences. Several of these observations, including Proverbs 22:6, have been lifted out of that context and made to stand alone as promises from God. If we insist on that interpretation, then we must explain why so many other Proverbs do not inevitably prove accurate. For example:

Lazy hands make a man poor, but diligent hands bring wealth (10:4). (Have you ever met a diligent . . . but poor . . . Christian? I have.)

The blessing of the Lord brings wealth, and he adds no trouble to it (10:22).

The fear of the Lord adds length to life, but the years of the wicked are cut short (10:27). (I have watched some beautiful children die with a Christian testimony on their lips.)

No harm befalls the righteous, but the wicked have their fill of trouble (12:21).

Plans fail for lack of counsel, but with many advisers they succeed (15:22).

Gray hair is a crown of splendor; it is attained by a righteous life (16:31).

The lot is cast into the lap, but its every decision is from the Lord (16:33).

A tyrannical ruler lacks judgment, but he who hates ill-gotten gain will enjoy a long life (28:16).

We can all think of exceptions to the statements above. To repeat, they appear to represent likelihoods rather than absolutes with God's personal guarantee attached. This interpretation of the Proverbs is somewhat controversial among laymen, but less so among biblical scholars. For example, the *Bible Knowledge Commentary*, prepared by the faculty of the Dallas Theological Seminary, accepts the understanding I have suggested. This commentary is recognized for its intense commitment to the literal interpretation of God's Word, yet this is what the theologians wrote:

> . . . Some parents, however, have sought to follow this directive but without this result. Their children have strayed from the godly training the parents gave them. This illustrates the nature of a "proverb." A proverb is a literary device whereby a general truth is brought to bear on a specific situation. Many of the proverbs are not absolute guarantees for they express truths that are necessarily conditioned by prevailing circumstances. For example, verses 3–4, 9, 11, 16, 29 do not express promises that are always binding. Though the proverbs are generally and usually true, occasional exceptions may

be noted. This may be because of the self-will or deliberate disobedience of an individual who chooses to go his own way—the way of folly instead of the way of wisdom. For that he is held responsible. It is generally true, however, that most children who are brought up in Christian homes, under the influence of godly parents who teach and live God's standards, follow that training.°

Obviously, the humanistic concept of determinism has found its way even into the interpretation of Scripture. Those who believe Proverbs 22:6 offers a guarantee of salvation for the next generation have assumed, in essence, that a child can be programmed so thoroughly as to *determine* his course. The assignment for them is to bring him up "in the way that he should go." But think about that for a moment. Didn't the great Creator handle Adam and Eve with infinite wisdom and love? He made no mistakes in "fathering" them. They were also harbored in a perfect environment with none of the pressures we face. They had no in-law problems, no monetary needs, no frustrating employers, no television, no pornography, no alcohol or drugs, no peer pressure and no sorrow. They had *no excuses!* Nevertheless, they ignored the explicit warning from God and stumbled into sin. If it were ever possible to avoid the ensnarement of evil, it would have occurred in that sinless world. But it didn't. God in His love gave Adam and Eve a choice between good and evil and they abused it. Will He now withhold that same freedom from your children? No. Ultimately, they will decide for themselves. That time of decision is a breath-taking moment for parents, when everything they have taught appears to be on the line. But it must come for us all.

Q. *You obviously feel very strongly about this misinterpretation of Scripture. What are its implications?*

A. I am most concerned for dedicated and sincere Christian parents whose grown sons and daughters have rebelled against God and their own families. These mothers and fathers did the best they could to raise their children properly, but they lost them anyway. That situation produces enormous guilt in itself, quite apart from scriptural understandings. Then they read in the Book of Proverbs that God has promised—absolutely guaranteed—the spiritual welfare of children whose parents trained them up properly. What are they to conclude, then, in light of continued rebellion and sin in the next generation? The message is inescapable! It must be their fault. They have damned their own kids by failing to keep their half of the bargain. They have sent their beloved children to hell by their parenting failures. This thought is so terrible for a sensitive believer that it could actually undermine his sanity.

I simply do not believe God intended for the *total* responsibility for sin in the next generation to fall on the backs of vulnerable parents. When we look at the entire Bible, we find no support for that extreme position. Cain's murder of Abel was not blamed on his parents. Joseph was a godly man and his brothers were rascals, yet their father and mother (Jacob and Rachel) were not held accountable for the differences between them. The saintly Samuel raised rebellious children, yet he was not charged with their sin. And in the New Testament, the father of the Prodigal Son was never accused of raising his adventuresome son improperly. The boy was apparently old enough to make his own headstrong decision, and his father did not stand in his way. This good man never repented of any wrongdoing—nor did he need to.

It is not my desire to let parents off the hook when they have been slovenly or uncommitted during their child-rearing years. There is at least one biblical example of God's wrath falling on a father who failed to discipline and train his sons. That incident is described in 1 Samuel 2:22–36, where Eli, the priest, permitted his sons to desecrate the temple. All three were sentenced to death by the Lord. Obviously, He takes our parenting tasks seriously and expects us to do likewise. But He does not intend for us to grovel in guilt for circumstances beyond our control!

Q. *Referring to the point you made about young married couples who overcommit themselves, you warned against trying to do too much too soon. I don't want to make that mistake, yet I do hope to get married and go on to graduate school. Would you be more specific about the advice you would offer to people like me?*

A. It seems only yesterday that I was faced with some similar questions in my own life. I was a third-year student in college, hoping to earn a Ph.D., get married, have children, buy a home and earn a living in the next few years. Because I was young, I thought there were no limits to what I could accomplish. But then my aunt, Lela London, heard a Christian psychologist named Clyde Narramore speak one day, and he offered to spend an afternoon with any promising student who wanted to enter the field of mental health. "We need Christians in this work," he said, "and I'll help those who are interested." I called Dr. Narramore a few days later and he graciously agreed to see me. This busy man gave me two hours of his time in the living room of his home. I still remember his words thirty years later. Among other things, he warned me not to get married too quickly if I wanted to get through school and become a practicing psychologist.

He said, "A baby will come along before you know it and you will find yourself under heavy financial pressure. That will make you want to quit. You'll sit up nights caring for a sick child and then spend maybe $300 in routine medical bills. Your wife will be frustrated and you will be tempted to abandon your dreams. Don't put yourself in that strait jacket."

I accepted Dr. Narramore's advice and waited until I was twenty-four years old and had almost finished my master's degree before Shirley and I were married. We then delayed our first child for five more years until I had completed the coursework for my doctorate. It was a wise choice, although today I am listed in the *Guinness Book of Records* as "Oldest Living Father of a Teenager." Life is a trade-off, as they say.

Though Dr. Narramore did not say so, I assure you that marital problems are almost inevitable when couples overcommit themselves during the early years. The bonding that should occur in the first decade requires time together—time that cannot be given if it is absorbed elsewhere. My advice to you is to hold onto your dreams, but take a little longer to fulfill them. Success will wait, but a happy family will not. To achieve the former and lose the latter would be an empty victory, at best.

Let me toss in this afterthought. I read an article in the *Los Angeles Times* recently about a man named J. R. Buffington. His goal in life was to produce lemons of record-breaking size from the tree in his back yard. He came up with a formula to do just that. He fertilized the tree with ashes from the fireplace, some rabbit-goat manure, a few rusty nails and plenty of water. That spring, the scrawny little tree gave birth to two gigantic lemons, one weighing over five pounds. But every other lemon on the tree was shriveled and misshapen. Mr. Buffington is still working on his formula.

Isn't that the way it is in life? Great investments in a particular endeavor tend to rob others of their potential. I'd rather have a tree covered with juicy lemons than a record-breaking but freakish crop, wouldn't you? *Balance* is the word. It is the key to successful living . . . and parenting.

Keep trying, Mr. Buffington. Have you thought about using licorice?

Q. *My three-year-old son can be counted on to behave like a brat whenever we are in the mall or in a restaurant. He seems to know I will not punish him there in front of other people. How should I handle this tactic?*

A. They tell me that a raccoon can usually kill a dog if he gets him in a lake or river. He will simply pull the hound underwater until he drowns. Most other animals would also prefer to do battle on the turf of their own choosing. It works that way with young children too. If they're going to pick a fight with Mom or Dad, they'd rather stage it in a public place, such as a supermarket or in the church foyer. They are smart enough to know that they are "safer" in front of other people. They will grab candy or speak in disrespectful ways which would never be attempted at home. Again, the most successful military generals are those who surprise the enemy in a terrain advantageous to their troops. Public facilities represent the "high ground" for a rambunctious preschooler.

You may be one of the parents who has fallen into this trap. Rather than having to discipline in public, you have inadvertently created "sanctuaries" where the old rules are not enforced. It is a certainty that your strong-willed son or daughter will behave offensively and disrespectfully in those neutral zones. There is something within the child that almost forces him to "test the limits" in situations where the resolve of adults is in question. Therefore, I recommend that you issue a stern warning *before* you enter those public arenas, making it clear that the same rules will apply. Then if he misbehaves, simply take him back to the car or around the corner and do what you would have done at home. His public behavior will improve dramatically.

Q. *I could use some advice about a minor problem we're having. Tim, my six-year-old, greatly loves to use silly names whenever he speaks to my husband and me. For example, this past week it's been "you big Hot Dog." Nearly every time he sees me now he says, "Hi, Hot Dog." Before that it was "dummy," then "moose" (after he studied M for moose in school).*

I know it's silly and it's not a huge problem, but it gets so annoying after such a long time. He's been doing this for a year now. How can we get him to talk to us with more respect, calling us Mom or Dad, instead of hot dog and moose?

Thank you for any advice you can offer.

A. What we have here is a rather classic power game, much like those we have discussed before. And contrary to what you said, it is not so insignificant. Under other circumstances, it would be a minor matter for a child to call his parents a playful name. That is not the point here. Rather, strong-willed Tim is continuing to do something that he knows is irritating to you and your husband, yet you are unable to stop him. That is the issue. He has been using humor as a tactic of defiance for a full year. It is time for you to sit down and have a quiet little talk with young Timothy. Tell him that he is being disrespectful and that the next time he calls either you or his father a name of any kind, he will be punished. You must then be prepared to deliver on the promise, because he will continue to challenge you until it ceases to be fun. That's the way he is made. If that response never comes, his insults will probably become more pronounced, ending in adolescent nightmares. Appeasement for a strong-willed child is an invitation to warfare.

Never forget this fact: the classic strong-willed child craves power from his toddler years and even earlier. Since Mom is the nearest adult who is holding the reins, he will hack away at her until she lets him drive his own buggy. I remember a mother telling me of a confrontation with her tough-minded four-year-old daughter. The child was demanding her own way and the mother was struggling to hold her own.

"Jenny," said the mother, "you are just going to have to do what I tell you to do. I am your boss. The Lord has given me the responsibility for leading you, and that's what I intend to do!"

Jenny thought that over for a minute and then asked, "How long does it have to be that way?"

Doesn't that illustrate the point beautifully? Already at four years of age, this child was anticipating a day of *freedom* when no one could tell her what to do. There was something deep within her spirit that longed for control. Watch for the same phenomenon in your child. If he's a toughie, it will show up soon.

Q. *You have explained the dangers of power to both children and adults. But there's no great virtue in being completely powerless either, is there? What does it do to a* *person to be without influence or credibility in today's society?*

A. You've asked an insightful question. There is reason to be concerned about those who have been stripped of all social power in this day. The elderly, the handicapped, the poverty-stricken, the homeless, the sick and the dying are often among that number.

My father was given a glimpse of their plight toward the end of his life. I'll never forget visiting him in the hospital for the final time after his massive heart attack. I flew in from Cincinnati that night and rushed to his bedside. I sat with him through the late hours and talked about his circumstances. He was in a contemplative mood. Dad told me that the medical staff had given him good care, but they somehow managed to convey disrespect for him. He was not angry and he didn't ask me to intercede on his behalf. That was not his point. He had simply made an observation that troubled him. He said the young doctors and nurses responded to him as though he were an old man. He was only sixty-six years of age then and was still engaged full time as a college professor. He had been a very energetic man until the pruning knife of time did its dastardly work. Now, life was rapidly winding down and he seemed to know it.

Then he said, "I have seen during these past few days what it is like to experience the absolute powerlessness of old age—where you are totally dependent on someone who does not value you as a person. I understand for the first time the disrespect that accompanies advanced age in this country. It is a frightening thing."

Millions of older people know precisely what my dad was trying to express. Being powerless is difficult even when accompanied by love and acceptance. Dependency is terrifying when surrounded by disrespect. I believe this is why Jesus came to help the down-and-outers—the wounded, lame and sick. He touched the leper who had not been approached in years. And He told His disciples, "It is not the healthy who need a doctor, but the sick . . ." (Mark 2:17). He admonished us all, ". . . I tell you the truth, whatever you did for one of the least of these brothers of mine, you did for me" (Matthew 25:40). What incredible compassion He had for those who hurt— for the powerless people of the world. I wish I could point them all to Him. He is a friend who will stick closer than a brother.

Q. *The greatest power struggle in our home is schoolwork, which you mentioned, and especially homework. Our fifth grader simply will not do it! When we force him to study, he sits and stares, doodles, gets up for water and just kills time. Furthermore, we never know for sure what his assignments are. What would you recommend?*

A. Let me offer a short discourse on school achievement, based on years of interaction with parents. I served as a teacher and I've worked as a high school counselor. Believe me, I know the agitation that mothers and fathers feel when their kids will not use the abilities God has given them. This is the situation with which they are faced: the kind of self-discipline necessary to succeed in school appears to be distributed among children on a continuum from one extreme to the other. Students at the positive end of the scale (Type I, I'll call them) are by nature rather organized individuals who care about details. They take the educational process very seriously and assume full responsibility for assignments given. They also worry about grades, or at least, they recognize their importance. To do poorly on a test would depress them for several days. They also like the challenge offered in the classroom. Parents of these children do not have to monitor their progress to keep them working. It is their way of life . . . and it is consistent with their temperament.

At the other end of the continuum are the boys and girls who do not fit in well with the structure of the classroom (Type II). If their Type I siblings emerge from school cum laude, these kids graduate "Thank You, Laude!" They are sloppy, disorganized and flighty. They have a natural aversion to work and love to play. They can't wait for success and they hurry on without it. Like bacteria that gradually become immune to antibiotics, the classic underachievers become impervious to adult pressure. They withstand a storm of parental protest every few weeks and then, when no one is looking, they slip back into apathy. They don't even hear the assignments being given in school and seem not to be embarrassed when they fail to complete them. And, you can be sure, they drive their parents to distraction.

There are several important understandings about Type I and II kids that may help parents deal with their differences. First, these characteristics are not highly correlated with intelligence. By that I mean there are bright children who are at the flighty end of the scale, and there are slow-learning individuals who are highly motivated. The primary difference between them is a matter of temperament and maturity, rather than IQ.

Second, Type II kids are not inferior to Type I. Yes, it would be wonderful if every student used the talent he possessed to best advantage. But each child is a unique individual. All don't have to fit the same mold. I know education is important today, and we want our children to go as far as they can, academically. But let's keep our goals in proper perspective. It is possible that the low achiever will outperform the academic superstar in the long run. There are countless examples of that occurring in the real world (Einstein, Edison, Roosevelt, etc.). Don't write off that disorganized, apparently lazy kid as a lifelong loser. He may surprise you.

Third, you will *never* turn a Type II youngster into a Type I scholar by nagging, pushing, threatening and punishing. It isn't in him. If you try to squeeze him into something he's not, you will only produce aggravation for yourself and anger from the child. That effort can fill a house with conflict. I have concluded that it is simply not worth the price it extracts.

On the other hand, I certainly do not recommend that children be allowed to float through life, avoiding responsibility and wasting their opportunities. My approach to the underachiever can be summarized in these suggestions: (1) He lacks the discipline to structure his life. Help him generate it. Systematize his study hours. Look over his homework to see that it is neat and complete, etc. (2) Maintain as close contact with the school as possible. The more you and your child's teacher communicate, the better. Only then can you provide the needed structure. (3) Avoid anger in the relationship. It does not help. Those parents who become most frustrated and irritated usually believe their child's irresponsibility is a deliberate thing. Usually it is not. Approach the problem as one of temperament rather than acts of defiance. (4) Having done what you can to help, accept what comes in return. Go with the flow and begin looking for other areas of success for your child. Let me say it once more: not every individual can be squeezed into the same mold. There is room in this world for the creative "souls" who long to breathe free. I'll bet some of you as parents approached life from the same direction.

Q. *How do you feel about homework being given by schools? Do you think it is a good idea? If so, how much and how often?*

A. Having written several books on discipline and being on the record as an advocate of parental authority, my answer may surprise you: I believe homework can be destructive and counterproductive if it is not handled very carefully. I am especially concerned about large quantities of homework that are given routinely during elementary school. Little kids are asked to sit for six or more hours a day doing formal classwork. Then they take that tiring bus ride home and guess what? They're placed at a desk and told to do more assignments. For a wiry, hyperactive child or even for a fun-loving youngster, that is asking too much. Learning for them becomes an enormous bore, instead of the exciting panorama that it should be.

I remember a mother coming to see me because her son was struggling in school. "He has about five hours of homework per night," she said. "How can I make him *want* to do it?"

"Are you kidding?" I told his mother. "*I* wouldn't do that much homework!"

Upon investigation, I found that the private school which he attended vigorously denied giving him that many assignments. Or rather, they didn't give the *other* students that much work. They did expect the slower boys and girls to complete the assignments they didn't get done in the classroom each day plus finish the homework. For the plodders like this youngster, that meant up to five hours of work nightly. There was no escape from books throughout their entire day. What a mistake!

Excessive homework during the elementary school years also has the potential of interfering with family life. In our home, we were trying to do many things with the

limited time we had together. I wanted our kids to participate in church activities, have some family time and still
be able to kick back and waste an hour or two. Children
need opportunities for unstructured play—swinging on
the swings and throwing rocks and playing with basket-
balls. Yet by the time that homework was done, darkness
had fallen and dinnertime had arrived. Then baths were
taken and off they went to bed. Something didn't feel
right about that kind of pace. That's why I negotiated
with our children's teachers, agreeing that they would
complete no more than one hour per night of supervised
homework. It was enough!

Homework also generates a considerable amount of
stress for parents. Their kids either won't do the assignments or they get tired and whine about it. Tensions
build and angry words fly. I'm also convinced that child
abuse occurs right at that point for some children. When
Shirley was teaching the second grade, one little girl
came to school with both eyes black and swollen. She said
her father had beaten her because she couldn't learn her
spelling words. That is illegal now, but it wasn't then.
The poor youngster will remember those beatings for a
lifetime and will always think of herself as "stupid."

Then there are the parents who do the assignments
for their kids just to get them over the hump. Have you
ever been guilty of that illegality? Shame on you! More
specifically, have you ever worked for two weeks on
a fifth-grade geography project for your nonacademic
eleven-year-old—and then learned later that you got a C
on it?! That's the ultimate humiliation.

In short, I believe homework in elementary school
should be extremely limited. It is appropriate for learning
multiplication tables, spelling words and test review. It is
also helpful in training kids to remember assignments,
bring books home and complete them as required. But to

load them down night after night with monotonous book-work is to invite educational burnout.

In junior high classes, perhaps an hour of homework per night should be the maximum. In high school, those students who are preparing for college may handle more work. Even then, however, the load should be reasonable. Education is a vitally important part of our children's lives, but it is only *one* part. Balance between these competing objectives is the key word.

Q. *May I go back to the story of the undisciplined toddler on the airplane? You described her as being unruly and unwilling to be buckled in her seat. How would you have handled that situation?*

A. Well, I think I mentioned that a few sharp slaps on the legs would have curtailed her temper tantrum and given control back to the mother. On the other hand, the crisis need never have developed. The mother should have anticipated that situation and brought some sugarless mints and a few interesting toys or playthings. That would have been so easy to do. Instead, mom and daughter were like two freight trains coming together on the same track. A violent collision was inevitable. I just happened to be there to witness the crash.

Q. *You've made a big deal over the issue of newborns and whether or not they come into the world with complex temperaments or as "blank slates." When all is said and done, what difference does it make? Children are children, and we take them as we find them. Why does it matter whether they began with "something" or with "nothing"?*

A. It is easy to see how you could assume that this issue is of academic interest only, with no practical application. Nothing could be further from the truth. These contrasting ways of perceiving children have far-reaching implications and will influence parenting techniques throughout the developmental years. Let me explain.

The "blank slate" theory holds that children are born neutral but with a penchant for "good." Their natural tendency is to love, give, work, cooperate and learn. The failure of the individual to behave in these positive ways does not result from any internal flaw, but rather from a corrupt and misguided society. Bad *experiences* are responsible for bad behavior. Therefore, it is the task of parents to provide a loving environment and then stay out of the way. Natural goodness will flow from it. As long as major mistakes are avoided, there will be no negative stimuli to distort or warp the developing individual. Rebellion and disobedience do not emanate from love. Thus, parental discipline is of lesser significance because there is no inner nature to be confronted.

This is the humanistic perspective on childish nature. Millions of Americans and Canadians, the majority no doubt, believe it to be true. Most psychologists have also accepted and taught it throughout the twentieth century. There is only one thing wrong with the concept: it is entirely inaccurate.

It is impossible to understand human nature without consulting the "Owners Manual." Only the Creator of children can tell us how He made them, and He has done that in Scripture. It teaches that we are born in sin, having inherited a disobedient nature from Adam. King David said, ". . . in sin did my mother *conceive* me" (Psalm 51:5), meaning that this tendency to do wrong was transmitted genetically. It has infected every person who ever lived. "For *all* have sinned and come short of the glory of God" (Romans 3:23). Therefore, with or without bad experiences, a child is naturally inclined toward rebellion, selfishness, dishonesty, aggression, exploitation and greed. He does not have to be taught these behaviors. They are inevitable expressions of his humanness.

Although this perspective on man is mocked in the secular world today, abundant evidence attests to its accuracy. How else do we explain the pugnacious and perverse nature of every society on earth? Bloody warfare has been the centerpiece of world history for more than 5,000 years. People of every race and creed around the globe have tried to rape, plunder, burn, blast and kill each other century after century. Peace was merely a momentary pause when they stopped to reload! Plato said more than 2,350 years ago, "Only dead men have seen an end to war." He was right, at least until the Prince of Peace comes.

Furthermore, in the midst of these warring nations we find a depressing incidence of murder, drug abuse, child molestation, prostitution, adultery, homosexuality and dishonesty. How do we explain this pervasive evil in a world of people who are naturally inclined toward good? Have they really drifted into these antisocial behaviors despite their inborn tendencies? If so, surely *one* society in all the world has been able to preserve the goodness with which children are born. Where is it? Does such a place exist? No, even though some societies are more moral than others, none reflects the harmony which might be expected from the "blank slate" theorists. Why not? Because the premise is wrong.

What, then, does this biblical understanding mean for parents? Are they to look on their babies as guilty before they have done wrong? Of course not. Children are not responsible for their sins until they reach an age of accountability—and that time frame is known best to God. On the other hand, parents would be wise to anticipate and deal with rebellious behavior when it occurs. And it *will* occur, probably by the eighteenth month or before. Anyone who has watched a toddler throw a violent temper tantrum when he doesn't get his way must be hard-pressed to explain how that particular "blank slate" got so mixed up! Did his mother or father model the tantrum for him, falling on the floor, slobbering, kicking, crying and screaming? I would hope not. Either way, the kid needs no demonstration. Rebellion comes naturally to him.

Parents can, and must, train, shape, mold, correct, guide, punish, reward, instruct, warn, teach and love their kids during the formative years. Their purpose is to control that inner nature and keep it from tyrannizing the entire family. Ultimately, however, only Jesus Christ can cleanse it and make it "wholly acceptable" to the Master.

You know what? I believe I've preached a sermon. And I'm not even a minister.

Q. *Generally speaking, what kind of discipline do you use with a teenager who is habitually miserable to live with?*

A. In addition to what I've already written on this subject, let me offer this thought: the general rule is to use action—not anger—to reach an understanding. Any time you can get teenagers to do what is necessary without becoming furious at them, you are ahead of the game. Let me provide a few examples of how this might be accomplished.

(1) In Russia, I'm told that teenagers who are convicted of using drugs are denied driver's licenses for years. It is a very effective approach.

(2) When my daughter was a teenager, she used to slip into my bathroom and steal my razor, my shaving cream, my toothpaste or my comb. Of course, she never brought them back. Then after she had gone to school, I

would discover the utensils missing. There I was with wet hair or "fuzzy" teeth, trying to locate the confiscated item in *her* bathroom. It was no big deal, but it was irritating at the time. Can you identify?

I asked Danae a dozen times not to do this, but to no avail. Thus, the phantom struck without warning one cold morning. I hid everything she needed to put on her "face," and then left for the office. My wife told me she had never heard such wails and moans as were uttered that day. Our daughter plunged desperately through bathroom drawers looking for her toothbrush, comb and hair dryer. The problem has never resurfaced.

(3) A family living in a house with a small hot-water tank was continually frustrated by their teenager's endless showers. Screaming at him did no good. Once he was locked behind the bathroom door, he stayed in the steamy stall until the last drop of warm water had been drained. Solution? In mid-stream, Dad stopped the flow of hot water by turning a valve at the tank. Cold water suddenly poured from the nozzle. Junior popped out of the shower in seconds.

(4) A single mother couldn't get her daughter out of bed in the morning until she announced a new policy: The hot water would be shut off promptly at 6:30 A.M. The girl could either get up on time or bathe in ice water. Another mother had trouble getting her eight-year-old out of bed each morning. She then began pouring bowls of frozen marbles under the covers with him each morning. He arose quite quickly.

(5) Instead of standing in the parking lot and screaming at students who drive too fast, school officials now put huge bumps in the road that jar the teeth of those who ignore them. It does the job quite nicely.

(6) You as the parent have the car that a teenager

needs, the money that he covets and the authority to grant or withhold privileges. If push comes to shove, these chips can be exchanged for commitments to live responsibly, share the work load at home and stay off little brother's back. This bargaining process works for younger kids, too. I like the "one to one" trade-off for television viewing time. It permits a child to watch one minute of television for every minute spent reading.

The possibilities are endless.

Q. *Would you ever, under any circumstances, permit a son or daughter to bring a roomie of the opposite sex into your home to live?*

A. No. It would be dishonoring to God and a violation of the moral principles on which Shirley and I have staked our lives. I will bend for my kids, but never that far.

Q. *Are there times when good, loving parents don't like their own kids very much?*

A. Yes, just as there are times in a good marriage when husbands and wives don't like each other for a while. What you should do in both situations is hang tough. Look for ways to make the relationship better, but never give up your commitment to one another. That is especially true during the teen years, when the person we see will be *very* different in a few years. Wait patiently for him to grow up. You'll be glad you did.

NOTE: The following item was originally published in my earlier book, *Straight Talk to Men and Their Wives*, but it is also being included here because of its relevancy to the topic. *Someone* needs to read this message! Is it you?

Q. *My wife and I are new Christians, and we now realize that we raised our kids by the wrong principles.*

They're grown now, but we continue to worry about the past and we feel great regret for our failures as parents. Is there anything we can do at this late date?

A. Let me deal, first, with the awful guilt you are obviously carrying. There's hardly a parent alive who does not have some regrets and painful memories of failures as a mother or a father. Children are infinitely complex as I've indicated, and we cannot be perfect parents any more than we can be perfect human beings. The pressures of living are stressful and we get tired and irritated; we are influenced by our physical bodies and our emotions, which sometimes prevent us from saying the right things and being the model we should be. We don't always handle our children as unemotionally as we wish we had, and it's very common to look back a year or two later and see how wrong we were in the way we approached a problem.

All of us experience these failures! That's why each of us should get alone with the Creator of parents and children and say: "Lord, You know my inadequacies. You know my weaknesses, not only in parenting, but in every area of my life. I did the best I could, but it wasn't good enough. As You broke the fishes and the loaves to feed the five thousand, now take my meager effort and use it to bless my family. Make up for the things I did wrong. Satisfy the needs that I have not satisfied. Wrap Your great arms around my children, and draw them close to You. And be there when they stand at the great crossroads between right and wrong. All I can give is my best, and I've done that. Therefore, I submit to You my children and myself and the job I did as a parent. The outcome now belongs to You."

I know God will honor that prayer, even for parents whose job is finished. The Lord does not want you to suffer from guilt over events you can no longer influence.

The past is the past. Let it die, never to be resurrected. Give the situation to God, once and for all time. I think you'll be surprised to learn that you're no longer alone! ". . . forgetting what is behind and straining toward what is ahead, I press on toward the goal to win the prize for which God has called me heavenward in Christ Jesus" (Philippians 3:13-14).

For the benefit of the discouraged mother of a strong-willed toddler who feels like she's about to lose her mind, I am herewith providing a portion of two letters sent to me a few years ago. The first was written by an exasperated mother who felt she did not get the help she needed in my book, *The Strong-willed Child.* The second letter came from the same woman, five years later. The first letter, written October 14, 1978:

> Dear Dr. Dobson,
> After purchasing your new book I must tell you I was disappointed. The beginning was encouraging, but then the rest was devoted to general child-rearing techniques. I thought the entire book was written about the strong-willed child. Are you sure you know what one is? Nearly every child is strong-willed, but not every child is *strong-willed!*
> Our third (and last) daughter is *strong-willed!* She is twenty-one months old now, and there have been times when I thought she must be abnormal. If she had been my firstborn child there would have been no more in this family. She had colic day and night for six months, then we just quit calling it that. She was simply unhappy all the time. She began walking at eight months and she became a merciless bully with her sisters. She pulled hair, bit, hit, pinched and pushed with all her might. She yanked out a handful of her sister's long black hair.

NOTE: This mother went on to describe the characteristics of her tyrannical daughter which I have heard thousands of times. She then closed, advising me to give greater emphasis to the importance of corporal punishment for this kind of youngster. I wrote her a cordial letter in reply and told her I understood her frustration. Five years later, she wrote to me again, as follows:

February 2, 1983

Dear Dr. Dobson,

This letter is long overdue, but, thank you! Thank you for a caring reply to what was probably not a very nice letter from a discouraged mom. Thank you for your positive remarks, the first I had had in a long time.

Perhaps you would be interested in an update on our Sally Ann. Back when I wrote to you, she was probably a perfect "10" when it came to strong-willed-ness. "Difficult" hardly scratches the surface of descriptive words for her babyhood. As Christian parents, we tried every scriptural method we could find for dealing with her. I had decided she was abnormal. Something so innocent as offering her her morning juice (which she loved) in the wrong glass threw her into thirty minutes of tantrums—and this was before she could really talk! Family dinners were a nightmare.

Before she turned two, Sally Ann would regularly brutalize her older sisters, ages four, eight, and twelve, even having the twelve-year-old in tears many times. A spanking from me did not deter her in the least. Finally, in prayer one day the Lord plainly showed me that her sisters must be allowed to retaliate, something I was strictly against (and still am!). However, in this case, all I can say is that it worked. I carefully and clearly told my four girls (little Sally Ann in my lap) what they were to do the next time they were attacked by their littlest sister: they were to give her a good smack on the top of her chubby little leg, next to her diaper. Sally got the point: within two days the attacks ceased.

Disciplining our youngest was never easy, but with God's help, we persevered. When she had to be spanked, we could expect up to an hour of tantrums. It would have been so easy to give in and ignore the misbehavior, but I am convinced that, without it, our Sally would have become at best a holy terror, and at worst, mentally ill. Tell your listeners that discipline *does* pay off, when administered according to the Word of God.

Sally today is a precious six-year-old and a joy to her family. She is still rather strong-willed, but it is well within normal limits now! She is very bright and has a gentle, creative, and sympathetic nature unusual in one so young. I know the Lord has great plans for her. She has already asked Jesus into her life and knows how to call upon Him when she has a need (like fear from a nightmare, etc.).

In conclusion, though I still don't think you went far enough in your book, loving discipline certainly is the key. With perseverance!

Thank you and may God's continued blessing be upon you and your household and your ministry, through Jesus Christ our Lord.

In His love,
Mrs. W. W.

FINAL NOTE: Thank you too, Mrs. W. It was a special treat to hear from you again. You're on the right track with Sally Ann. Discipline with love was God's idea. Oh, and by the way, *this* book was written for you. Did I get it said this time?

James Dobson

°John Walvoord and Roy Zuck, eds., *Bible Knowledge Commentary, Old Testament* (Wheaton, IL: Victor Books, 1985), 953.

Releasing Your Grown Child

11

We come now to the final task assigned to mothers and fathers . . . that of releasing grown children and launching them into the world of adulthood. It is also one of the most difficult. Several years ago, we explored this topic by conducting another informal poll of the Focus on the Family radio listeners. I asked them to react to this question: "What are the greatest problems you face in dealing with your parents or in-laws, and how will you relate differently to your grown children than your parents have to you?" An avalanche of mail flooded my offices in the next few days, eventually totaling more than 2,600 detailed replies.

We read every letter and catalogued the responses according to broad themes. As is customary in such inquiries, the results surprised our entire staff. We fully expected in-law complaints to represent the most common category of concerns. Instead, it ranked fifth in frequency, representing only 10 percent of the letters we received. The fourth most commonly mentioned problem, at 11 percent, related to sickness, dependency, senility and other medical problems in the older generation. In third place, at 19 percent, was general concern for the spiritual welfare of un-Christian parents. The second most common reply, representing 21 percent, expressed irritation and frustration at parents who didn't care about their children or grandchildren. They never came to visit, wouldn't baby-sit, and seemed to follow a "me-first" philosophy.

That brings us to the top of the hit parade of problems between adults and their parents. May I have the envelope please? (Drum roll in background.) And the winner is, the inability or unwillingness of parents to release their grown children and permit them to live their own lives. An incredible 44 percent of the letters received made reference to this failure of older adults to let go. It was as though some of the writers had been waiting for years for that precise question to be asked. Here are a few of their comments:

1. "Mother felt my leaving home was an insult to her. She couldn't let go, couldn't realize I needed to become an independent person, couldn't understand that I no longer needed her physical help, although I did need her as a person. Quite unintentionally she retarded my growing up by 35 years."

2. "One of the greatest problems is to have my parents see me as an adult, not as a child who doesn't know the best way to do things. As a child, I played a specific role in my family. Now as an

adult, I wish to change my role, but they will not allow it."

3. "Our parents never seemed able to grasp the reality of the fact that we had grown from dependent children, to capable, responsible adults. They did not recognize or appreciate our abilities, responsibilities or contributions to the outside world."

4. "I am 54 years old but when I visit my mother I am still not allowed to do certain things such as peel carrots, etc. because I do not do them correctly. Our relationship is still child-parent. I am still regularly corrected, criticized, put-down and constantly reminded of what terrible things I did 50 years ago. Now we are not talking about major criminal acts, just normal childish disobedience during the pre-school years. I was the youngest of five and the only daughter and I still hear, 'I would rather have raised another four boys than one daughter.' Pray for me, please. I need Jesus to help me forgive and forget."

We received literally hundreds of letters expressing this general concern. The writers wanted desperately to be free, to be granted adult status, and especially, to be respected by their parents. At the same time, they were saying to them, "I still love you. I still need you. I still want you as my friend. But I no longer need you as the authority in my life."

I remember going through a similar era in my own life. My parents handled me wisely in those years and it was rare to have them stumble into common parental mistakes. However, we had been a very close-knit family and it was difficult for my mother to shift gears when I graduated from high school. During that summer, I traveled 1,500 miles from home and entered a college in California. I will never forget the exhilarating feeling of freedom that swept over me that fall. It was not that I wanted to do anything evil or previously forbidden. It was simply that I felt accountable for my own life and did not have to explain my actions to my parents. It was like a fresh, cool breeze on a spring morning. Young adults who have not been properly trained for that moment sometimes go berserk in the absence of authority, but I did not. I did, however, quickly become addicted to that freedom and was not inclined to give it up.

The following December, my parents and I met for Christmas vacation at the home of some relatives. Suddenly, I found myself in conflict with my mom. She was responding as she had six months earlier when I was still in high school. By then, I had journeyed far down the path toward adulthood. She was asking me what time I would be coming in at night, and urging me to drive the car safely, and watching what I ate. No offense was intended, mind you. My mother had just failed to notice that I had changed and she needed to get with the new program, herself.

Finally, there was a brief flurry of words between us and I left the house in a huff. A friend picked me up and I talked about my feelings as we rode in the car. "Darn it, Bill!" I said. "I don't *need* a mother anymore!"

Then a wave of guilt swept over me, as though I had said, "I don't love my mother anymore." I meant no such thing. What I was feeling was the desire to be friends with my parents instead of accepting a line of authority from them. My wish was granted by my mom and dad very quickly thereafter.

Most parents in our society do not take the hint so

easily. I'm convinced that mothers and fathers in North America are among the very best in the world. We care passionately about our kids and would do anything to meet their needs. But we are among the worst when it comes to letting go of our grown sons and daughters. In fact, those two characteristics are linked. The same commitment that leads us to do so well when the children are small (dedication, love, concern, involvement), also causes us to hold on too tightly when they are growing up. I will admit to my own difficulties in this area. I understood the importance of turning loose before our kids were born. I wrote extensively on the subject when they were still young. I prepared a film series in which all the right principles were expressed. But when it came time to open my hand and let the birds fly, I struggled mightily!

Why? Well, fear played a role in my reluctance. We live in Los Angeles where weird things are done by strange people every day of the year. For example, our daughter was held at gunpoint on the campus of the University of Southern California late one night. Her assailant admonished Danae not to move or make a noise. She figured her chances of survival were better by defying him right then than by cooperating. She fled. The man did not shoot at her, thank God. Who knows what he had in mind for her?

A few days later, my son was walking his bicycle across a busy road near our home when a man in a sportscar came around the curve at high speed. Skid marks later showed he was traveling in excess of 80 miles per hour. Ryan saw that he was going to be hit, and he jumped over the handlebars and attempted to crawl to safety. The car was fishtailing wildly and careening toward our son. It came to a stop just inches from his head, and then the driver sped off without getting out. Perhaps he was on PCP or cocaine. Thousands of addicts live here in Los Angeles, and innocent people are victimized by them every day.

Such near-misses make me want to gather my children around me and never let them experience risk again. Of course, that is impossible and would be unwise even if they submitted to it. Life itself is a risk, and parents must let their kids face reasonable jeopardy on their own. Nevertheless, when Danae or Ryan leave in the car, I'm still tempted to say, "Be sure to keep the shiny side up and the rubber side down!"

What are *your* reasons for restricting the freedom of your grown or nearly grown children? In some cases, if we're honest, we need them too much to let them go. They have become an extension of ourselves, and our egos are inextricably linked to theirs. Therefore, we not only seek to hold them to us, but we manipulate them to maintain our control. As described in Chapter 7, we use guilt, bribery, threats, intimidation, fear and anger to restrict their freedom. And sadly, when we win at this game, we *and* our offspring are destined to lose.

Many of the letters we received in response to our poll were written by young adults who had not yet broken free. Some stories they told were almost hard to believe in a culture which legally emancipates its children at such a young age. Consider this excerpt from a young lady with very possessive parents:

> I'm 23 and the eldest of 3 children. My parents are still overprotective. They won't let go. I have a career and a very stable job but they will not allow me to move out on my own. They still try to discipline me with a spanking using a belt and hold me to a 10:00 P.M. curfew. Even if it is a church activity, I must be home by 10:00 P.M. If it's out of town or impossible for me to be home by that time,

I'm not allowed to go. I have high Christian moral standards and they trust me, but they are just overprotective.

Can you imagine these parents spanking this twenty-
three-year-old woman for her minor infractions and
disobediences? Though I do not know the girl or her parents, it would appear that they have a classic dependency
problem occurring commonly with a very compliant
child. No self-respecting strong-willed individual would
tolerate such dominance and disrespect. A compliant girl
might, while harboring deep resentment all the while.

In a sense, this twenty-three-year-old is equally responsible for her lack of freedom. She has permitted
her parents to treat her like a child. First Corinthians
13:11 says, " When I was a child, I talked like a child,
I thought like a child, I reasoned like a child. When I
became a man, I put childish ways behind me." What
could be more childish than for a woman in her twenties
to yield to a physical thrashing for arriving home after
10:00 P.M.? Of course, I believe young adults should
continue to listen to the accumulated wisdom of their
parents and to treat them with respect. However, the
relationship must change when adolescence is over. And
if the parents will not or cannot make that transformation, the son or daughter is justified in respectfully insisting that it happen. For the very compliant child, that
tearing loose is extremely difficult to accomplish!

Parents who refuse to let go often force their sons
or daughters to choose between two bad alternatives.
The first is to accept their domination and manipulation.
That is precisely what the twenty-three-year-old girl
had done. Instinctively, she knew her parents were
wrong, but she lacked the courage to tell them so. Thus,
she remained under their authoritative umbrella for a
couple of years too long. She was like an unborn baby in

the tenth or eleventh month of pregnancy. Granted, the womb was safe and warm, but she could grow no more until she got past the pain and indignities of childbirth. She was overdue for "delivery" into the opportunities and responsibilities of adulthood.

To repeat our now familiar theme, it is the very compliant child who often yields to the tyranny of intimidation. Some remain closeted there for forty years or more. Even if they marry, their parents will not grant emancipation without a struggle, setting the stage for lifelong in-law problems.

The other alternative is to respond like a mountainous volcano which blows its top. Hot lava descends on everything in its path. Great anger and resentment characterize the parent-child relationship for years, leaving scars and wounds on both generations. The strong-willed individual typically chooses this response to parental domination. He isn't about to let anyone hem him in, but in the process of breaking free, he loses the support and fellowship of the family he needs.

The legendary Beatles rock group often sang about drug usage and revolution, among other antiestablishment themes. But occasionally, their music was devastatingly incisive. One of their best renditions was recorded in 1967. It went to the heart of this matter of breaking free. The lyrics described a young woman whose parents had held on too long, forcing her to steal away in the early morning hours. Perhaps you will feel the pain of her confused parents as you read the words to *She's Leaving Home*.

> Wedn'sday morning at five o'clock as the day begins
> Silently closing her bedroom door
> Leaving the note that she hoped would say more

She goes downstairs to the kitchen clutching
   her handkerchief
Quietly turning the backdoor key
Stepping outside, she is free.
She (We gave her most of our lives)
Is leaving (Sacrificed most of our lives)
Home (We gave her everything money could buy).
She's leaving home after living alone
   for so many years. Bye-Bye.

Father snores as his wife gets into her dressing gown
Picks up the letter that's lying there
Standing alone at the top of the stairs
She breaks down and cries to her husband,
"Daddy, our baby's gone!"
Why would she treat us so thoughtlessly?
How could she do this to me?
She (We never thought of ourselves)
Is leaving (Never a thought for ourselves)
Home (We struggled hard all our lives to get by).
She's leaving home after living alone
   for so many years. Bye-Bye.

Friday morning at nine o'clock she is far away
Waiting to keep the appointment she made
Meeting a man from the motor trade
She (What did we do that was wrong?)
Is having (We didn't know it was wrong)
Fun (Fun is the one thing that money can't buy).
Something inside that was always denied
   for so many years. Bye-Bye.
She's leaving home. Bye-Bye.°

There must be a better way to launch a postadolescent son or daughter, and of course there is. It is the
responsibility of parents to release the grip and set
the fledgling adult free to make it on his own. But alas,

independence sometimes fails not because parents have withheld it, but because immature sons and daughters refuse to accept it. They have no intention of growing up. Why should they? The nest is too comfortable at home. Food is prepared, temperature is regulated, clothes are laundered and all bills are paid. There is no incentive to face the cold world of reality, and they are determined not to budge. Some even refuse to work. They keep hours like hamsters, staying up (and out) all night and then sleeping half the day. They sit around the house listening to electronic music and waiting for a dish to rattle in the kitchen. Three months worth of dirty underwear and who knows what else are stuffed under the bed. Life is a lark, albeit a boring one. Even when they do move away for a time, they inevitably run out of money and come dragging home at mealtime. Their parents remind me of a man with a new boomerang. He would have made it fine except he went crazy trying to throw the old one away.

I received a letter from the mother of one of these perpetual freeloaders a few years ago. Let me share what she asked and how I replied:

Q. We have a twenty-one-year-old who is still living at home. He does not want to come under our authority and he breaks all the rules we have set up as minimum standards of behavior. He plays his stereo so loudly that it drives me crazy, and he comes in every night after 1 A.M. I know he needs his freedom, but I worry about our younger children who are trying to get away with the same things their big brother does. How would you balance the rights and privileges of this young adult with our needs as a family?

A. It is very difficult for a strong-willed twenty-one-year-old to continue living at home, and it will become even more unsettling with every year that passes. The demand for independence and freedom in such cases is almost always in conflict with the parents' expectations and wishes. Your son's unwillingness to respect your reasonable requests is a sure-fire indication that he needs to face life on his own. Also, the bad modeling he is providing for your younger siblings is a serious matter. I think it is time to help him pack. At the very least, he should be made to understand that his continued residency at home is conditional. Either live with the rules—or live with the YMCA.

I know it's difficult to dislodge a home-bound son or daughter. They are like furry puppies who hang around the back door waiting for a warm saucer of milk. How can you yell "Shoo!" at someone so lost and needy? But to let them stay year after year, especially if they are pursuing no career goals or if they are disrespectful at home, is to cultivate irresponsibility and dependency. That is not love, even though it may feel like it.

We are agreed, then, that independence and freedom must be granted to those who have passed through the far side of adolescence. But how is that accomplished? The Amish have a unique approach to it. Their children are kept under the absolute authority of their parents throughout childhood. Very strict discipline and harsh standards of behavior are imposed from infancy. When they turn sixteen years of age, however, they enter a period called "Rumspringa." Suddenly, all restrictions are lifted. They are free to drink, smoke, date, marry, or behave in ways that horrify their parents. Some do just that. But most don't. They are even granted the right to leave the Amish community if they choose. But if they stay, it must be in accordance with the rules of convention. The majority accept the heritage of their forefathers, not because they must, but because they wish to.

Although I admire the Amish and many of their approaches to child-rearing, I believe the Rumspringa concept is too precipitous. To take a child overnight from total domination to absolute freedom is an invitation to anarchy. Perhaps it works in the controlled environment of Amish country, but it is usually disastrous for the rest of us. I've seen families emulate this "instant adulthood" idea, lifting parental governance overnight. The result has been similar to what occurred in African colonies when European leadership was suddenly withdrawn. Bloody revolutions were often fought in the heady spirit of freedom.

It is better, I believe, to begin releasing your children during the preschool years, granting independence that is consistent with their age and maturity. When a child can tie his shoes, let him—yes, require him—to do it. When he can choose his own clothes within reason, let him make his own selection. When he can walk safely to school, allow him the privilege. Each year, more *responsibility* and *freedom* (they are companions) are given to the child so that the final release in early adulthood is merely the final relaxation of authority. That is the theory, at least. Pulling it off is sometimes quite difficult.

However you go about transferring the reins of authority—the rudiments of power—to your children, the task should be completed by 20 and no later than 22 years of age. To hold on longer is to invite revolution.

° "She's Leaving Home" by John Lennon and Paul McCartney. © 1967 NORTHERN SONGS LIMITED. All rights in the USA, CANADA, MEXICO, and the PHILIPPINES controlled and administered by BLACKWOOD MUSIC INC., under license from ATV Music (MACLEN). All rights reserved. International copyright secured. Used by permission.

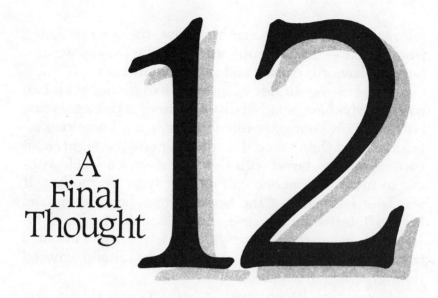

A
Final
Thought

Perhaps we can summarize our discussion of parenthood and its tougher dimensions by answering a question posed to me recently by a puzzled mother. It went something like this:

"Tell me why it is that some kids with every advantage and opportunity seem to turn out bad, while others raised in terrible homes become pillars in the community? I know one young man, for example, who grew up in squalid circumstances, yet he is such a fine person today. How did his parents manage to raise such a responsible son when they didn't even seem to care?"

Curious cases of this type are not so uncommon around us and they validate the theme of this book. As we have seen, environmental influences in themselves will not account for the behavior we observe in our fellowman. There is something else there—something from within—that also operates to make us who we are. Some behavior is caused and some plainly isn't.

Just last month, for example, I had dinner with two parents who have unofficially "adopted" a thirteen-year-old boy. This youngster followed their son home one afternoon, and then asked if he could spend the night. As it turned out, he stayed with them for almost a week without so much as a phone call coming from his mother. It was later learned that she works sixteen hours a day and has no interest in her son. Her alcoholic husband divorced her several years ago and left town without a trace. The boy had been abused, unloved and ignored through much of his life.

Given this background, what kind of kid do you think he is today—a druggie? A foul-mouthed delinquent? A lazy, insolent bum? No. He is polite to adults; he is a hard worker; he makes good grades in school and he enjoys helping around the house. This boy is like a lost puppy who desperately wants a good home. He has begged the family to adopt him officially so he could have a real father and a loving mother. His own mom couldn't care less.

How is it that this teenager could be so well-disciplined and polished despite his lack of training? I don't know. It is simply within him. He reminds me of my wonderful friend, David Hernandez. David and his parents came to America illegally from Mexico more than forty years ago and nearly starved to death before they found work. They eventually survived by helping to harvest the potato crop throughout the state of California. During this era, David lived under trees or in the open fields. His father made a stove out of an oil drum half-filled with dirt. The open campfire was their home.

David never had a roof over his head until his parents finally moved into an abandoned chicken coop. His mother covered the boarded walls with cheap wallpaper and David thought they were living in luxury. Then one day, the city of San Jose condemned the area and David's "house" was torn down. He couldn't understand why the community would destroy so fine a place.

Given this beginning, how can we explain the man that Dave Hernandez became? He graduated near the top of his class in high school and was granted a scholarship to college. Again, he earned high marks and four years later entered Loma Linda University School of Medicine. Once more, he scored in the top 10 percent of his class and continued in a residency in obstetrics and gynecology. Eventually, he served as a professor of OB/GYN at both Loma Linda University and the University of Southern California Medical Schools. Then at the peak of his career, his life began to unravel.

I'll never forget the day Dr. Hernandez called me on the telephone. He had just been released from hospital care following a battery of laboratory tests. The diagnosis? Sclerosing cholangitis, a liver disorder that is invariably fatal. We lost this fine husband, father and friend six years later at the age of forty-three. I loved him like a brother and I still miss him today.

Again, I ask, how could such discipline and genius come from these infertile circumstances? Who would have thought that this deprived Mexican boy sitting out there in the dirt would someday become one the most loved and respected surgeons of his era? Where did the motivation originate? From what bubbling spring did his ambition and thirst for knowledge flow? He had no books, took no educational trips, knew no scholars. Yet he reached for the sky. Why did it happen to David Hernandez and not the youngster with every advantage and opportunity? Why have so many children of prominent and loving parents grown up in ideal circumstances, only to reject it all for the streets of San Francisco or New York? Good answers are simply not available. It apparently comes down to this: God chooses to use some individuals in unique ways. Beyond that mysterious relationship, we must simply conclude that some kids seem born to make it and others are determined to fail. Someone reminded me recently that the same boiling water that softens the carrot also hardens the egg. Likewise, some individuals react positively to certain circumstances and others negatively. We don't know why.

One thing is clear to me: behavioral scientists have been far too simplistic in their explanation of human behavior. We are more than the aggregate of our experiences. We are more than the quality of our nutrition. We are more than our genetic heritage. We are more than our biochemistry. And certainly, we are more than our parents' influence. God has created us as unique individuals, capable of independent and rational thought that is not attributable to *any* source. That is what makes the task of parenting so challenging and rewarding. Just when you think you have your kids figured out, you had better brace yourself! Something new is coming your way.

I've spent more than half my life studying children, yet my own kids continue to surprise and fascinate me. I remember calling home some years ago from a city in Georgia where I had traveled for a speaking engagement. Danae, who was then thirteen years of age, picked up the phone and we had a warm father-daughter chat. Then she said, "Oh, by the way, Dad, I'm going to be running in a track meet next Saturday."

"Really?" I said. "What distance have you chosen?"

"The 880," she replied.

I gasped. "Danae, that is a very grueling race. Do you know how far 880 yards is?"

"Yes," she said. "It's a half mile."

"Have you ever run that far before?" I asked.

She said that she hadn't, even in practice. I continued to probe for information and learned that nine schools would be competing in the meet, which was only three days away. My daughter intended to compete against a field of other runners who presumably had been training for weeks. I was concerned.

"Danae," I said, "you've made a big mistake. You're about to embarrass yourself and I want you to think it over. You should go to your coach and ask to run a shorter race. At that speed 880 yards will kill you!"

"No, Dad," she said with determination. "No one else signed up for the 880 and I want to run it."

"Okay," I replied, "but you're doing it against my better judgment."

I thought about that beloved kid the rest of the week and wondered what humiliation was in store for her. I called again on Saturday afternoon.

"Guess what, Dad!" Danae said cheerfully. "I won the race today!" She had indeed finished in first place, several yards ahead of her nearest competitor. The following year, also without training, she won the same race by 50 yards and set a school record that may still be standing.

Wow! I said to myself. *The kid has talent. She'll be a great runner someday.* Wrong again. She ran and won two races in the ninth grade, came in second in the next, and then lost interest in track. End of story.

So much for fatherly wisdom in all its glory.

Obviously, I am deeply respectful of the human personality and the stunning complexity of even our youngest members. In a sense, this entire book has been a testimony to them and to those of you as parents who are dedicated to their care. I admire each of you greatly and I hope we have been of assistance in fulfilling your awesome responsibility. Now in these concluding paragraphs, I would like to express two or three final thoughts directly to the mothers and fathers of very rebellious kids. I am especially concerned about you.

First, I know your task is difficult and there are times when you feel like throwing in the towel. But you must remain steady. Someday, you will look back on this difficult period of conflict and be thankful that you stayed on course—that you continued to do what was right for those children whom God loaned to you for a season. This era will pass so quickly, and the present stresses will seem insignificant and remote. What will matter to you then will be the loving relationships you built with your family, even when other parents ran away or buried themselves in work. You will also have the knowledge of a job well done in the eyes of the Creator Himself.

Therefore, I hope you will resist the temptation to feel cheated or deprived because of the difficult temperament of your son or daughter. You are certainly not alone. In an earlier survey of 3,000 parents, we found that 85 percent of families had at least one strong-willed child. So, you are not an exception or the butt of some cruel cosmic joke. This *is* parenthood. This is human nature. Most of us who have raised two or more kids have gone through some of the same stresses you are experi-

encing. We survived, and you will too. You *can* handle
the assignment.

Let me review the concepts we have considered in
our meandering discussion of children:

1. You are not to blame for the temperament with
which your child was born. He is simply a tough kid to
handle and your task is to rise to the challenge.

2. He *is* in greater danger because of his inclination
to test the limits and scale the walls. Your utmost dili-
gence and wisdom will be required to deal with him.

3. If you fail to understand his lust for power and
independence, you can exhaust your resources and bog
down in guilt. It will benefit no one.

4. If it is not already too late, by all means, take
charge of your babies. Hold tightly to the reins of authority in the early days, and build an attitude of respect
during your brief window of opportunity. You will need
every ounce of "awe" you can get during the years to
come. Once you have established your right to lead, begin to let go systematically, year by year.

5. Don't panic, even during the storms of adolescence. Better times are ahead. A radical turnaround usually occurs in the early twenties.

6. Stay on your child's team, even when it appears to
be a *losing* team. You'll have the rest of your life to enjoy
mutual fellowship if you don't overreact to frustration
now.

7. Give him time to find himself, even if he appears
not to be searching.

8. Most importantly, I urge you to hold your children before the Lord in fervent prayer throughout their
years at home. I am convinced that there is no other
source of confidence and wisdom in parenting. There is

not enough knowledge in the books, mine or anyone else's, to counteract the evil that surrounds our kids today. Our teenagers are confronted by drugs, alcohol, sex and foul language wherever they turn. And, of course, the peer pressure on them is enormous. We must bathe them in prayer every day of their lives. The God who made your children *will* hear your petitions. He has promised to do so. After all, He loves them more than you do.

Finally, I have a word of encouragement prepared especially for those of you who are depressed today. It is a message written by a loving mother named Joan Mills, who must be a very special lady. She expressed her feelings about her children in an article that initially appeared in a 1981 issue of *Reader's Digest*. It is called "Season of the Empty Nest," and I believe you will be touched by the warmth of these words.

> Remember when the children built blanket tents to sleep in? And then scrambled by moonlight to their own beds, where they'd be safe from bears? And how proud and eager they were to be starting kindergarten? But only up to the minute they got there? And the time they packed cardboard suitcases in such a huff? "You won't see us again!" they hollered. Then they turned back at the end of the yard because they'd forgotten to go to the bathroom.
>
> It's the same thing when they're 20 or 22, starting to make their own way in the grownup world. Bravado, pangs, false starts and pratfalls. They're half in, half out. "Good-by, good-by! Don't worry, Mom!" They're back the first weekend to borrow the paint roller and a fuse and a broom. Prowling the attic, they seize on the quilt the dog ate and the terrible old sofa cushions that smell

like dead mice. "Just what I need!" they cheer, loading the car.

"Good-by, good-by!" implying forever. But they show up without notice at suppertimes, sighing soulfully to see the familiar laden plates. They go away again, further secured by four bags of groceries, the electric frying pan and a cookbook.

They call home collect, but not as often as parents need to hear. And their news makes fast-graying hair stand on end: ". . . so he forgot to set the brake, and he says my car rolled three blocks backward down the hill before it was totaled!" ". . . simple case of last hired, first fired, no big deal. I sold the stereo, and . . ." "Mom! Everybody in the city has them! There's this roach stuff you put under the sink. It's . . ."

I gripped the phone with both hands in those days, wishing I could bribe my children back with everything they'd ever wanted—drum lessons, a junk-food charge account, anything. I struggled with an unbecoming urge to tell them once more about hot breakfasts and crossing streets and dry socks on wet days.

"I'm so impressed by how you cope!" I said instead.

The children scatter, and parents draw together, remembering sweetshaped infants heavy in their arms, patched jeans, chicken pox, the night the accident happened, the rituals of Christmases and proms. With wistful pride and a feeling for the comic, they watch over their progeny from an effortfully kept distance. It is the season of the empty nest.

Slowly, slowly, there are changes. Something wonderful seems to hover then, faintly heard, glimpsed in illumined moments. Visiting the children, the parents are almost sure of it.

A son spreads a towel on the table and efficiently irons a perfect crease into his best pants. (*Ironing boards*, his mother thinks, adding to a mental shopping list.) "I'm taking you to a French restaurant for dinner," the young man announces. "I've made reservations." "Am I properly dressed?" his mother asks, suddenly shy. He walks her through city streets within the aura of his assurance. His arm lies lightly around her shoulders.

Or a daughter offers her honored guest the only two chairs she has and settles into a harem heap of floor pillows. She has raised plants from cuttings, framed a wall full of prints herself, spent three weekends refinishing the little dresser that glows in a square of sun.

Her parents regard her with astonished love. The room has been enchanted by her touch. "Everything's charming," they tell her honestly. "It's a real home."

Now? Is it *now*? Yes. The something wonderful descends. The generations smile at one another, as if exchanging congratulations. The children are no longer children. The parents are awed to discover adults.

It *is* wonderful, in ways my imagination had not begun to dream on. How could I have guessed—how could they?—that of my three, the shy one would pluck a dazzling array of competencies out of the air and turn up, chatting with total poise, on TV shows? That the one who turned his adolescence into World War III would find his role in arduous, sensitive human service? Or that the unbookish, antic one, torment of his teachers, would evolve into a scholar, tolerating a student's poverty and writing into the night?

I hadn't suspected that my own young adults would be so ebulliently funny one minute, and so tellingly introspective the next: so openhearted and unguarded. Or that growing up would inspire them to buy life insurance and three-piece suits and lend money to the siblings they'd once robbed of lollipops. Or that walking into their houses, I'd hear Mozart on the tape player and find books laid out for me to borrow.

Once, long ago, I waited nine months at a time to

see who they would be, babes newly formed and wondrous. "Oh, *look*!" I said, and fell in love. Now my children are wondrously new to me in a different way. I am
in love again.

My daughter and I freely share the complex world
of our inner selves, and all the other worlds we know.
Touched, I notice how her rhythms and gestures are
reminding of her grandmother's or mine. We are linked
by unconscious mysteries and benignly watched by
ghosts. I turn my head to gaze at her. She meets my look
and smiles.

A son flies the width of the country for his one
vacation in a whole long year. He follows me around the
kitchen, tasting from the pots, handing down the dishes.
We brown in the sun. Read books in silent synchrony.
He jogs. I tend the flowers. We walk at the unfurled
edge of great waves. We talk and talk, and later play
cribbage past midnight. I'm utterly happy.

"But it's your vacation!" I remind him. "What shall
we do that's special?"

"This," he says. "Exactly this."

When my children first ventured out and away, I
felt they were in flight to outer space, following a curve
of light and time to such unknowns that my heart would
surely go faint with trying to follow. I thought this
would be the end of parenting. Not what it is—the best
part; the final, firmest bonding; the goal and the reward.°

Appendix

Questionnaire for Parents about Their Children Whom They Believe to Be Strong-Willed or Compliant

I. The items in this section ask general questions about you as a parent.

A. Individual completing this survey:
Mother ☐   Father ☐ Both parents together ☐

B. Mother (if you are the father answering for the mother, please circle the number you think she would have circled).
As a child, I was:

Very Strong-Willed	Strong-Willed	Neither	Compliant	Very Compliant
1	2	3	4	5

C. Father (if you are the mother answering for the father, please circle the number you think he would have circled):
As a child, I was:

Very Strong-Willed	Strong-Willed	Neither	Compliant	Very Compliant
1	2	3	4	5

II. Even though this questionnaire deals only with your oldest strong-willed or compliant child (if any), it is important to know how you evaluate the temperament of all your children. Please rate them on the scale below.

	First Born	Second Born	Third Born	Fourth Born	Fifth Born	Sixth Born	Seventh Born
Sex M/F	——	——	——	——	——	——	——
Current Age	——	——	——	——	——	——	——

Please circle one characteristic below:

Children	Very Compliant	Cooper-ative	Average	Uncooper-ative	Very Strong-Willed
First Born	1	2	3	4	5
Second Born	1	2	3	4	5
Third Born	1	2	3	4	5
Fourth Born	1	2	3	4	5
Fifth Born	1	2	3	4	5
Sixth Born	1	2	3	4	5
Seventh Born	1	2	3	4	5

III. The items in this section ask questions about your child(ren) whom you consider to be either strong-willed or compliant. It is possible that you had more than one child in each category. If so, please answer the questions for the *oldest* strong-willed child and/or the *oldest* compliant child. If you only had a child in one of the two categories, please ignore the other. If you had children who were neither strong-willed nor compliant, please place an "X" here _____, and return the questionnaire to us uncompleted.

	Strong-Willed Child	Compliant Child
A. Sex:	M ☐ F ☐	M ☐ F ☐
B. Current age:	_____	_____
C. Order of birth (1st, 2nd, . . .):	_____	_____

D. Age at which the temperament was first recognized:

	Strong-Willed Child	Compliant Child
Birth to 3 months:	_____	_____
3 to 6 months:	_____	_____
6 to 12 months:	_____	_____
1 to 3 years:	_____	_____
3 to 6 years:	_____	_____

E. Discipline of father (if you are the mother answering for the father, circle the number you think he would have circled):

Strong-Willed Child

Permissive	Rather Easy	Average	Rather Strict	Rigid and Severe
1	2	3	4	5

Compliant Child

Permissive	Rather Easy	Average	Rather Strict	Rigid and Severe
1	2	3	4	5

F. Discipline of mother (if you are the father answering for the mother, circle the number you think she would have circled):

Strong-Willed Child

Permissive	Rather Easy	Average	Rather Strict	Rigid and Severe
1	2	3	4	5

Compliant Child

Permissive	Rather Easy	Average	Rather Strict	Rigid and Severe
1	2	3	4	5

G. The amount of stress created for the parents by the child's temperament:

(Note: "1" indicates that the child was a joy to raise and caused virtually no disharmony or agitation for the parents; "2" means the child was generally pleasant and easy to raise; "3" means average; "4" means the child was generally difficult to raise; "5" means the child was unpleasant and caused great disharmony and agitation in the home.)

Strong-Willed Child

Total Joy	Generally Pleasant	Average	Difficult	Unpleasant
1	2	3	4	5

Compliant Child

Total Joy	Generally Pleasant	Average	Difficult	Unpleasant
1	2	3	4	5

H. Which parent related to and handled the child best at each age level?

Strong-Willed Child

Age	Mother	Father	Only One Parent Present	Neither Parent Did Well
0–2	1	2	3	4
2–4	1	2	3	4
4–6	1	2	3	4
6–13	1	2	3	4
13–20	1	2	3	4
20 to present	1	2	3	4

Compliant Child

Age	Mother	Father	Only One Parent Present	Neither Parent Did Well
0–2	1	2	3	4
2–4	1	2	3	4
4–6	1	2	3	4
6–13	1	2	3	4
13–20	1	2	3	4
20 to present	1	2	3	4

I. Degree of rebellion against adult authority and values at each age level:

Strong-Willed Child

Age	Complete Acceptance	Rather Cooperative	Average Response	Rather Defiant	Total Rejection
0–2	1	2	3	4	5
2–4	1	2	3	4	5
4–6	1	2	3	4	5
6–13	1	2	3	4	5
13–20	1	2	3	4	5
20 to present	1	2	3	4	5

Compliant Child

Age	Complete Acceptance	Rather Cooperative	Average Response	Rather Defiant	Total Rejection
0–2	1	2	3	4	5
2–4	1	2	3	4	5
4–6	1	2	3	4	5
6–13	1	2	3	4	5
13–20	1	2	3	4	5
20 to present	1	2	3	4	5

J. Describe the temperament of your child at *each* age level up to the present time (or to age 24, if applicable):

Strong-Willed Child

Age	Very Compliant	Cooperative	Average	Very Uncooperative	Defiant
1–2	1	2	3	4	5
3–4	1	2	3	4	5
5–6	1	2	3	4	5
7–8	1	2	3	4	5
9–10	1	2	3	4	5
11–12	1	2	3	4	5
13–14	1	2	3	4	5
15–16	1	2	3	4	5
17–18	1	2	3	4	5
19–20	1	2	3	4	5
21–22	1	2	3	4	5
23–24	1	2	3	4	5

Compliant Child

Age	Very Compliant	Cooper- ative	Average	Very Unco- operative	Defiant
1–2	1	2	3	4	5
3–4	1	2	3	4	5
5–6	1	2	3	4	5
7–8	1	2	3	4	5
9–10	1	2	3	4	5
11–12	1	2	3	4	5
13–14	1	2	3	4	5
15–16	1	2	3	4	5
17–18	1	2	3	4	5
19–20	1	2	3	4	5
21–22	1	2	3	4	5
23–24	1	2	3	4	5

K. Has your grown child (age 20 or older) accepted your values and established a good working relationship with you as his parents?

Strong-Willed Child

Yes	No	Somewhat	N/A
1	2	3	4

Compliant Child

Yes	No	Somewhat	N/A
1	2	3	4

L. Social adjustment at each age level:

Strong-Willed Child

Age	No Social Problems	Generally Liked	Average Response	Generally Disliked	Many Social Problems
4–6	1	2	3	4	5
6–13	1	2	3	4	5
13–20	1	2	3	4	5
20 to present	1	2	3	4	5

Compliant Child

Age	No Social Problems	Generally Liked	Average Response	Generally Disliked	Many Social Problems
4–6	1	2	3	4	5
6–13	1	2	3	4	5
13–20	1	2	3	4	5
20 to present	1	2	3	4	5

M. Influence of friends at each age level:

Strong-Willed Child

Age	No In-fluence by Peers	Little Influence by Peers	Average Response	Major Influence by Peers	Extremely Vulnerable to Peers
4–6	1	2	3	4	5
6–13	1	2	3	4	5
13–20	1	2	3	4	5
20 to present	1	2	3	4	5

Compliant Child

Age	No In-fluence by Peers	Little Influence by Peers	Average Response	Major Influence by Peers	Extremely Vulnerable to Peers
4–6	1	2	3	4	5
6–13	1	2	3	4	5
13–20	1	2	3	4	5
20 to present	1	2	3	4	5

N. Self-Concept:

Strong-Willed Child

Age	Excellent Self-Image	Generally Accepted Himself	Average Response	Generally Disliked Himself	Extreme Self-Hatred
4–6	1	2	3	4	5
6–13	1	2	3	4	5
13–20	1	2	3	4	5
20 to present	1	2	3	4	5

Compliant Child

Age	Excellent Self-Image	Generally Accepted Himself	Average Response	Generally Disliked Himself	Extreme Self-Hatred
4–6	1	2	3	4	5
6–13	1	2	3	4	5
13–20	1	2	3	4	5
20 to present	1	2	3	4	5

O. School achievement, generally, at each age level:
(Note: Scale the same as common grading scale in school: "A" outstanding; "C" average; "F" fail.)

	Strong-Willed Child	Compliant Child
Preschool	A B C D F	A B C D F
Grades 1–6	A B C D F	A B C D F
Grades 7–9	A B C D F	A B C D F
Grades 10–12	A B C D F	A B C D F
College	A B C D F	A B C D F
Post College	A B C D F	A B C D F

P. For your child who is now grown, how well has he or she achieved in life?

Strong-Willed Child

Highly Successful	Rather Successful	Average	Rather Unsuccessful	Very Unsuccessful
1	2	3	4	5

Compliant Child

Highly Successful	Rather Successful	Average	Rather Unsuccessful	Very Unsuccessful
1	2	3	4	5

Q. Speaking generally, circle the number of the sentence that best describes how you feel about raising your strong-willed child:
   1. It has been a struggle that has often left me depressed, guilt-ridden and exhausted.
   2. It has been difficult but exciting and rewarding, too.
   3. It has been a very positive experience.
   4. He/she was difficult in the early years, but the adolescent years were less stormy and difficult.

R. Speaking generally, select the sentence that best describes how you feel about raising your compliant child:
   1. It has been a struggle that has often left me depressed, guilt-ridden and exhausted.
   2. It has been difficult but exciting and rewarding, too.
   3. It has been a very positive experience.
   4. He/she was a joy in the early years, but adolescence was extremely stressful for both generations.

Thank you so much for your help in conducting this informal research project.